what did you eat yesterday? 6
fumi yoshinaga

D0834231

VERTICAL.

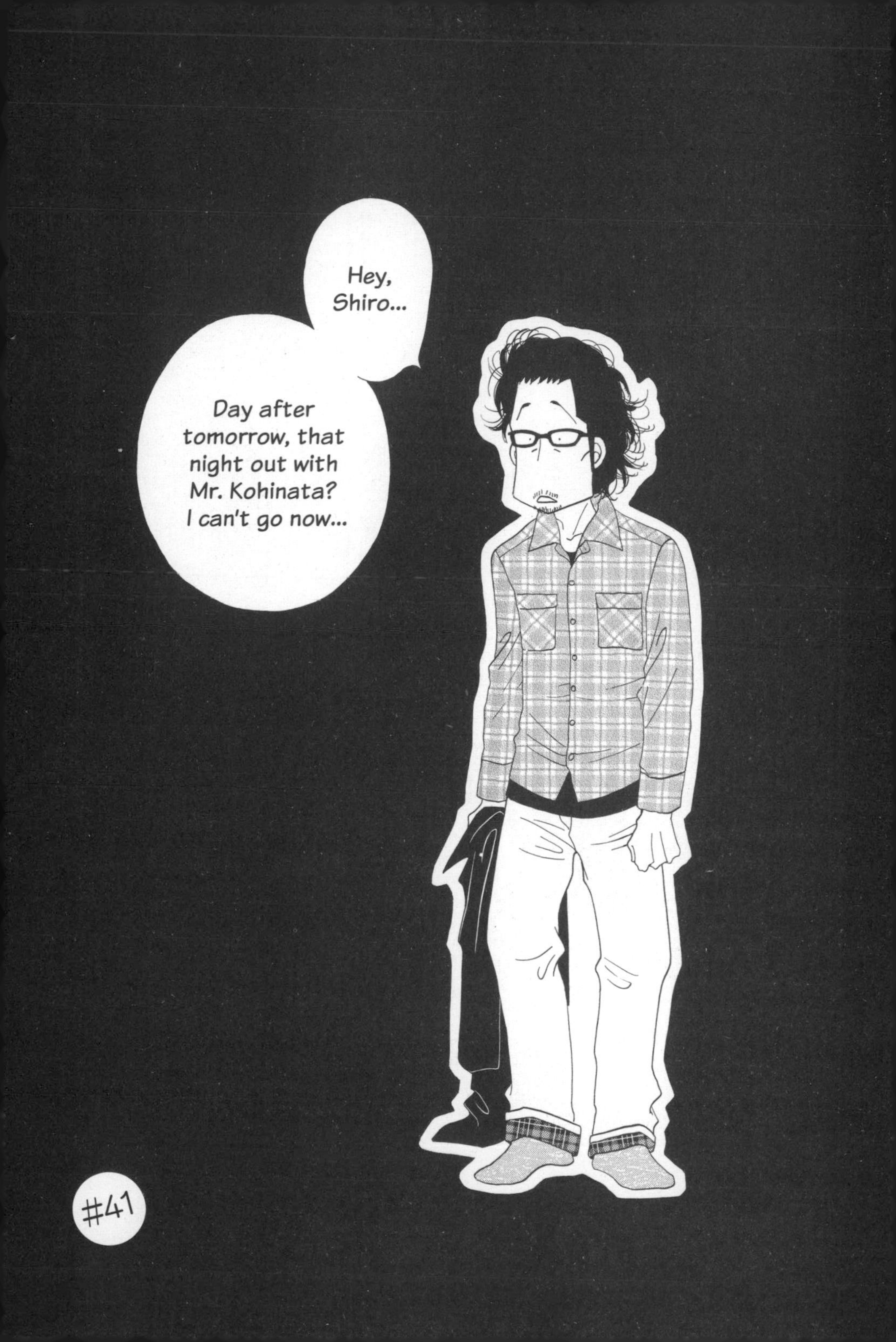
Hey, Shiro...
Day after tomorrow, that night out with Mr. Kohinata? I can't go now...
#41

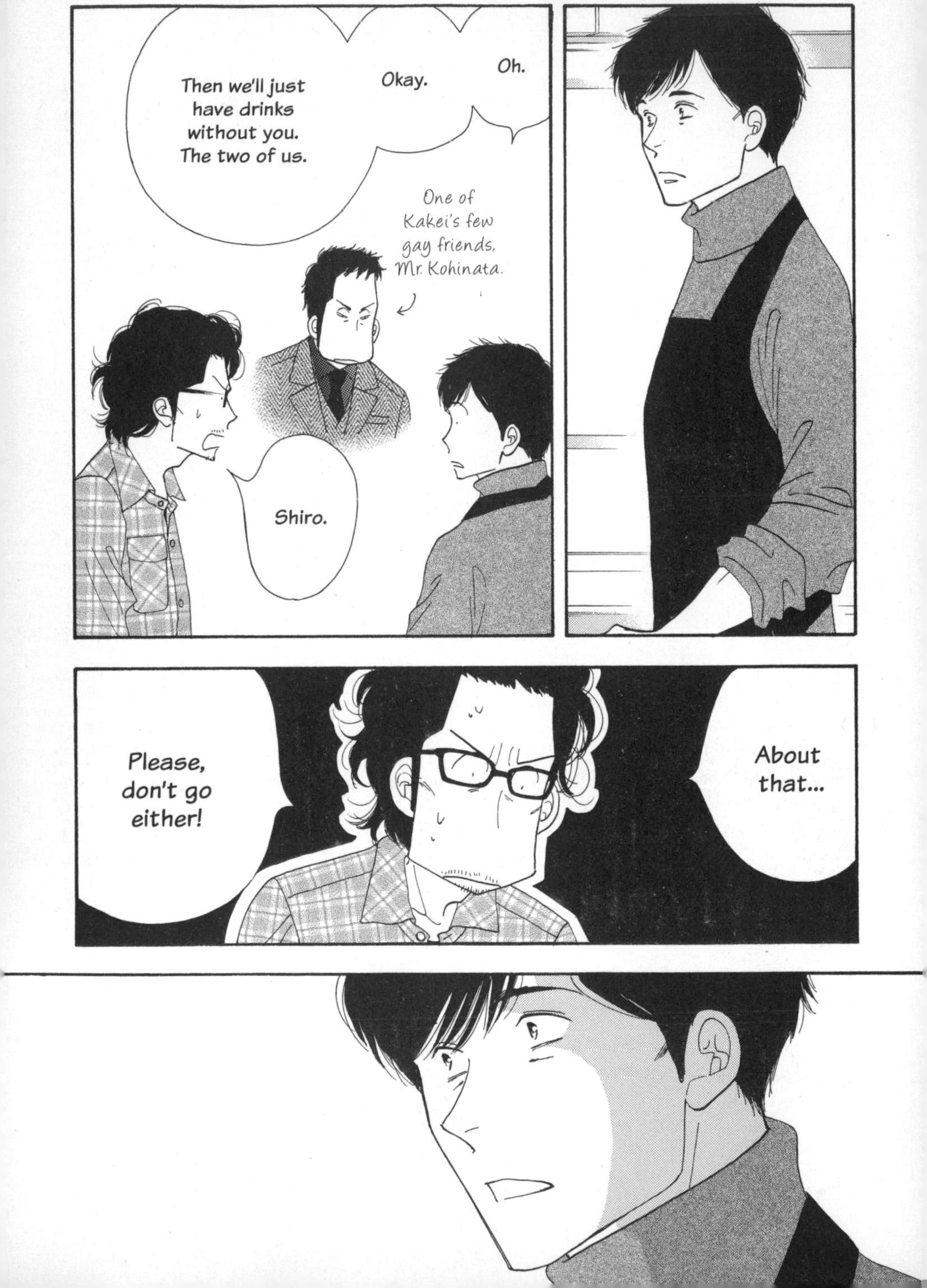
Oh.
Okay.
Then we'll just have drinks without you. The two of us.
One of Kakei's few gay friends, Mr. Kohinata.
Shiro.
About that...
Please, don't go either!

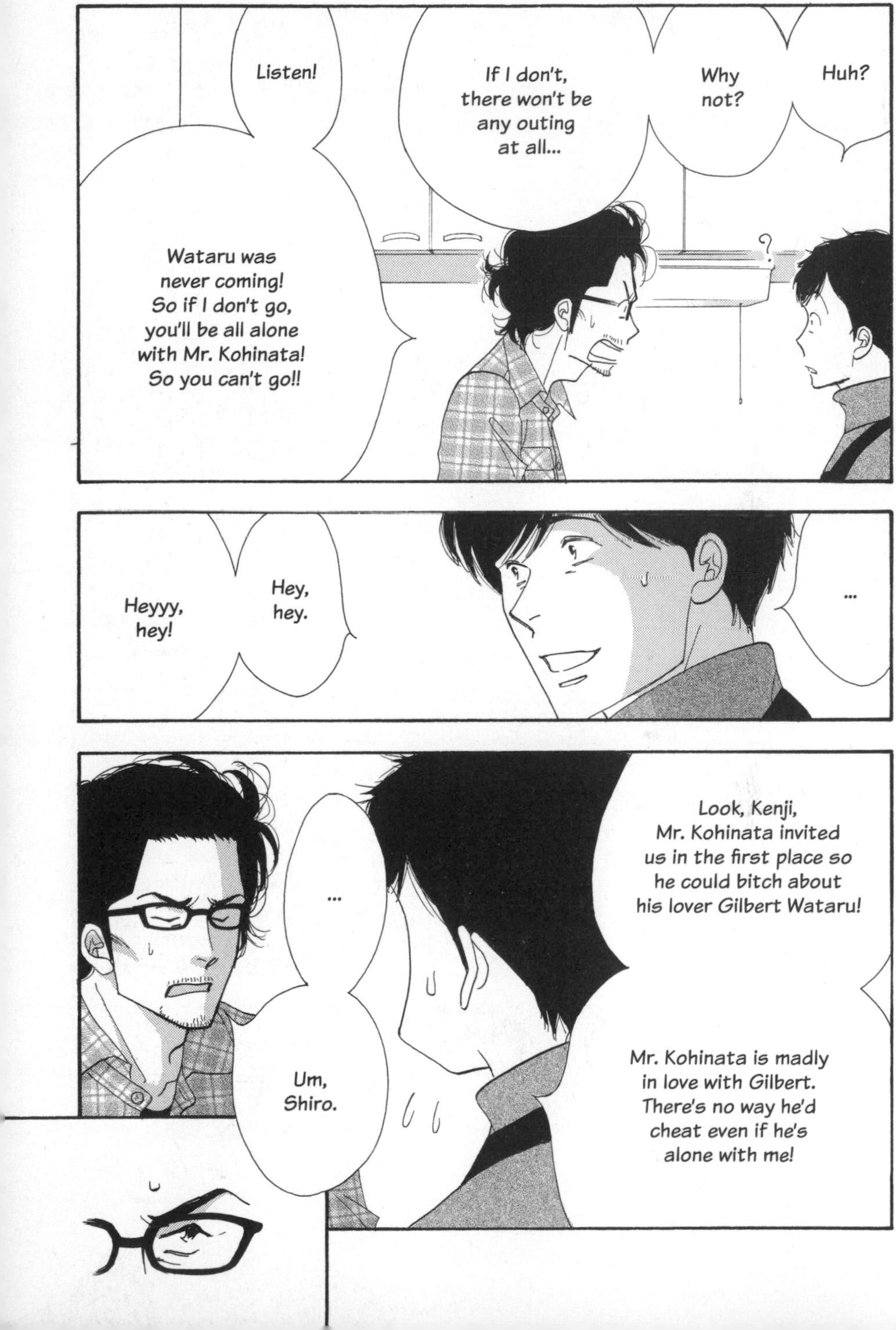
Huh?
Why not?
If I don't, there won't be any outing at all...
Listen!
Wataru was never coming! So if I don't go, you'll be all alone with Mr. Kohinata! So you can't go!!
...
Hey, hey.
Heyyy, hey!
Look, Kenji, Mr. Kohinata invited us in the first place so he could bitch about his lover Gilbert Wataru!
Mr. Kohinata is madly in love with Gilbert. There's no way he'd cheat even if he's alone with me!
...
Um, Shiro.

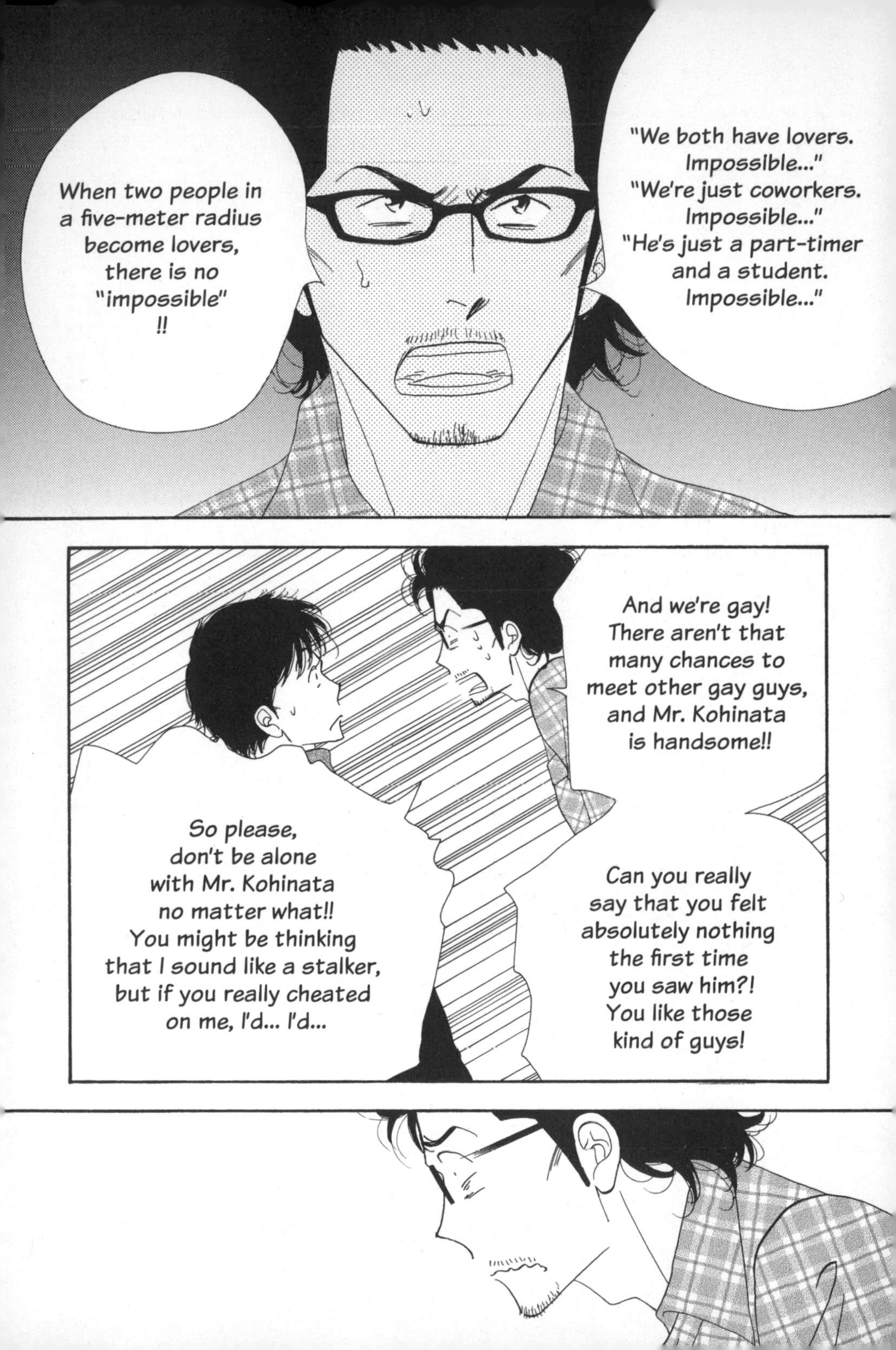
"We both have lovers. Impossible..." "We're just coworkers. Impossible..." "He's just a part-timer and a student. Impossible..."
When two people in a five-meter radius become lovers, there is no "impossible" !!
And we're gay! There aren't that many chances to meet other gay guys, and Mr. Kohinata is handsome!!
Can you really say that you felt absolutely nothing the first time you saw him?! You like those kind of guys!
So please, don't be alone with Mr. Kohinata no matter what!! You might be thinking that I sound like a stalker, but if you really cheated on me, I'd... I'd...

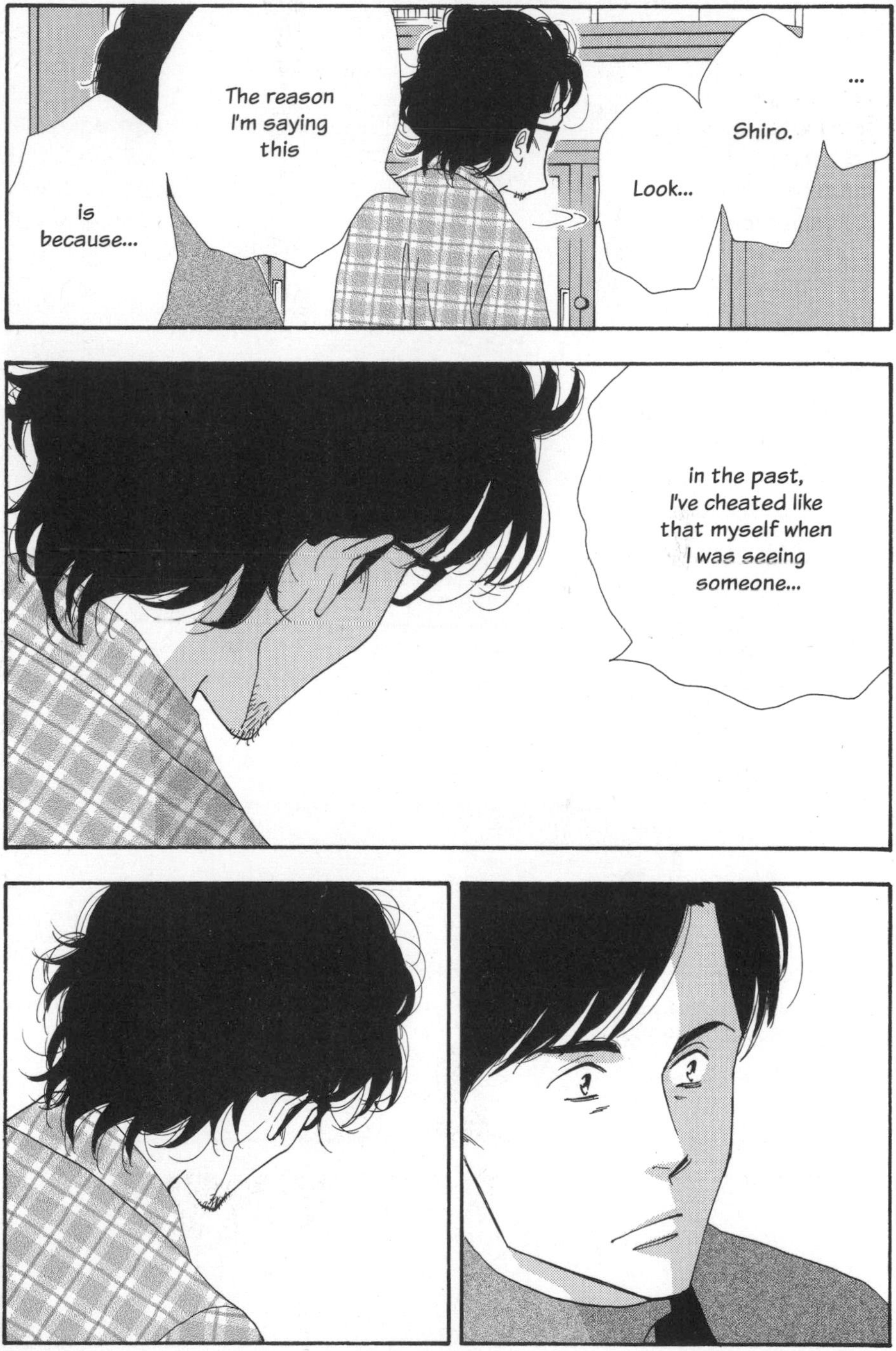
...
Shiro.
Look...
The reason I'm saying this
is because...
in the past, I've cheated like that myself when I was seeing someone...

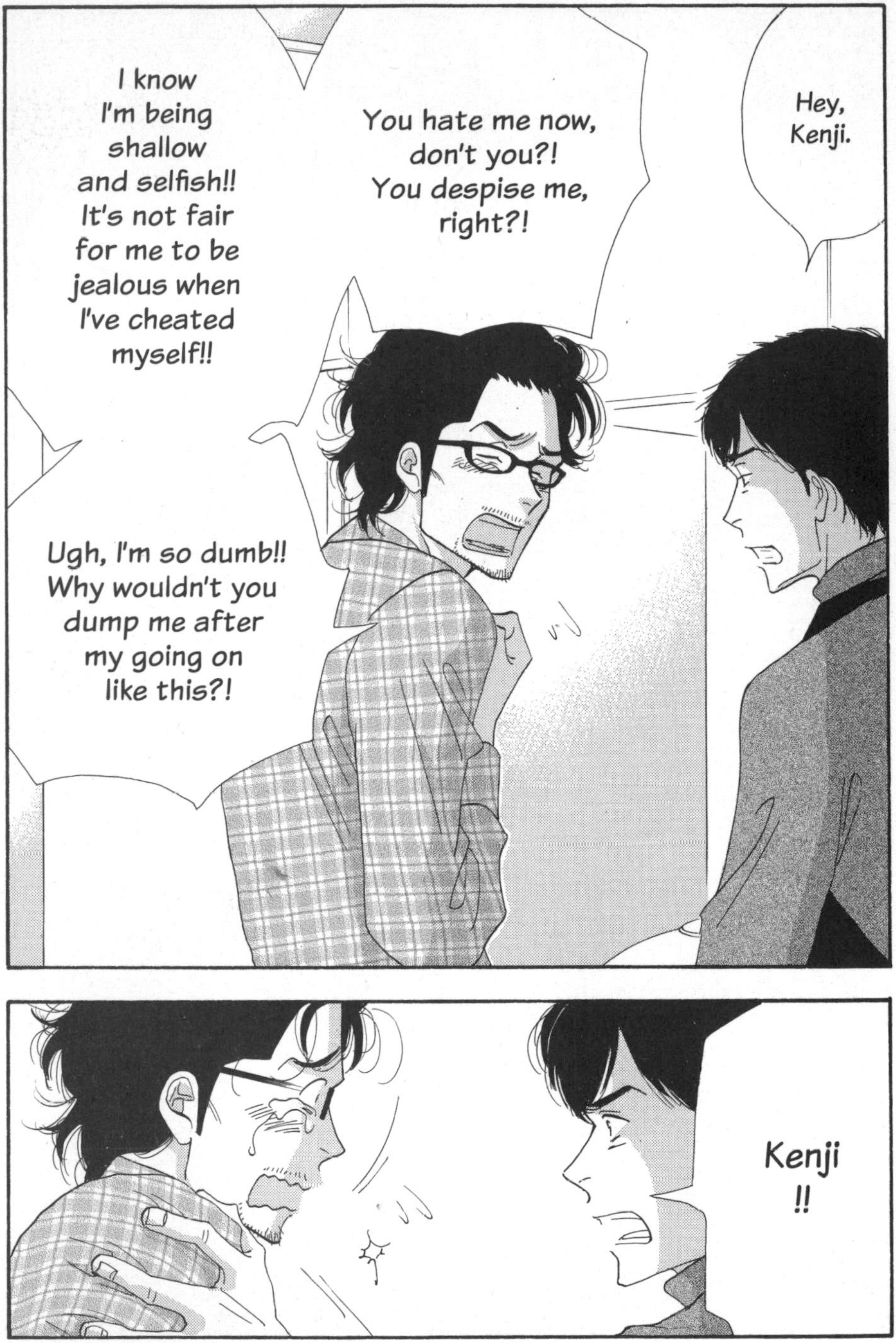
Hey, Kenji.
You hate me now, don't you?! You despise me, right?!
I know I'm being shallow and selfish!! It's not fair for me to be jealous when I've cheated myself!!
Ugh, I'm so dumb!! Why wouldn't you dump me after my going on like this?!
Kenji !!

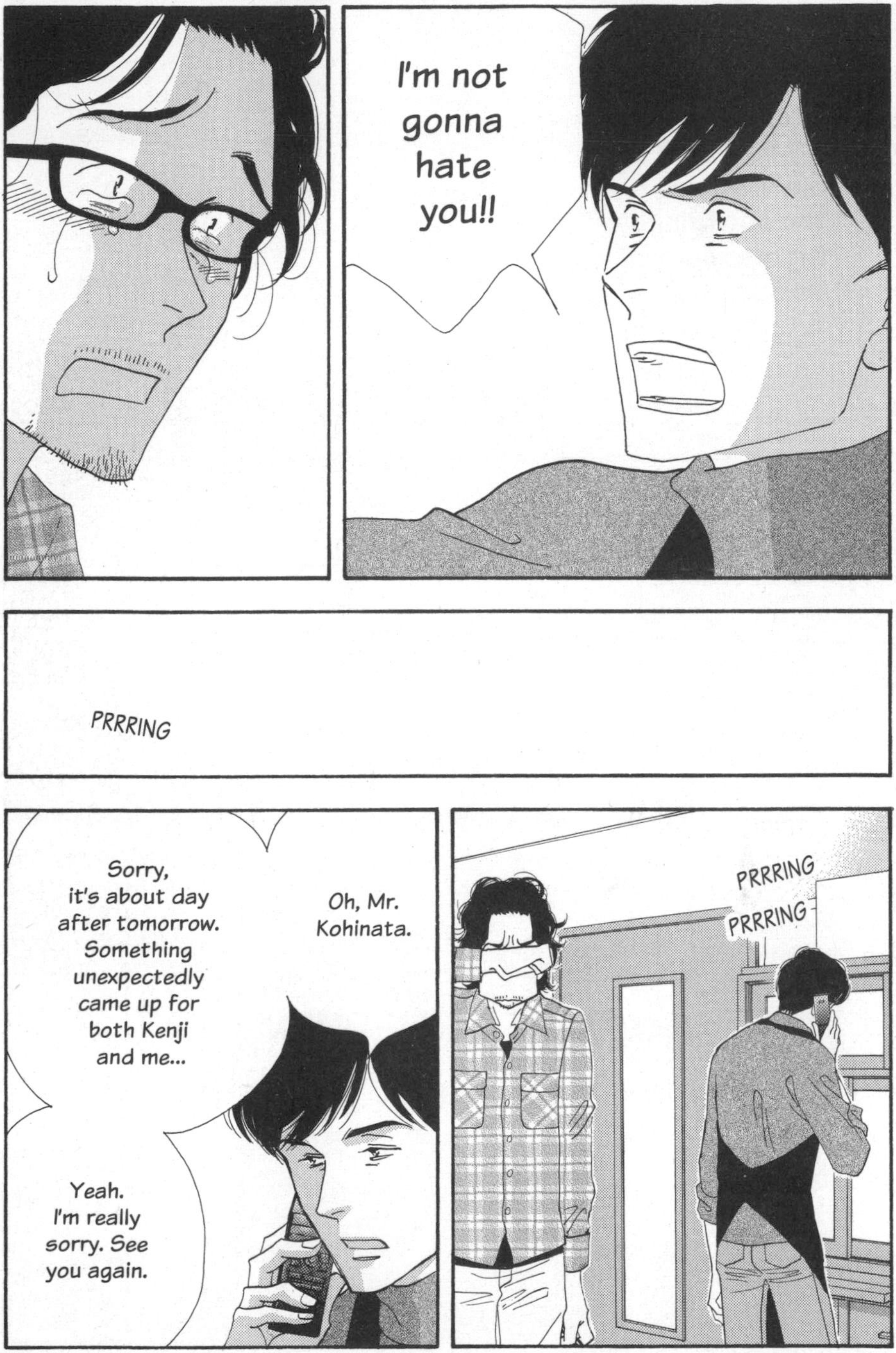
I'm not gonna hate you!!
PRRRING
PRRRING
PRRRING
Oh, Mr. Kohinata.
Sorry, it's about day after tomorrow. Something unexpectedly came up for both Kenji and me...
Yeah. I'm really sorry. See you again.

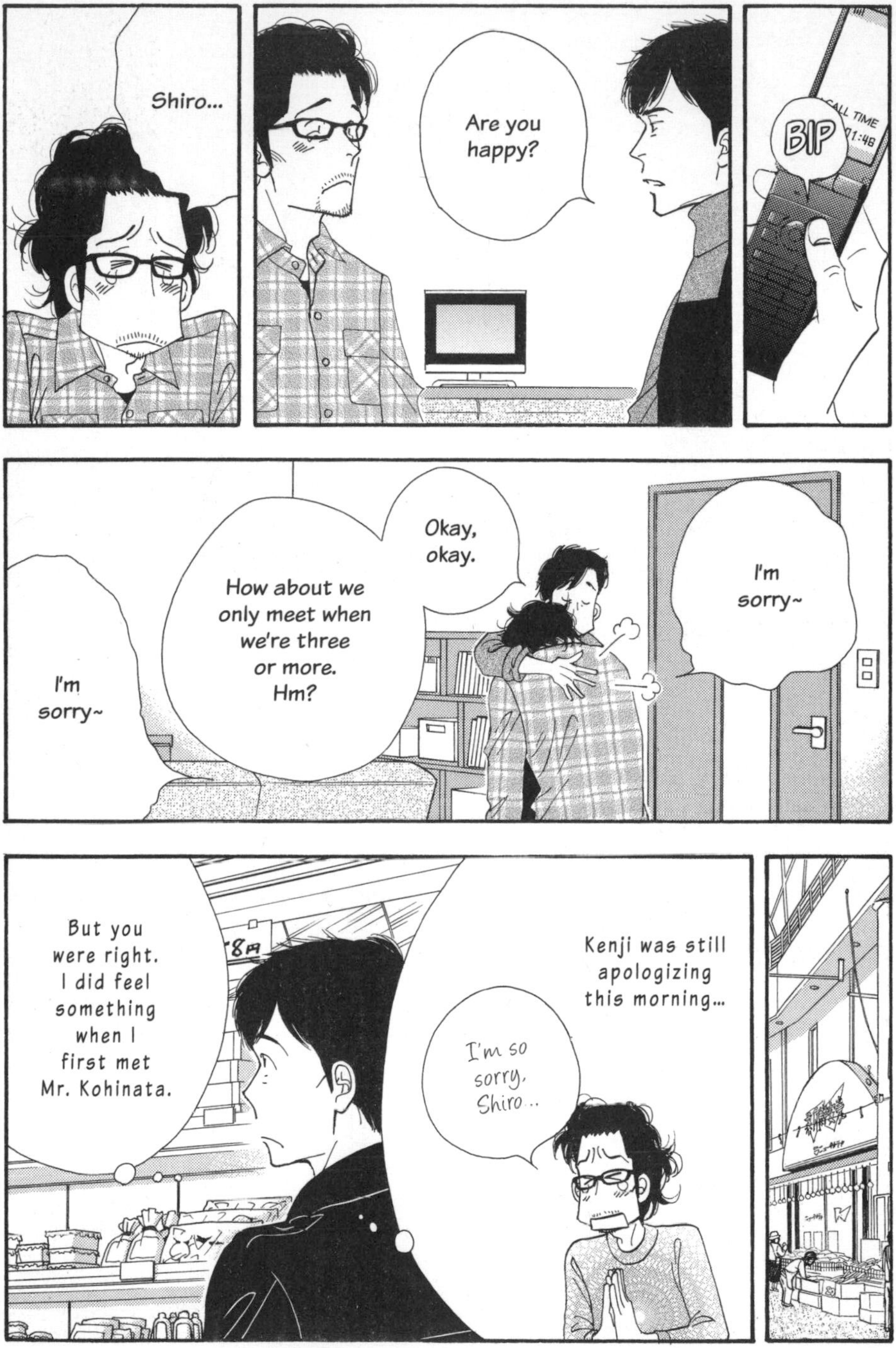
CALL TIME
BIP
Are you happy?
Shiro...
I'm sorry~
Okay, okay.
How about we only meet when we're three or more. Hm?
I'm sorry~
Kenji was still apologizing this morning...
I'm so sorry, Shiro...
But you were right. I did feel something when I first met Mr. Kohinata.

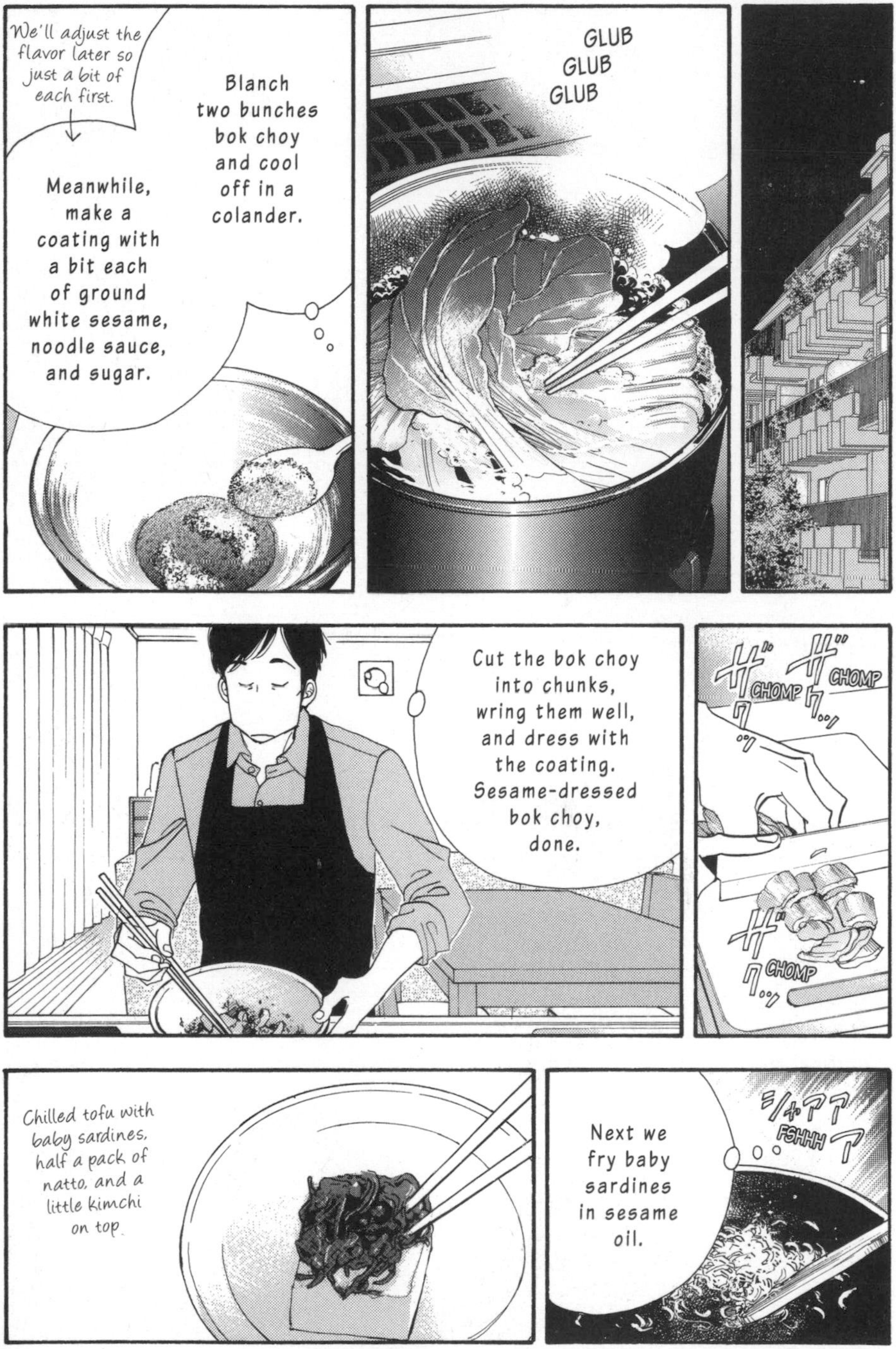
GLUB
GLUB
GLUB
Blanch two bunches bok choy and cool off in a colander.
We'll adjust the flavor later so just a bit of each first.
Meanwhile, make a coating with a bit each of ground white sesame, noodle sauce, and sugar.
CHOMP
CHOMP
CHOMP
Cut the bok choy into chunks, wring them well, and dress with the coating. Sesame-dressed bok choy, done.
FSHHH
Next we fry baby sardines in sesame oil.
Chilled tofu with baby sardines, half a pack of natto, and a little kimchi on top.

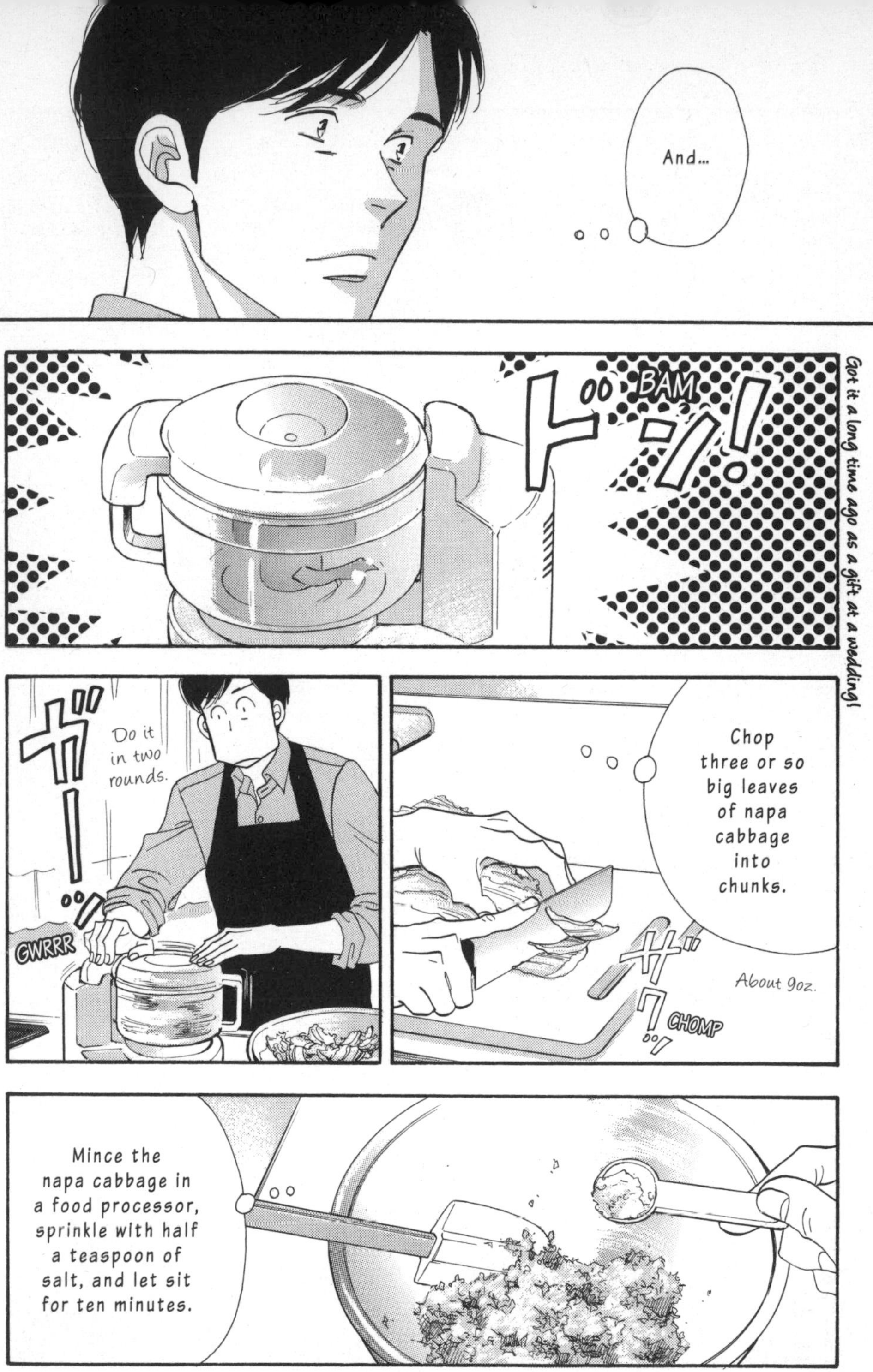
And...
BAM
Got it a long time ago as a gift at a wedding!
Chop three or so big leaves of napa cabbage into chunks.
About 9oz.
CHOMP
Do it in two rounds.
GWRRR
Mince the napa cabbage in a food processor, sprinkle with half a teaspoon of salt, and let sit for ten minutes.

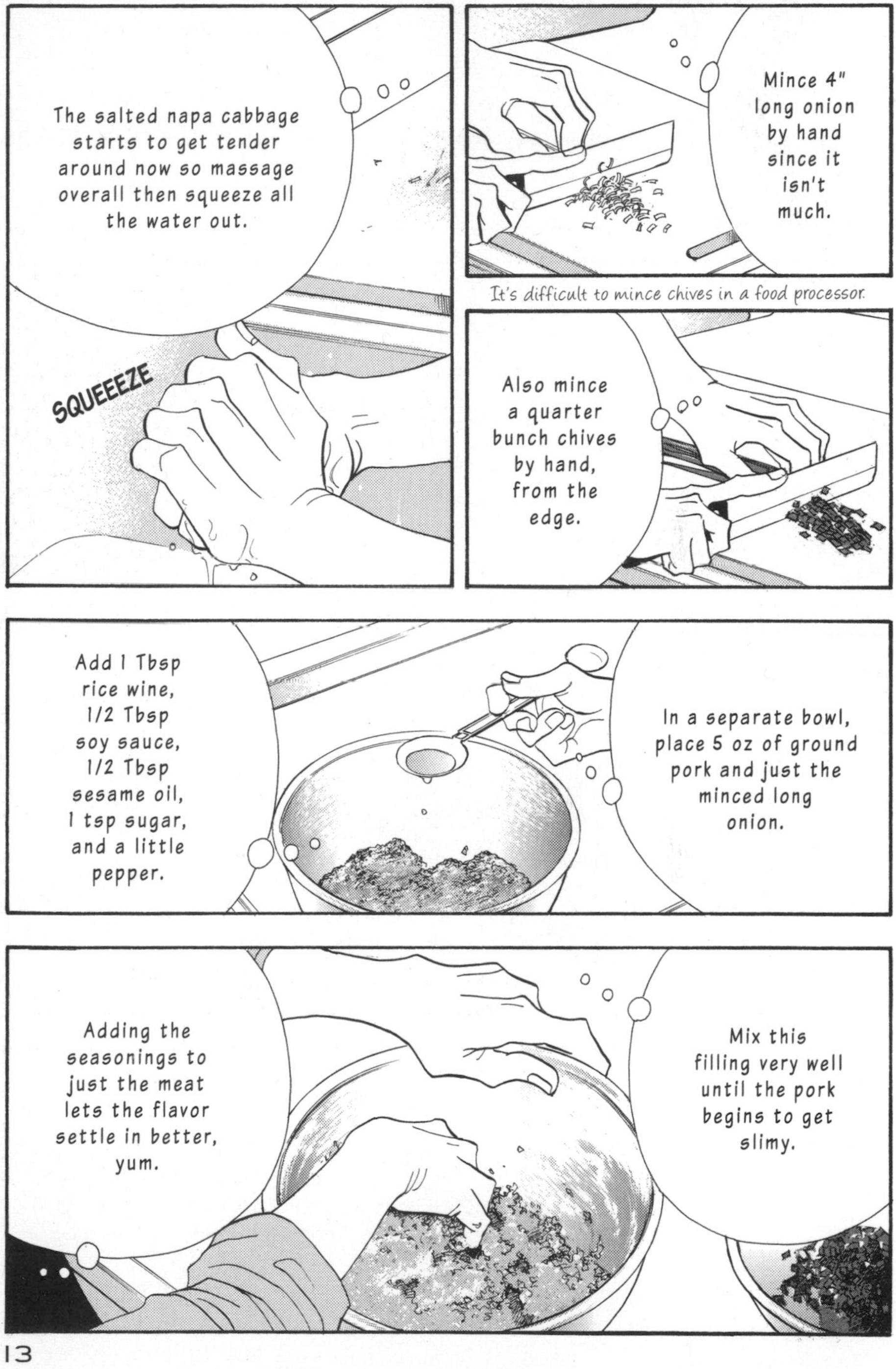
Mince 4" long onion by hand since it isn't much.
It's difficult to mince chives in a food processor.
Also mince a quarter bunch chives by hand, from the edge.
The salted napa cabbage starts to get tender around now so massage overall then squeeze all the water out.
SQUEEEZE
In a separate bowl, place 5 oz of ground pork and just the minced long onion.
Add 1 Tbsp rice wine, 1/2 Tbsp soy sauce, 1/2 Tbsp sesame oil, 1 tsp sugar, and a little pepper.
Mix this filling very well until the pork begins to get slimy.
Adding the seasonings to just the meat lets the flavor settle in better, yum.

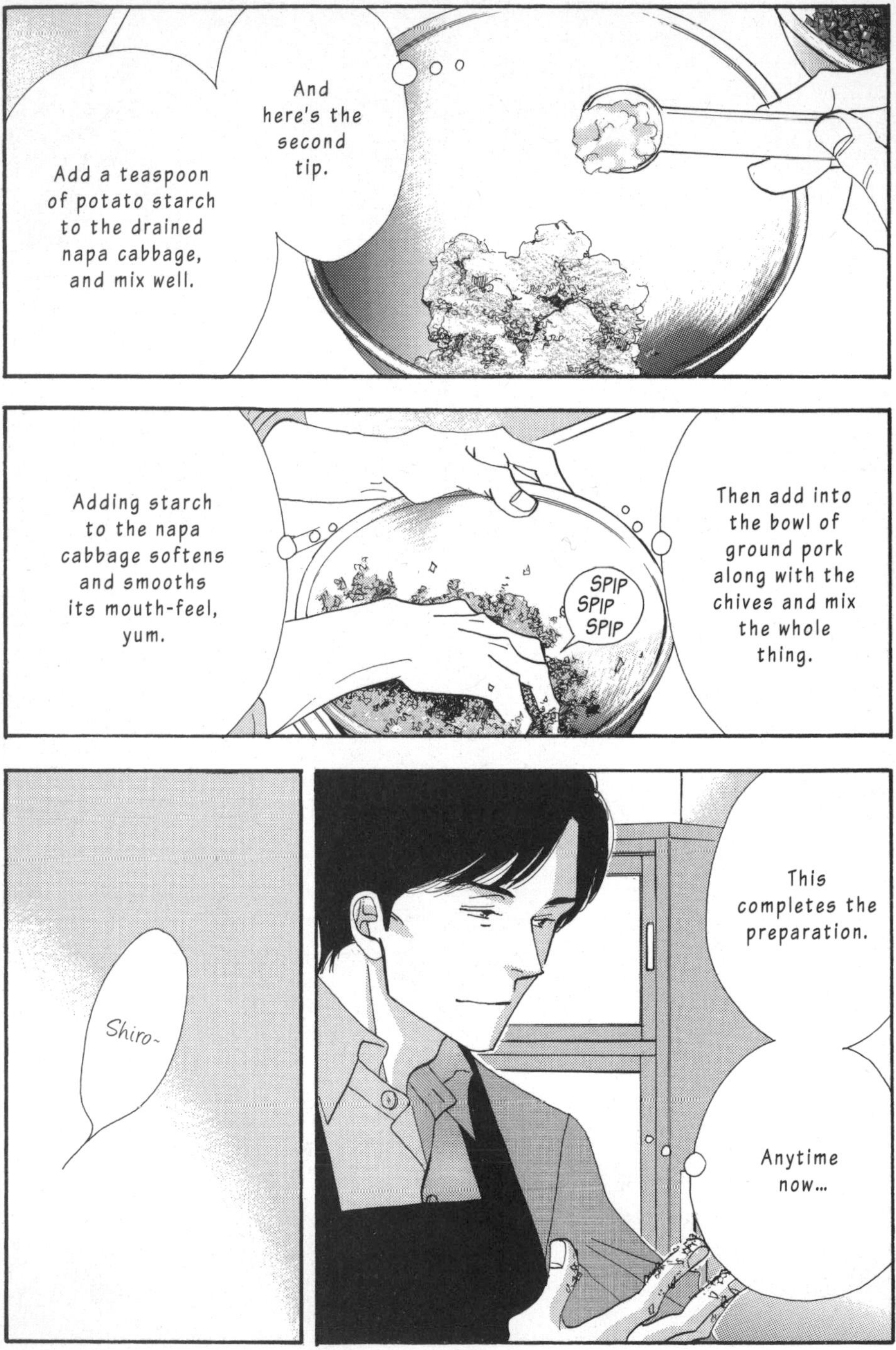
And here's the second tip.
Add a teaspoon of potato starch to the drained napa cabbage, and mix well.
Then add into the bowl of ground pork along with the chives and mix the whole thing.
SPIP SPIP SPIP
Adding starch to the napa cabbage softens and smooths its mouth-feel, yum.
This completes the preparation.
Anytime now...
Shiro~

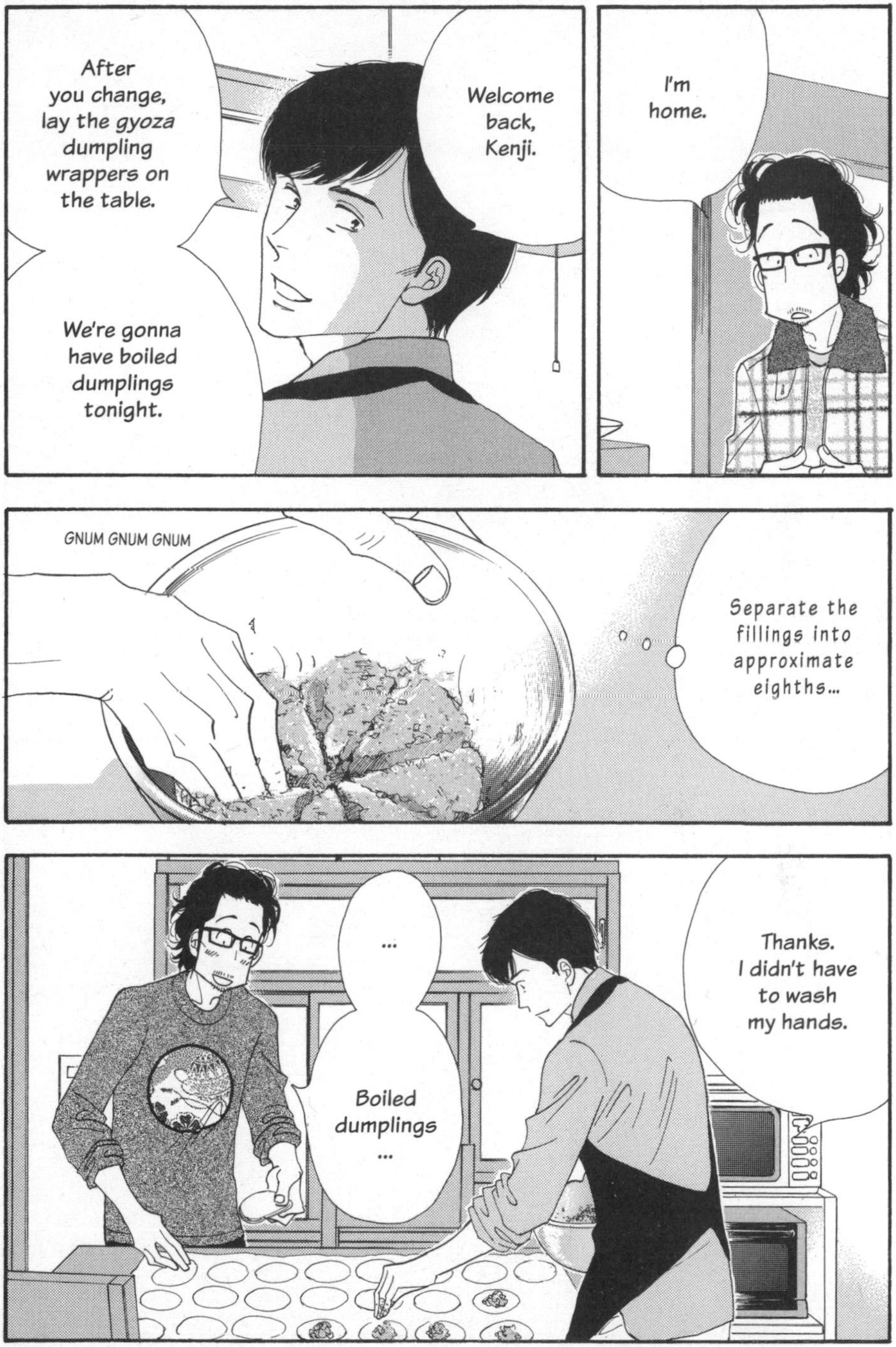
I'm home.
Welcome back, Kenji.
After you change, lay the *gyoza* dumpling wrappers on the table.
We're gonna have boiled dumplings tonight.
Separate the fillings into approximate eighths...
GNUM GNUM GNUM
Thanks. I didn't have to wash my hands.
...
Boiled dumplings ...

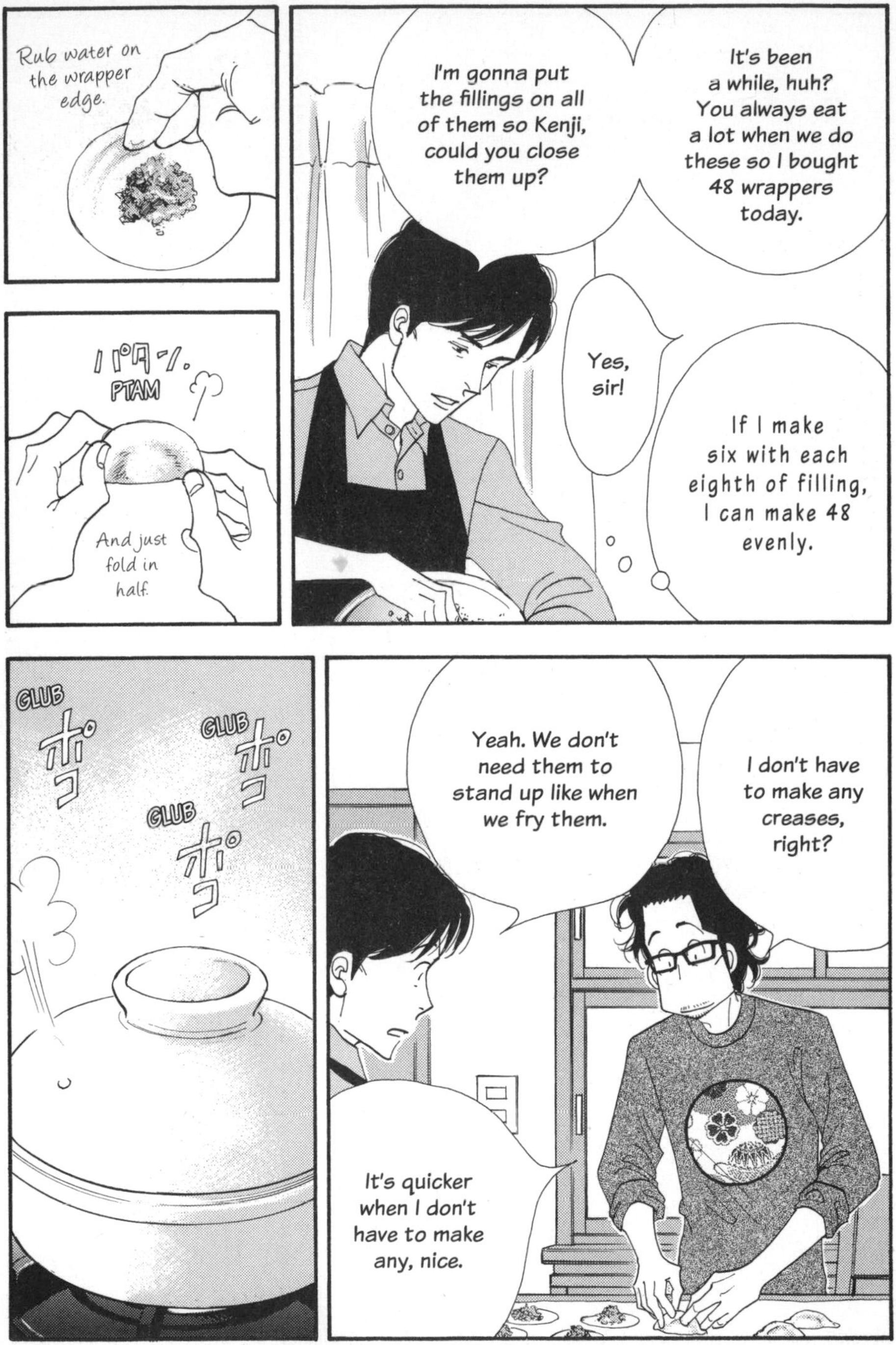
It's been a while, huh? You always eat a lot when we do these so I bought 48 wrappers today.
I'm gonna put the fillings on all of them so Kenji, could you close them up?
Yes, sir!
If I make six with each eighth of filling, I can make 48 evenly.
Rub water on the wrapper edge.
パタッ。
PTAM
And just fold in half.
I don't have to make any creases, right?
Yeah. We don't need them to stand up like when we fry them.
It's quicker when I don't have to make any, nice.
GLUB
ポコ
GLUB
ポコ
GLUB
ポコ

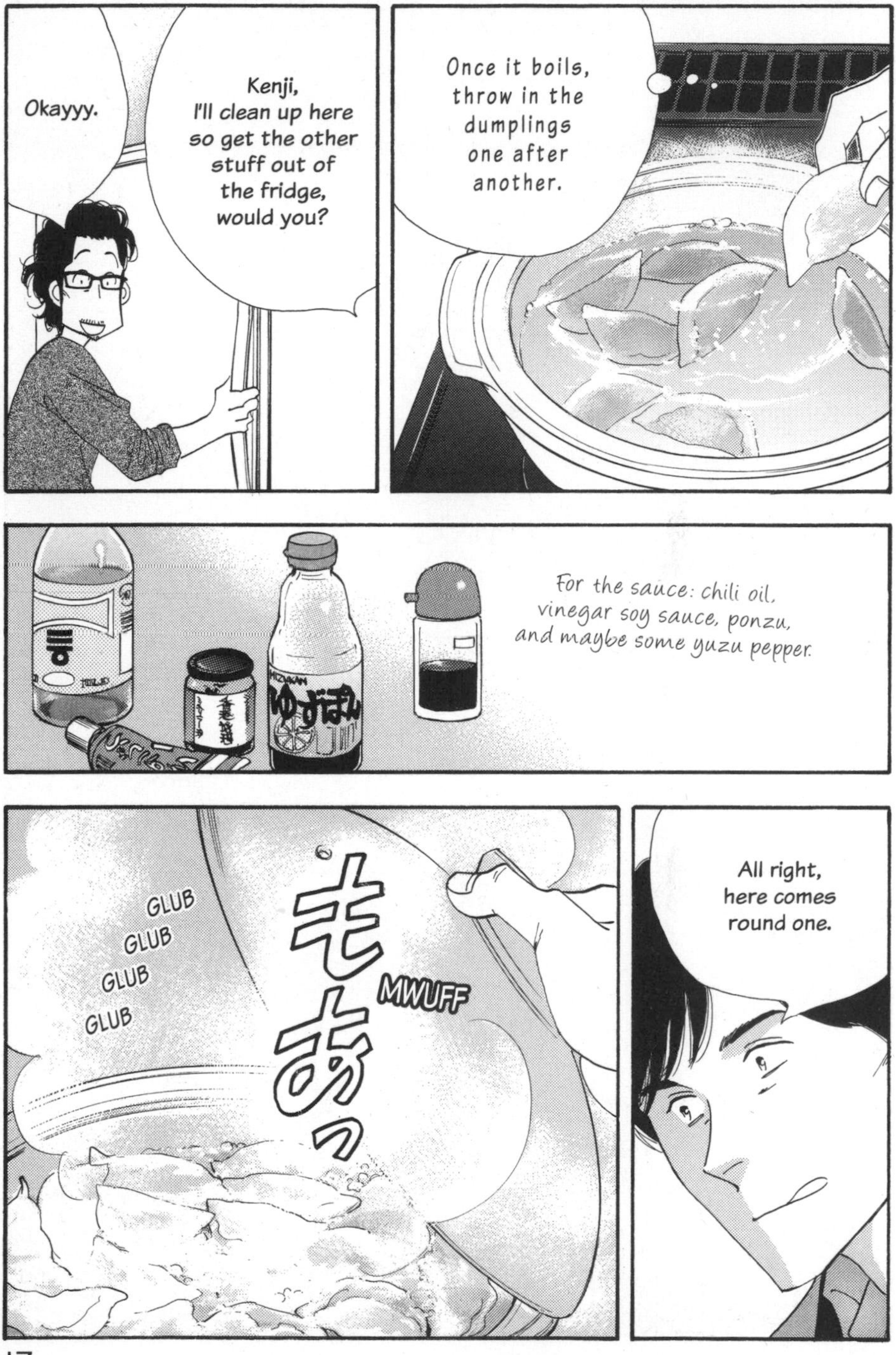
Once it boils, throw in the dumplings one after another.
Kenji, I'll clean up here so get the other stuff out of the fridge, would you?
Okayyy.
For the sauce: chili oil, vinegar soy sauce, ponzu, and maybe some yuzu pepper.
All right, here comes round one.
もあっ
MWUFF
GLUB
GLUB
GLUB
GLUB

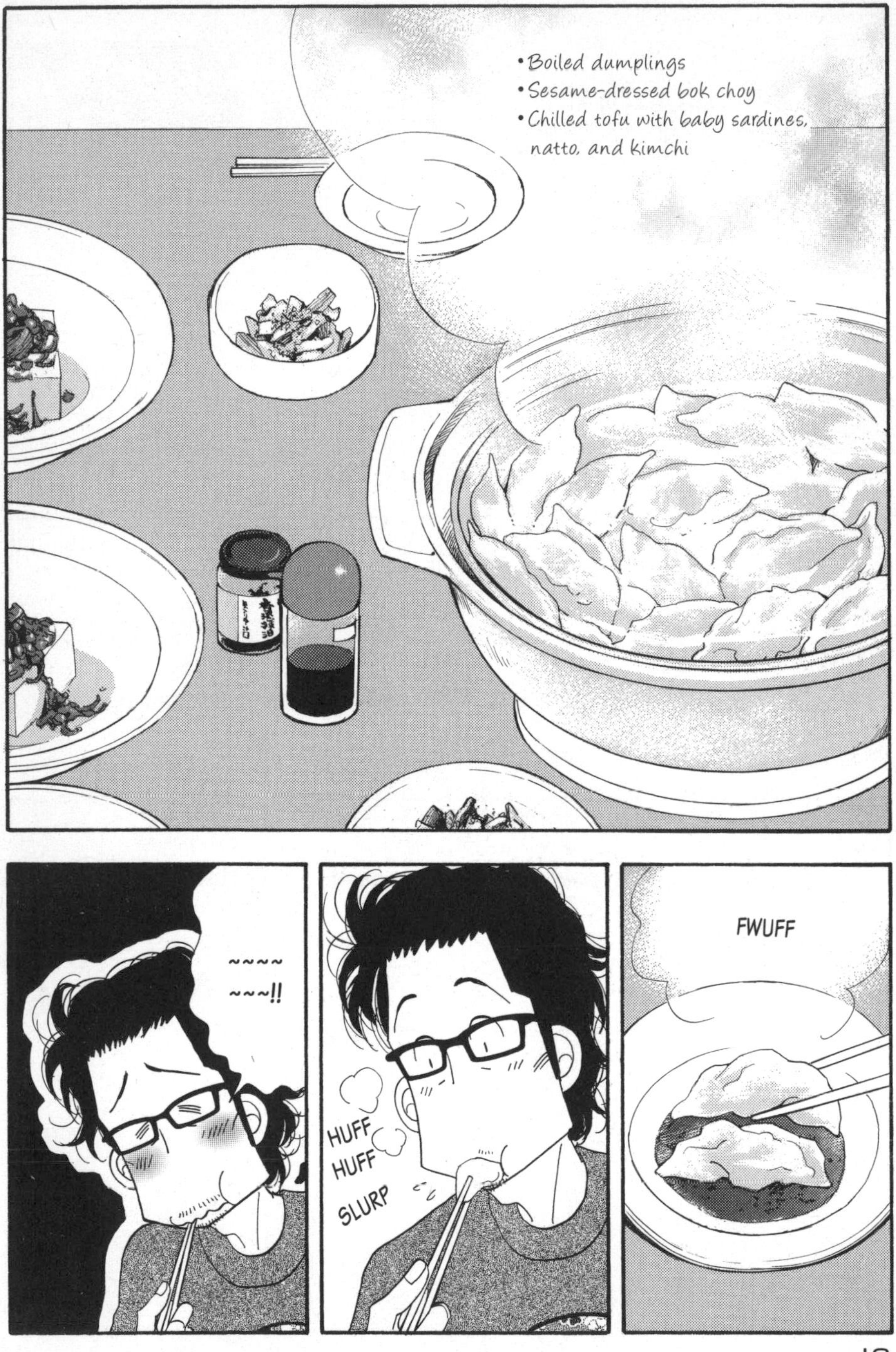
•Boiled dumplings
•Sesame-dressed bok choy
•Chilled tofu with baby sardines, natto, and kimchi
FWUFF
HUFF
HUFF
SLURP
~~~~
~~~!!

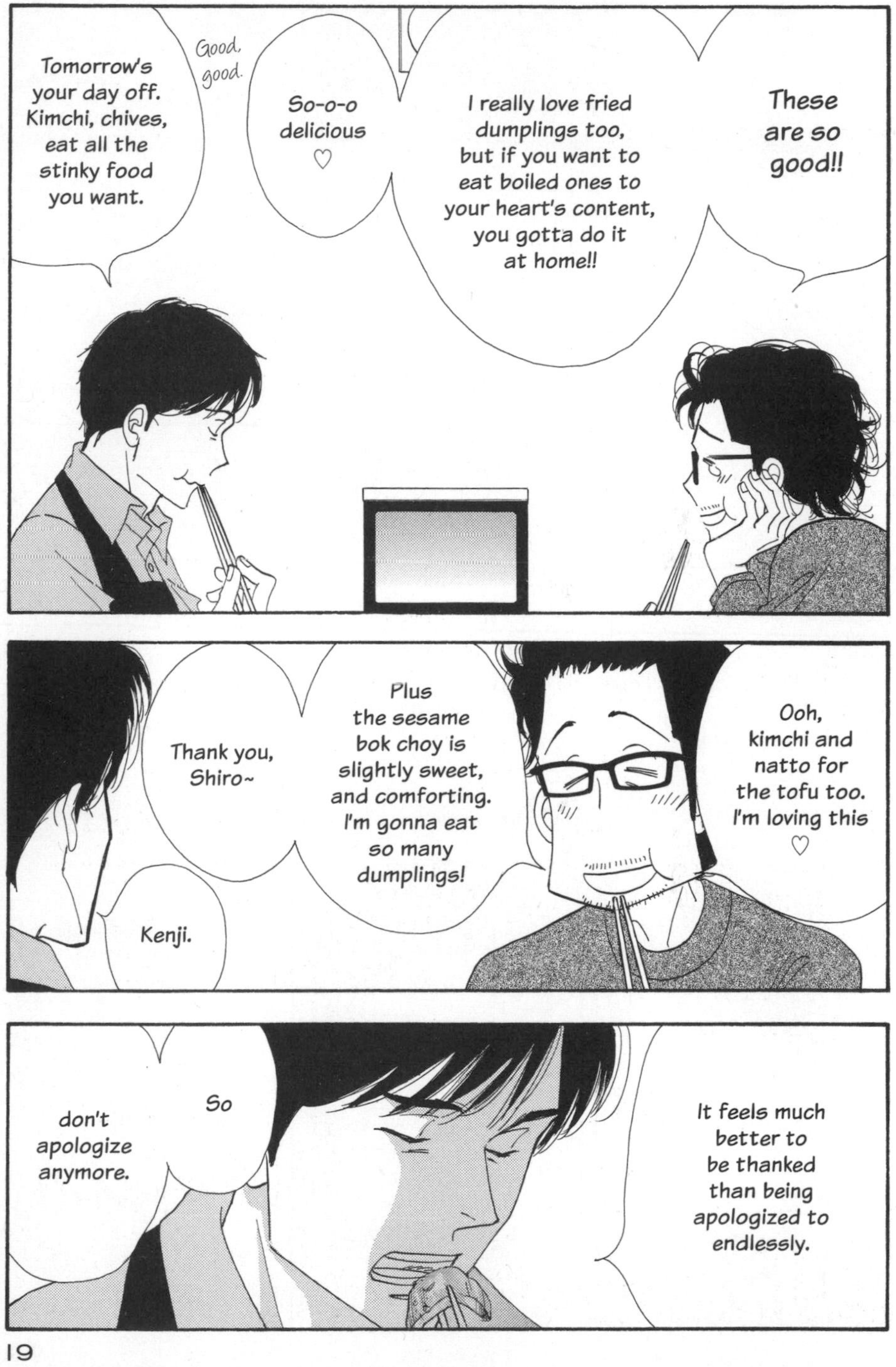
These are so good!!
I really love fried dumplings too, but if you want to eat boiled ones to your heart's content, you gotta do it at home!!
So-o-o delicious ♡
Good, good.
Tomorrow's your day off. Kimchi, chives, eat all the stinky food you want.
Ooh, kimchi and natto for the tofu too. I'm loving this ♡
Plus the sesame bok choy is slightly sweet, and comforting. I'm gonna eat so many dumplings!
Thank you, Shiro~
Kenji.
It feels much better to be thanked than being apologized to endlessly.
So
don't apologize anymore.

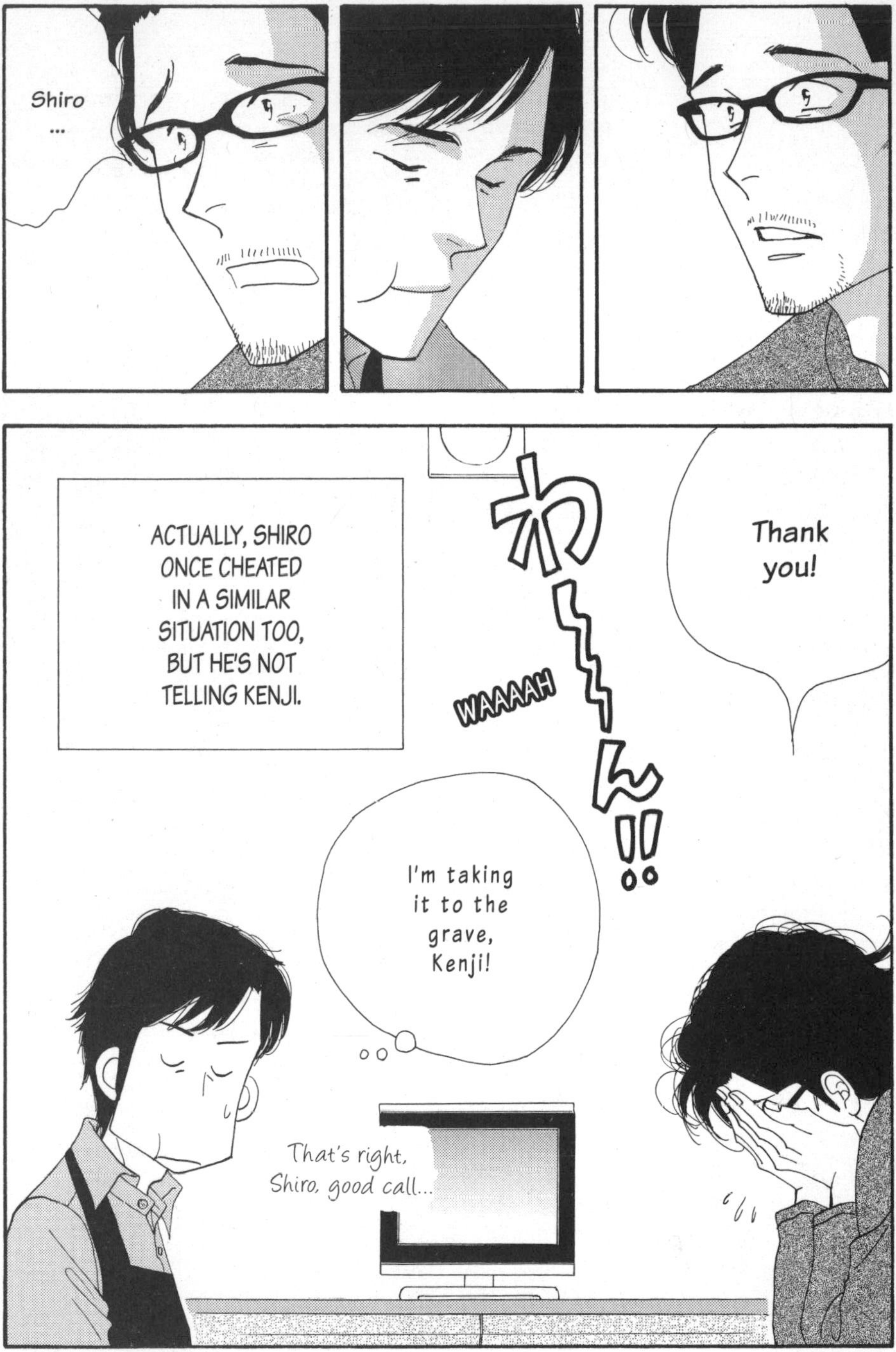
Shiro ...
Thank you!
わ〜〜ん!!
WAAAAH
ACTUALLY, SHIRO ONCE CHEATED IN A SIMILAR SITUATION TOO, BUT HE'S NOT TELLING KENJI.
I'm taking it to the grave, Kenji!
That's right, Shiro, good call...

Mincing napa cabbage without a food processor

Julienne each leaf diagonally from the base first, then slice into tiny pieces.

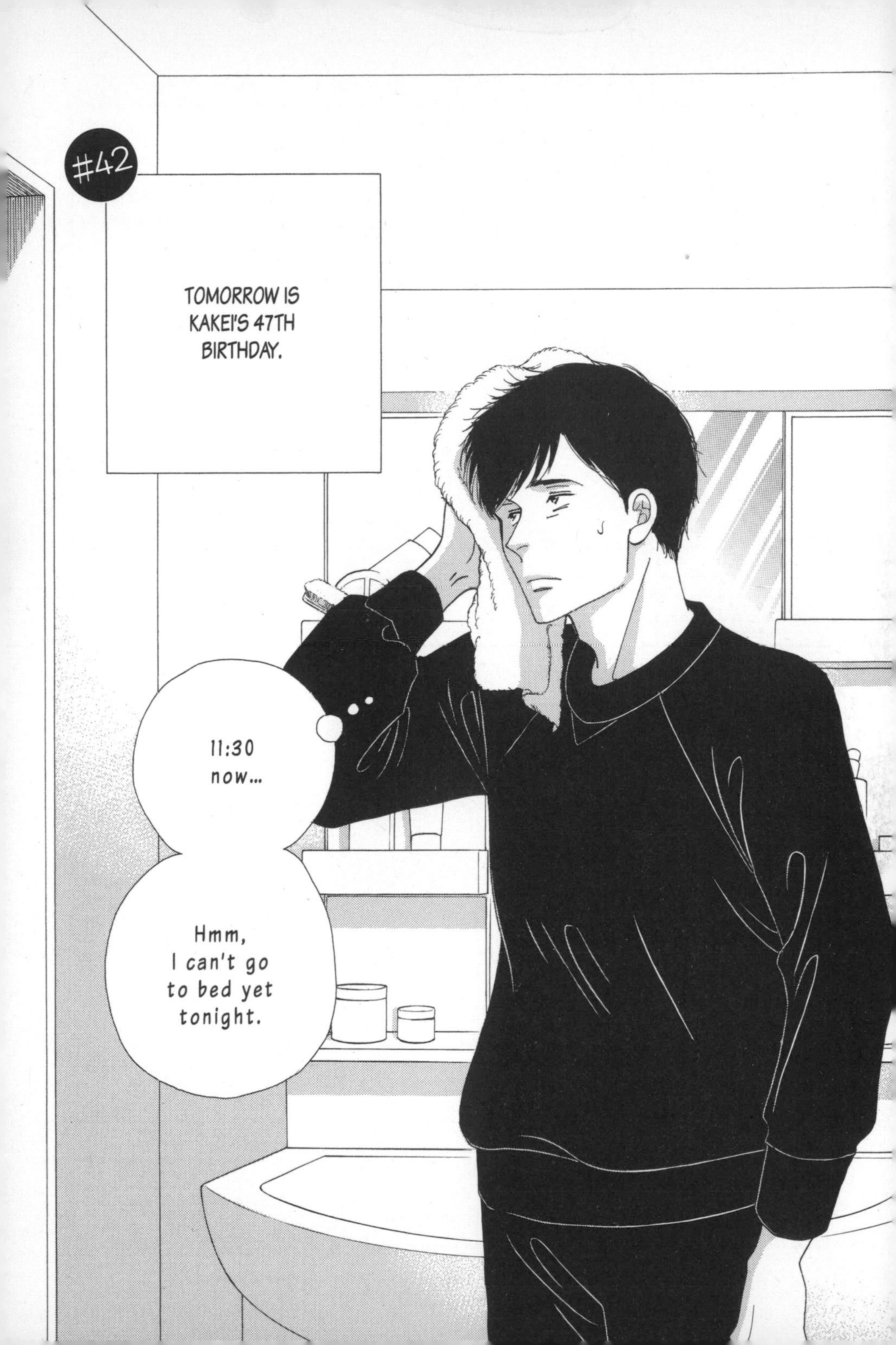
#42
TOMORROW IS KAKEI'S 47TH BIRTHDAY.
11:30 now...
Hmm, I can't go to bed yet tonight.

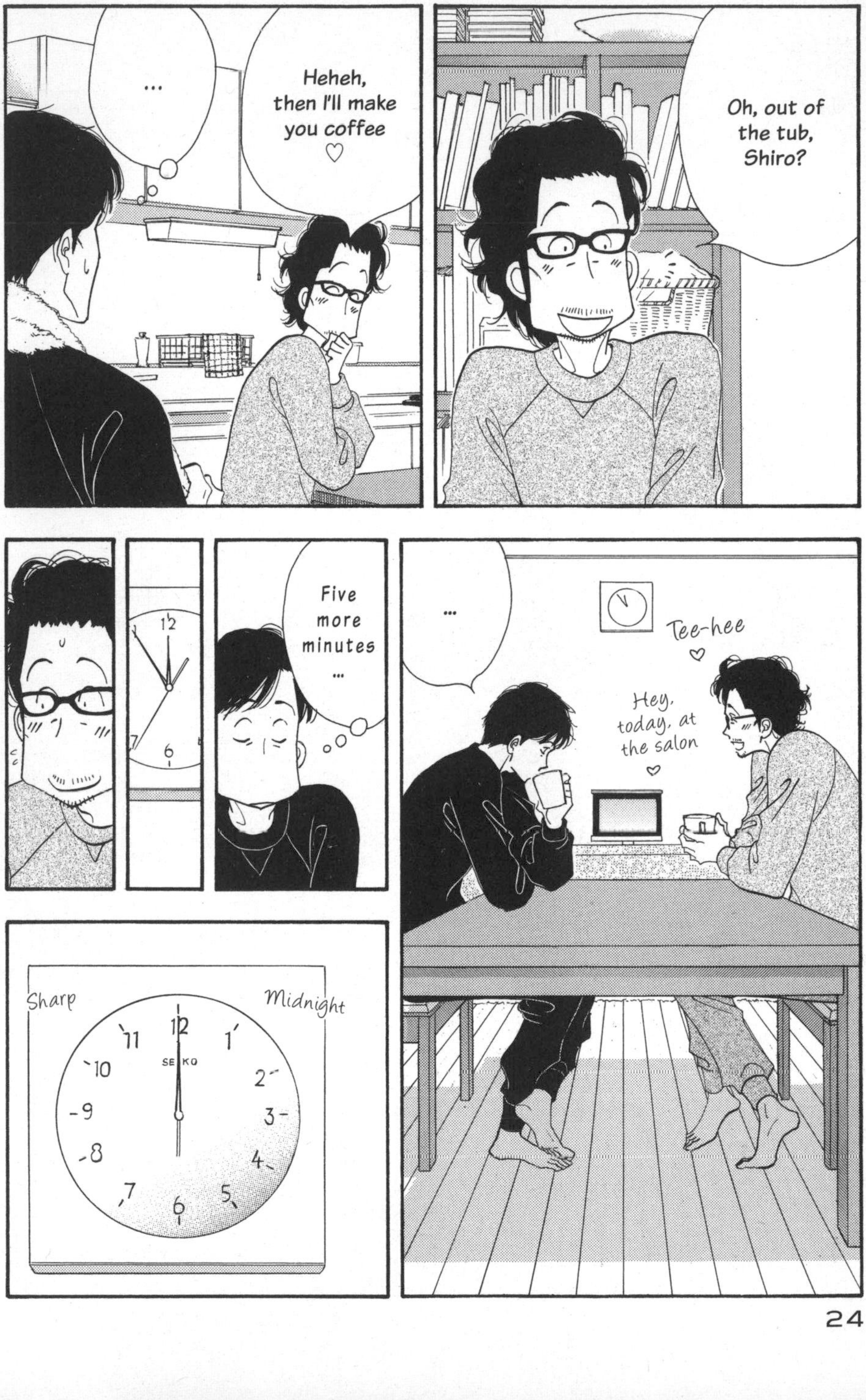

Oh, out of the tub, Shiro?
Heheh, then I'll make you coffee ♡
...
Tee-hee ♡
Hey, today, at the salon ♡
...
Five more minutes ...
Midnight
Sharp

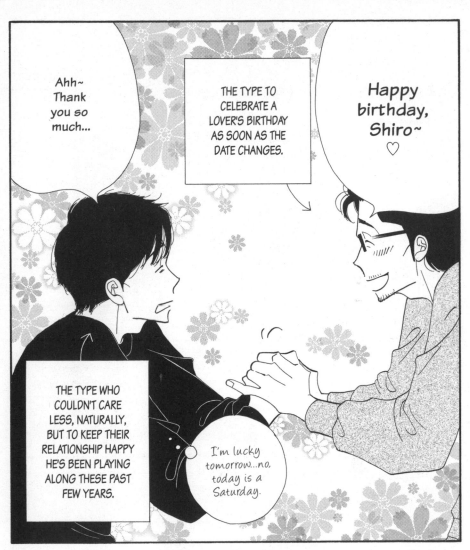

Happy birthday, Shiro~ ♡
THE TYPE TO CELEBRATE A LOVER'S BIRTHDAY AS SOON AS THE DATE CHANGES.
Ahh~ Thank you so much...
THE TYPE WHO COULDN'T CARE LESS, NATURALLY, BUT TO KEEP THEIR RELATIONSHIP HAPPY HE'S BEEN PLAYING ALONG THESE PAST FEW YEARS.
I'm lucky tomorrow...no, today is a Saturday.

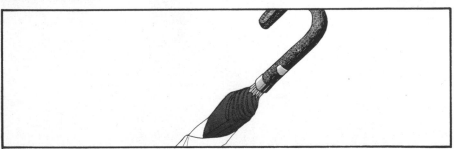

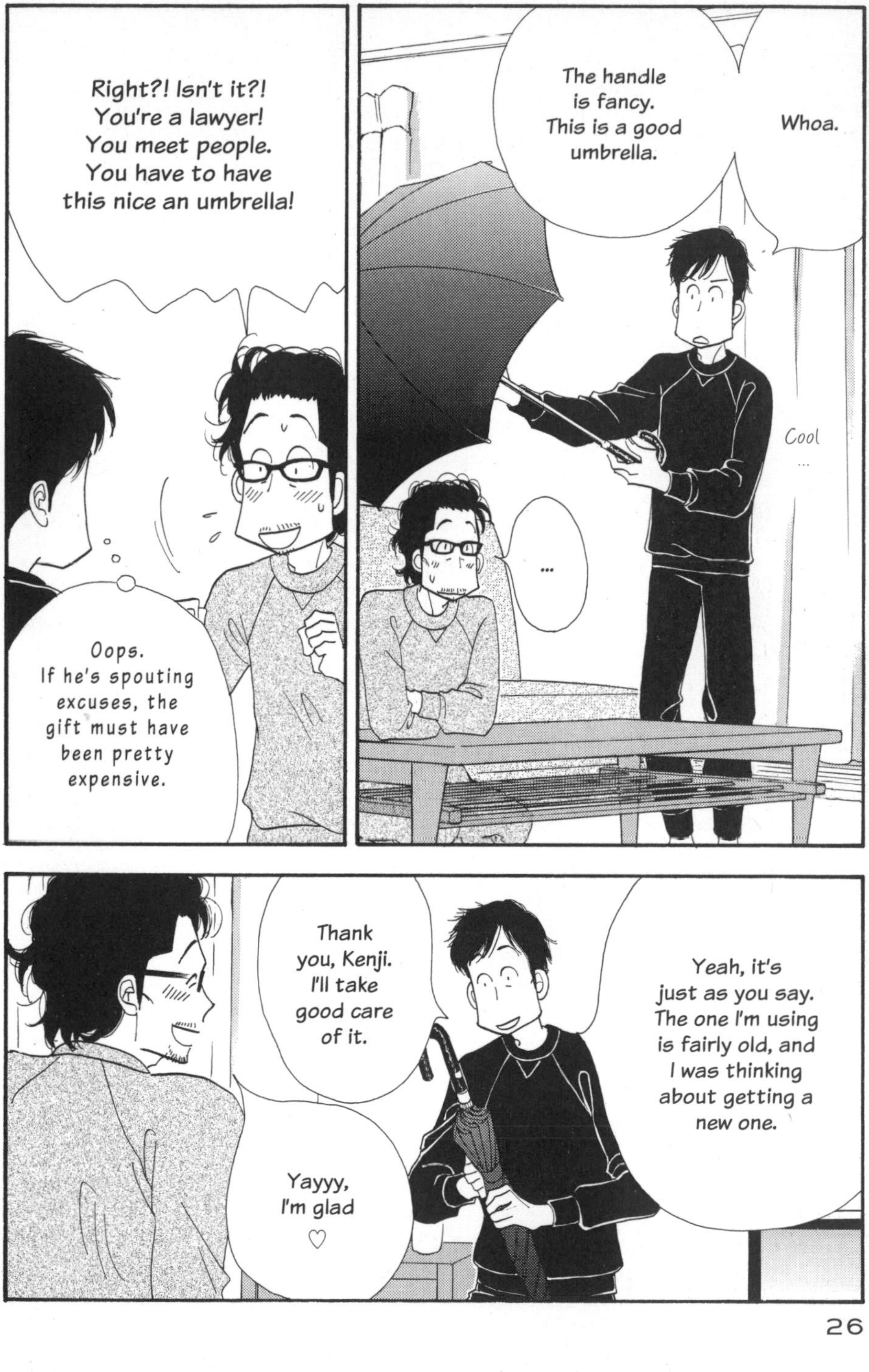
Whoa.
The handle is fancy. This is a good umbrella.
Cool ...
...
Right?! Isn't it?! You're a lawyer! You meet people. You have to have this nice an umbrella!
Oops. If he's spouting excuses, the gift must have been pretty expensive.
Yeah, it's just as you say. The one I'm using is fairly old, and I was thinking about getting a new one.
Thank you, Kenji. I'll take good care of it.
Yayyy, I'm glad ♡

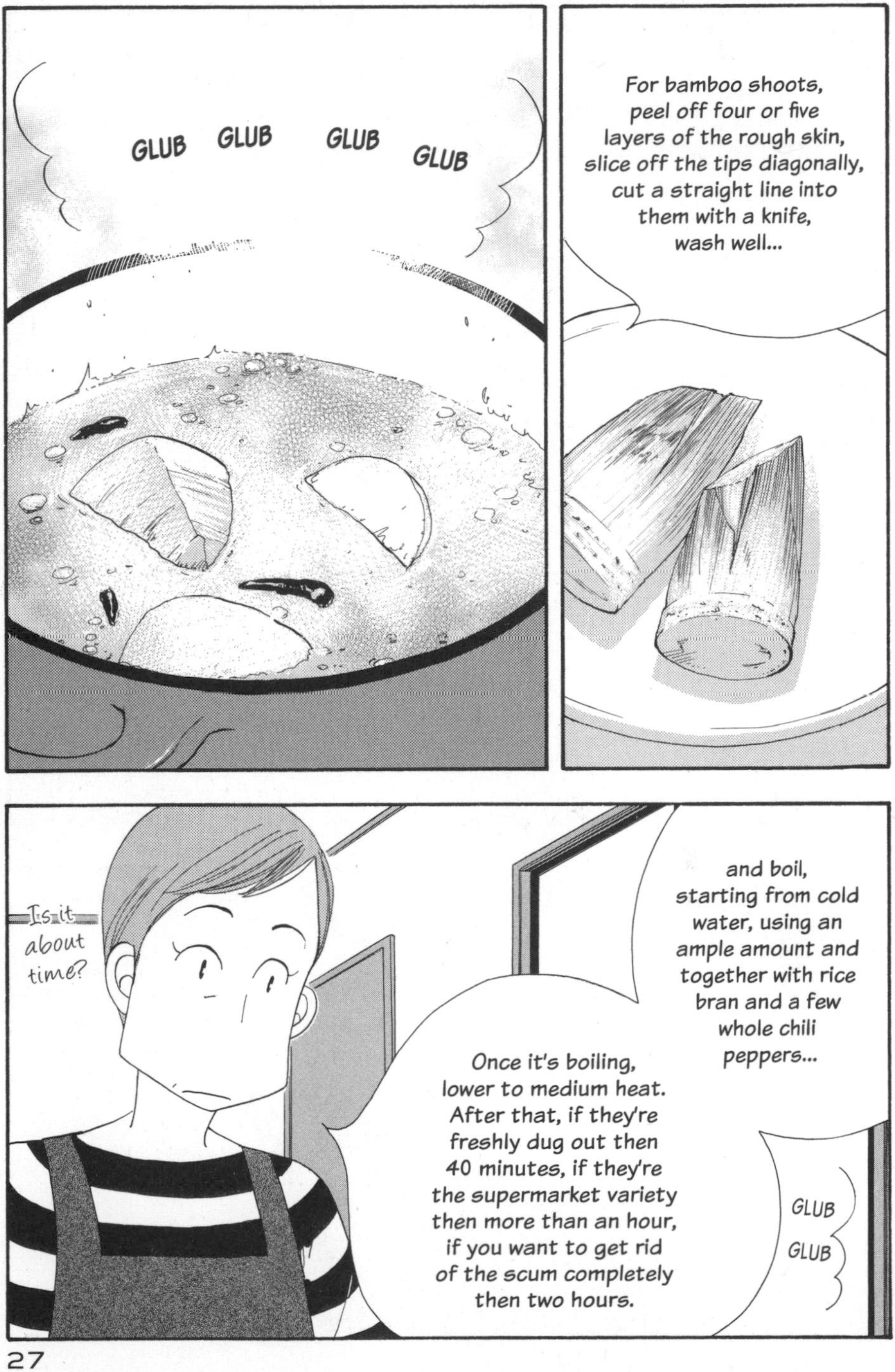
For bamboo shoots, peel off four or five layers of the rough skin, slice off the tips diagonally, cut a straight line into them with a knife, wash well...
GLUB GLUB GLUB GLUB
and boil, starting from cold water, using an ample amount and together with rice bran and a few whole chili peppers...
Once it's boiling, lower to medium heat. After that, if they're freshly dug out then 40 minutes, if they're the supermarket variety then more than an hour, if you want to get rid of the scum completely then two hours.
GLUB GLUB
Is it about time?

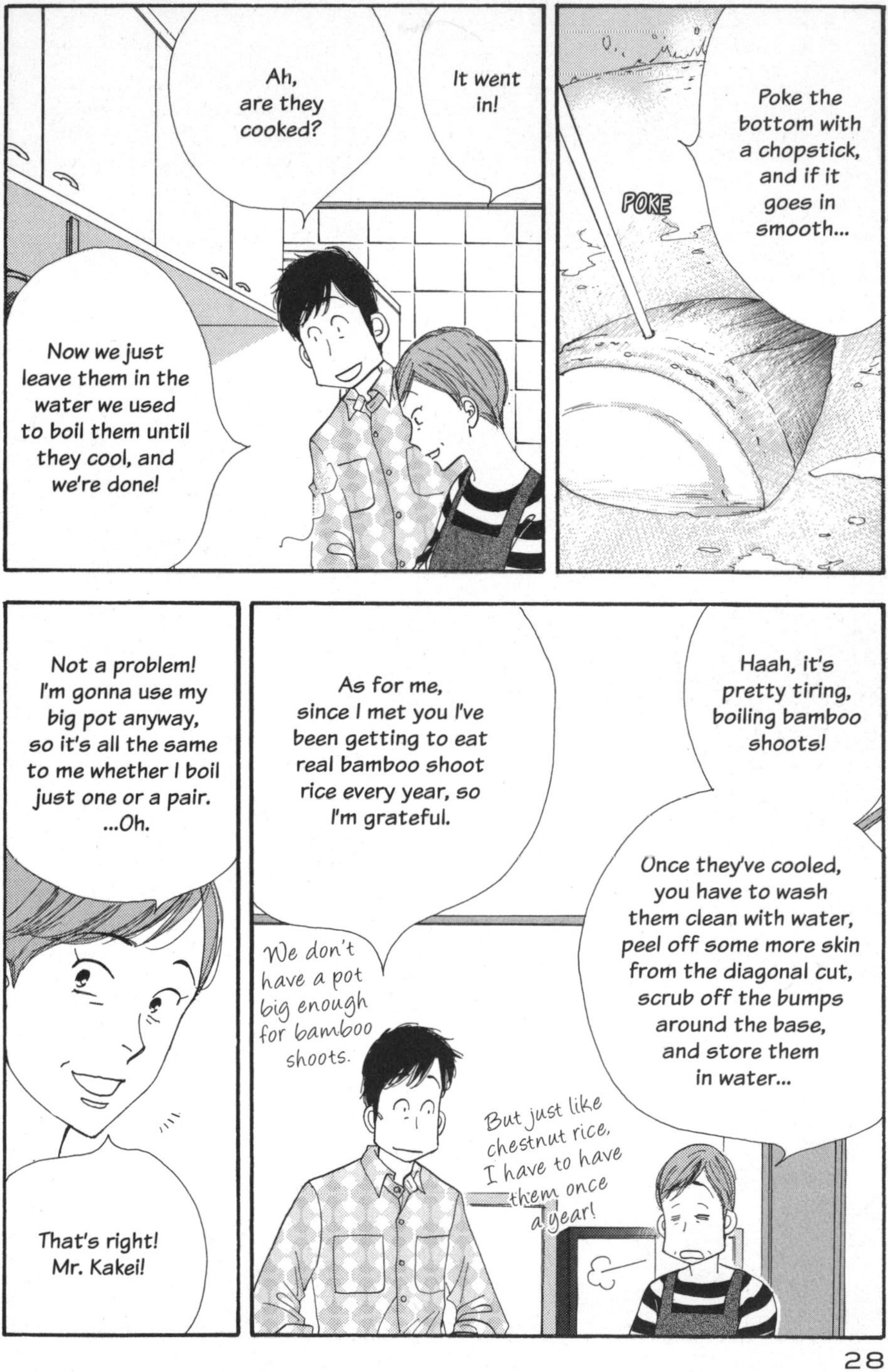
Poke the bottom with a chopstick, and if it goes in smooth...
POKE
It went in!
Ah, are they cooked?
Now we just leave them in the water we used to boil them until they cool, and we're done!
Haah, it's pretty tiring, boiling bamboo shoots!
Once they've cooled, you have to wash them clean with water, peel off some more skin from the diagonal cut, scrub off the bumps around the base, and store them in water...
As for me, since I met you I've been getting to eat real bamboo shoot rice every year, so I'm grateful.
We don't have a pot big enough for bamboo shoots.
But just like chestnut rice, I have to have them once a year!
Not a problem! I'm gonna use my big pot anyway, so it's all the same to me whether I boil just one or a pair. ...Oh.
That's right! Mr. Kakei!

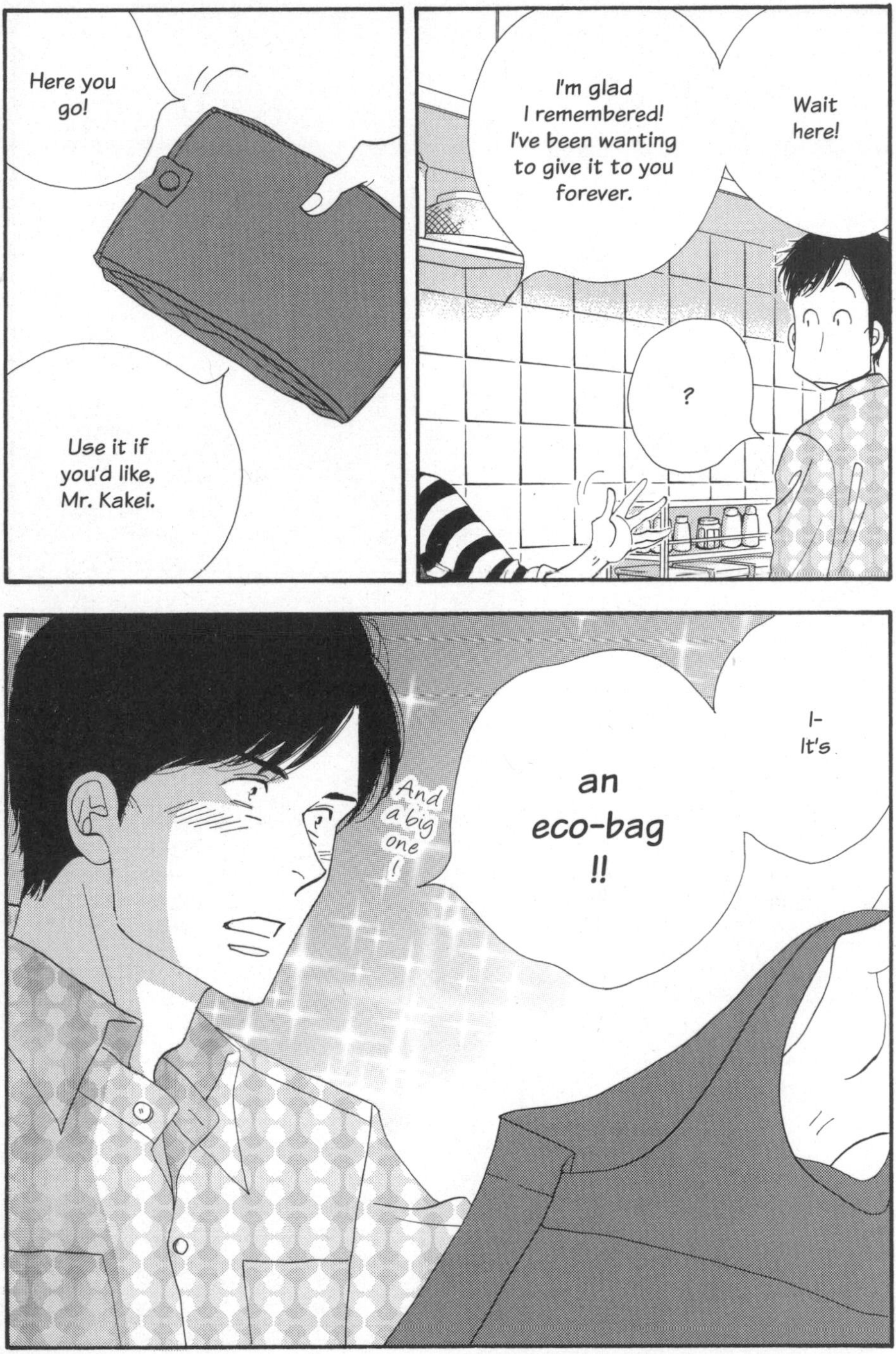
Wait here!
I'm glad I remembered! I've been wanting to give it to you forever.
?
Here you go!
Use it if you'd like, Mr. Kakei.
I- It's an eco-bag!!
And a big one!

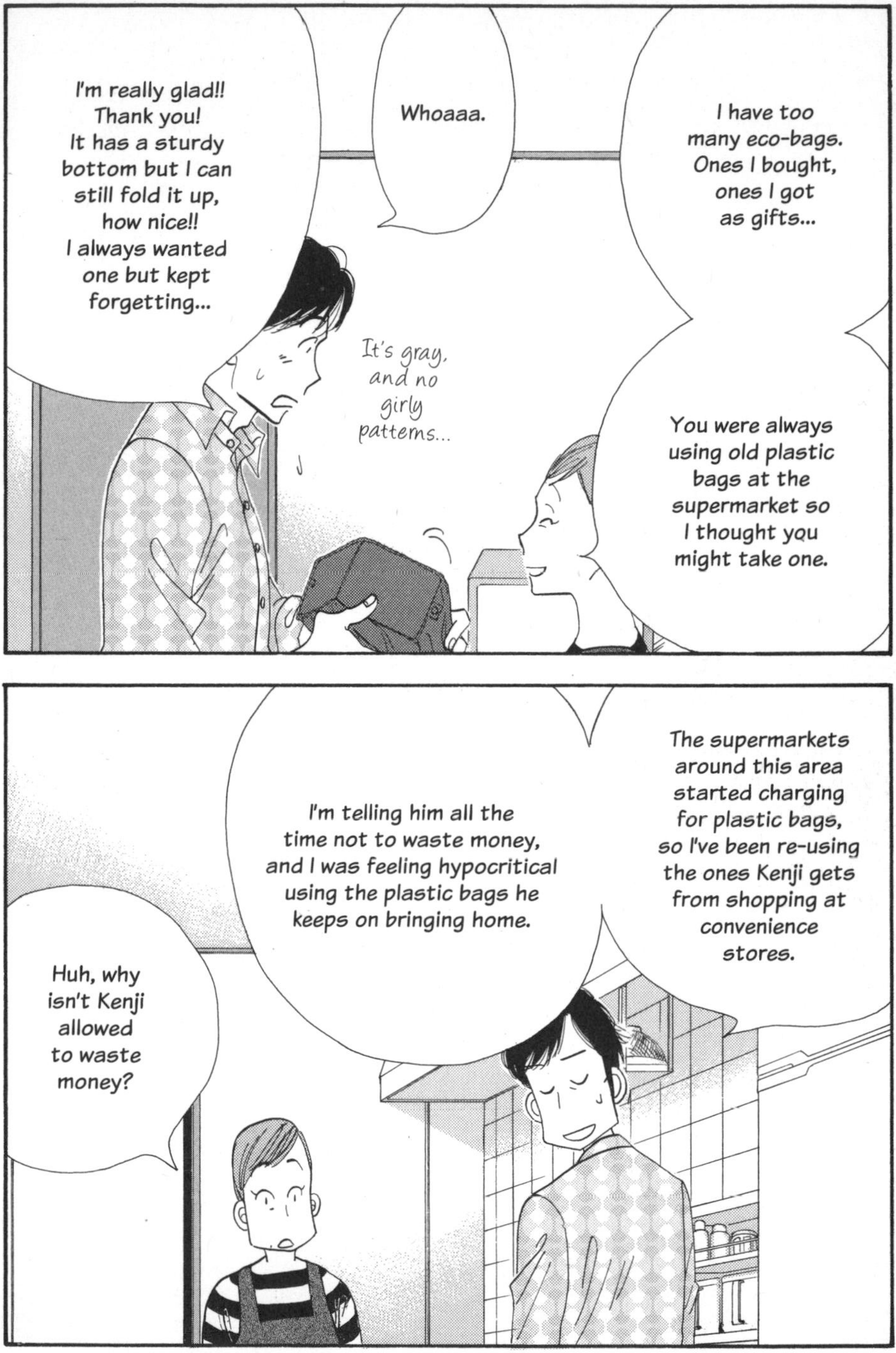
I have too many eco-bags. Ones I bought, ones I got as gifts...
You were always using old plastic bags at the supermarket so I thought you might take one.
Whoaaa.
It's gray, and no girly patterns...
I'm really glad!! Thank you! It has a sturdy bottom but I can still fold it up, how nice!! I always wanted one but kept forgetting...
The supermarkets around this area started charging for plastic bags, so I've been re-using the ones Kenji gets from shopping at convenience stores.
I'm telling him all the time not to waste money, and I was feeling hypocritical using the plastic bags he keeps on bringing home.
Huh, why isn't Kenji allowed to waste money?

Hear me out, Kayoko!
He has no plan whatsover to start his own shop, I mean, he has no interest in money to begin with, and I doubt he ever saved a penny in his life!
So at least now when he's paying only half the rent and sharing living expenses with me, I want him to save a little money...
...
Um, Mr. Kakei.
Could it be that
you're always so frugal because you want to have enough saved up for Kenji too when you retire?

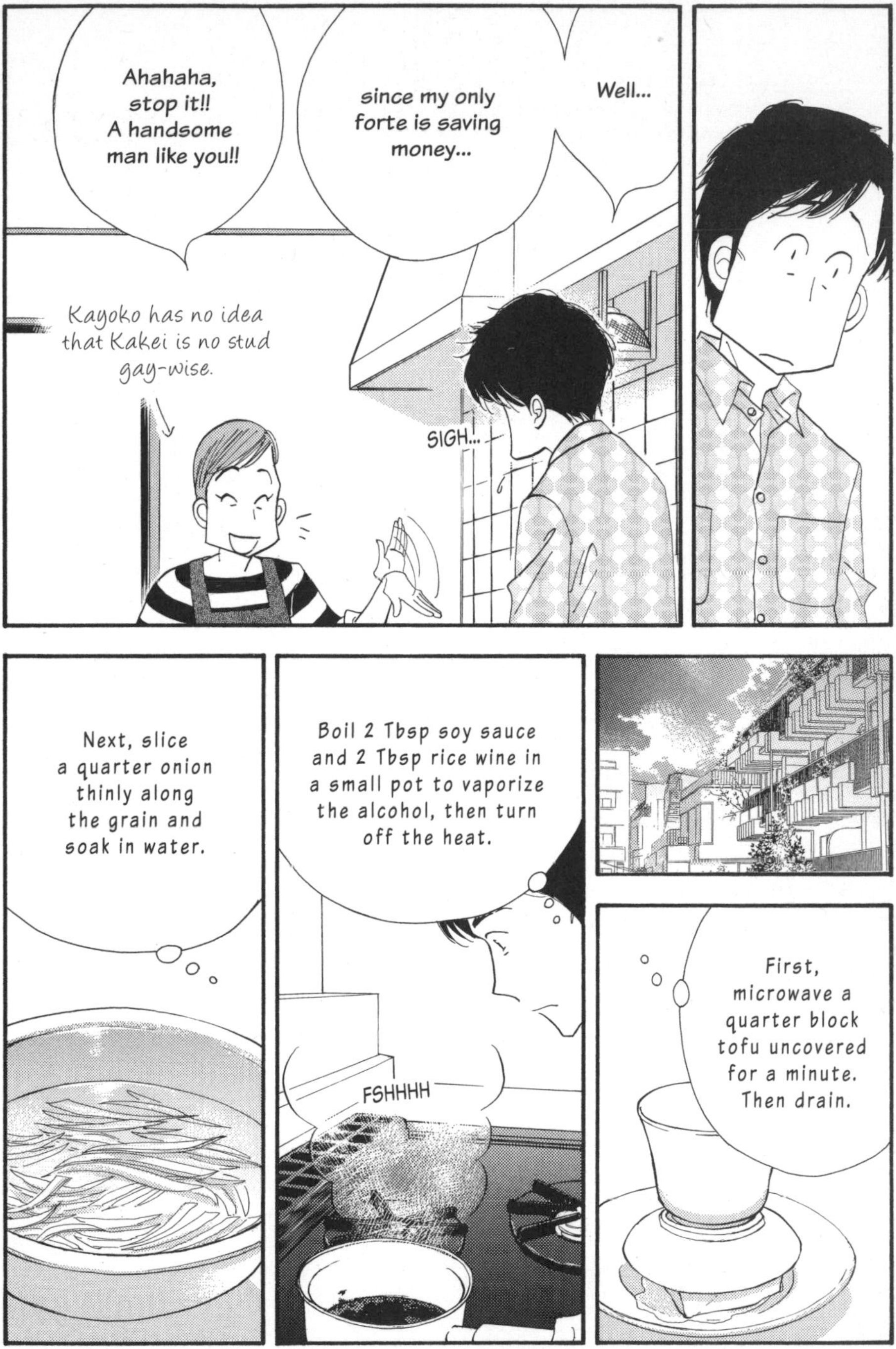
Well...
since my only forte is saving money...
SIGH...
Ahahaha, stop it!! A handsome man like you!!
Kayoko has no idea that Kakei is no stud gay-wise.
First, microwave a quarter block tofu uncovered for a minute. Then drain.
Boil 2 Tbsp soy sauce and 2 Tbsp rice wine in a small pot to vaporize the alcohol, then turn off the heat.
FSHHHH
Next, slice a quarter onion thinly along the grain and soak in water.

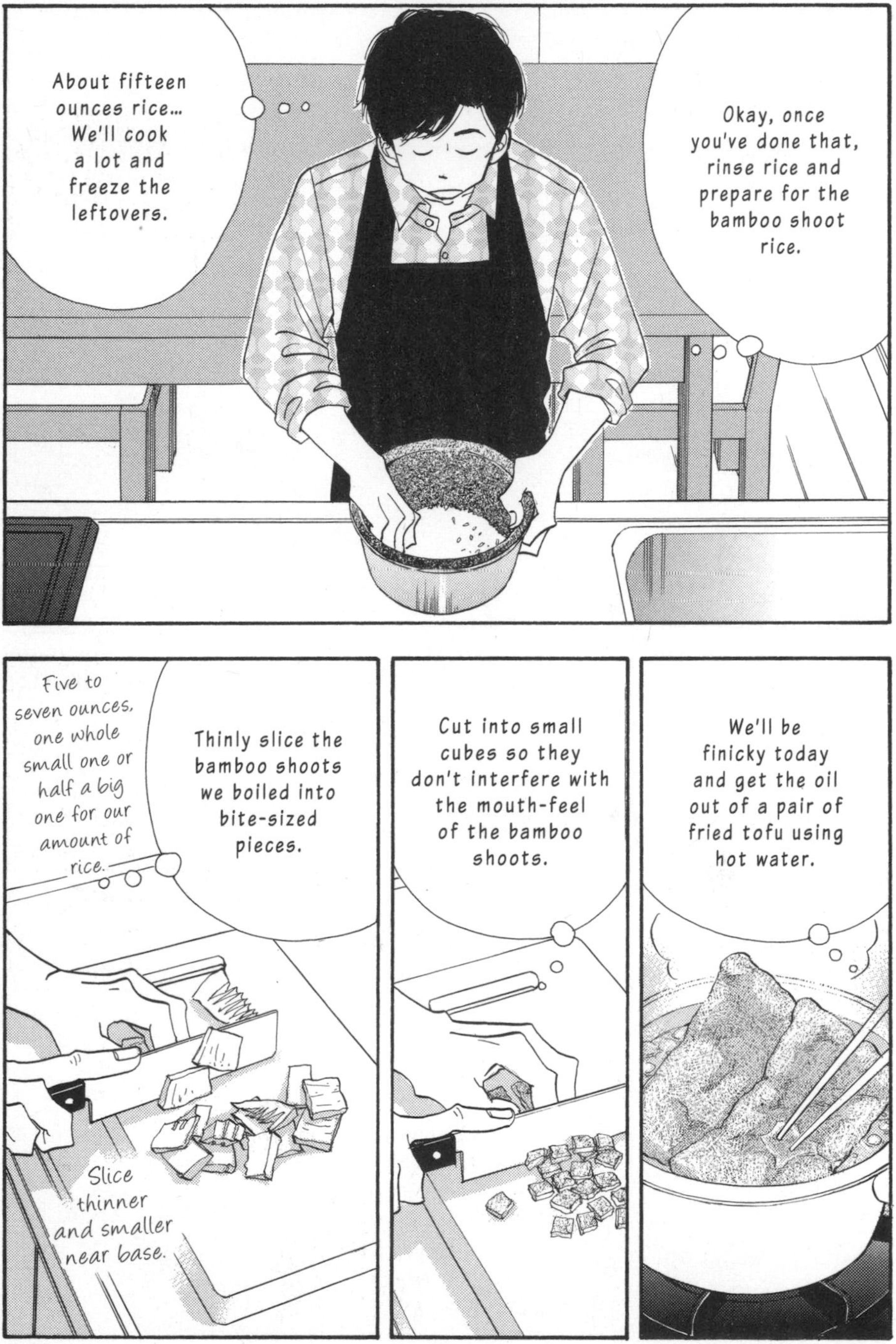
Okay, once you've done that, rinse rice and prepare for the bamboo shoot rice.
About fifteen ounces rice... We'll cook a lot and freeze the leftovers.
We'll be finicky today and get the oil out of a pair of fried tofu using hot water.
Cut into small cubes so they don't interfere with the mouth-feel of the bamboo shoots.
Thinly slice the bamboo shoots we boiled into bite-sized pieces.
Five to seven ounces, one whole small one or half a big one for our amount of rice.
Slice thinner and smaller near base.

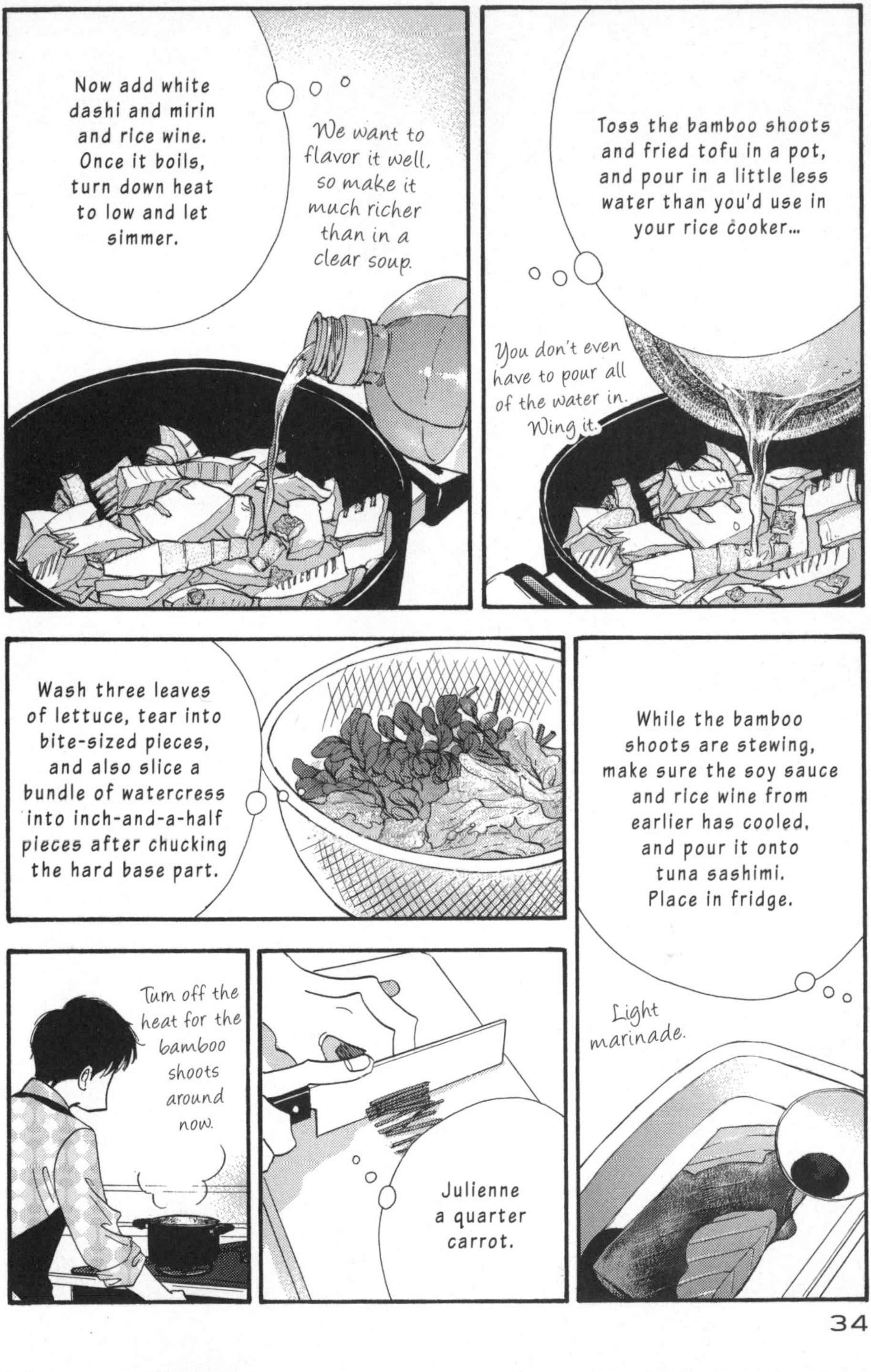
Toss the bamboo shoots and fried tofu in a pot, and pour in a little less water than you'd use in your rice cooker...
You don't even have to pour all of the water in. Wing it.
Now add white dashi and mirin and rice wine. Once it boils, turn down heat to low and let simmer.
We want to flavor it well, so make it much richer than in a clear soup.
While the bamboo shoots are stewing, make sure the soy sauce and rice wine from earlier has cooled, and pour it onto tuna sashimi. Place in fridge.
Light marinade.
Wash three leaves of lettuce, tear into bite-sized pieces, and also slice a bundle of watercress into inch-and-a-half pieces after chucking the hard base part.
Julienne a quarter carrot.
Turn off the heat for the bamboo shoots around now.

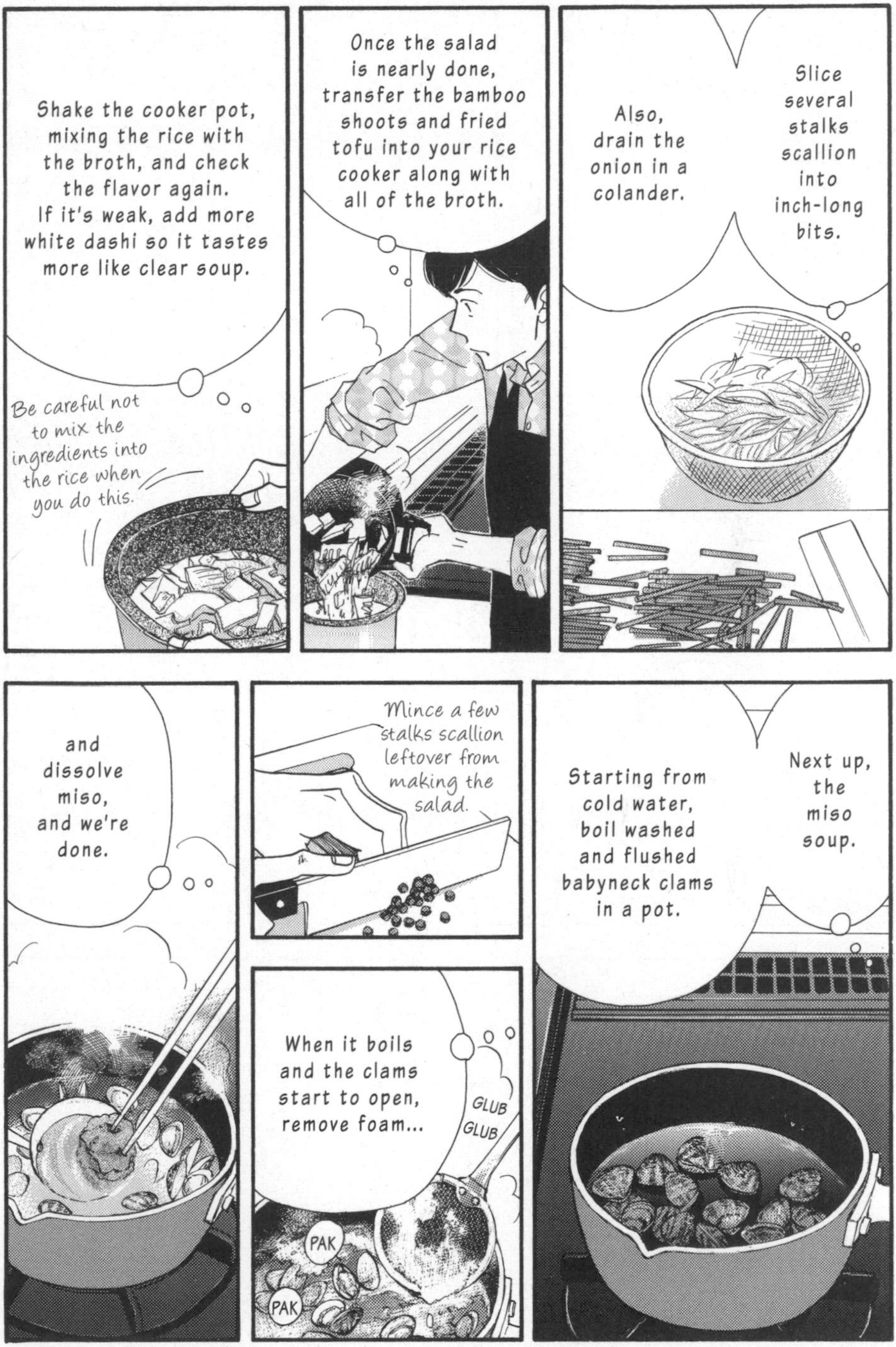
Slice several stalks scallion into inch-long bits.
Also, drain the onion in a colander.
Once the salad is nearly done, transfer the bamboo shoots and fried tofu into your rice cooker along with all of the broth.
Shake the cooker pot, mixing the rice with the broth, and check the flavor again. If it's weak, add more white dashi so it tastes more like clear soup.
Be careful not to mix the ingredients into the rice when you do this.
Next up, the miso soup.
Starting from cold water, boil washed and flushed babyneck clams in a pot.
Mince a few stalks scallion leftover from making the salad.
When it boils and the clams start to open, remove foam...
GLUB
GLUB
PAK
PAK
and dissolve miso, and we're done.

See Vol 2. #11 for how to boil them.

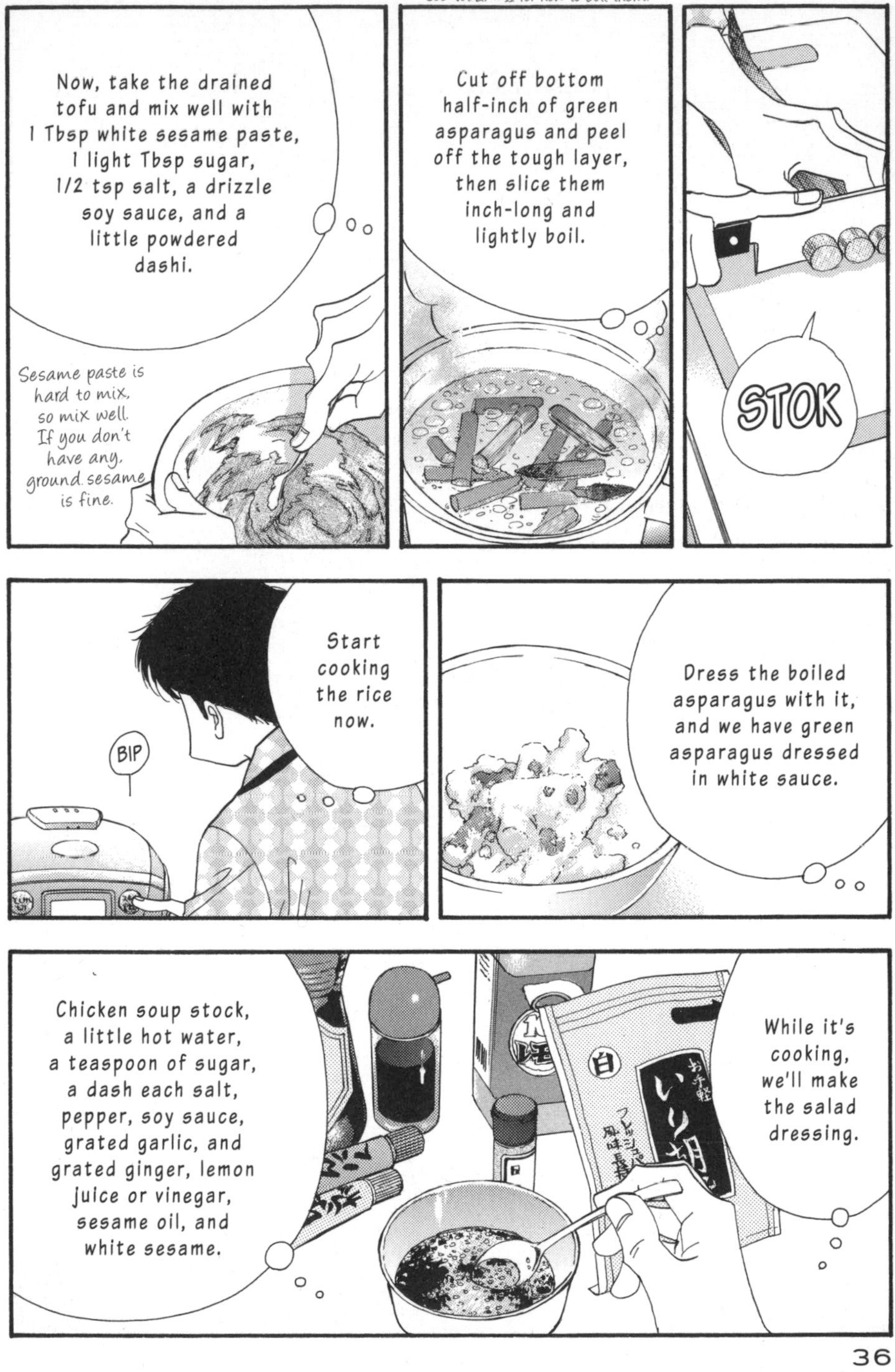

STOK
Cut off bottom half-inch of green asparagus and peel off the tough layer, then slice them inch-long and lightly boil.
Now, take the drained tofu and mix well with 1 Tbsp white sesame paste, 1 light Tbsp sugar, 1/2 tsp salt, a drizzle soy sauce, and a little powdered dashi.
Sesame paste is hard to mix, so mix well. If you don't have any, ground sesame is fine.
Dress the boiled asparagus with it, and we have green asparagus dressed in white sauce.
Start cooking the rice now.
BIP
While it's cooking, we'll make the salad dressing.
Chicken soup stock, a little hot water, a teaspoon of sugar, a dash each salt, pepper, soy sauce, grated garlic, and grated ginger, lemon juice or vinegar, sesame oil, and white sesame.

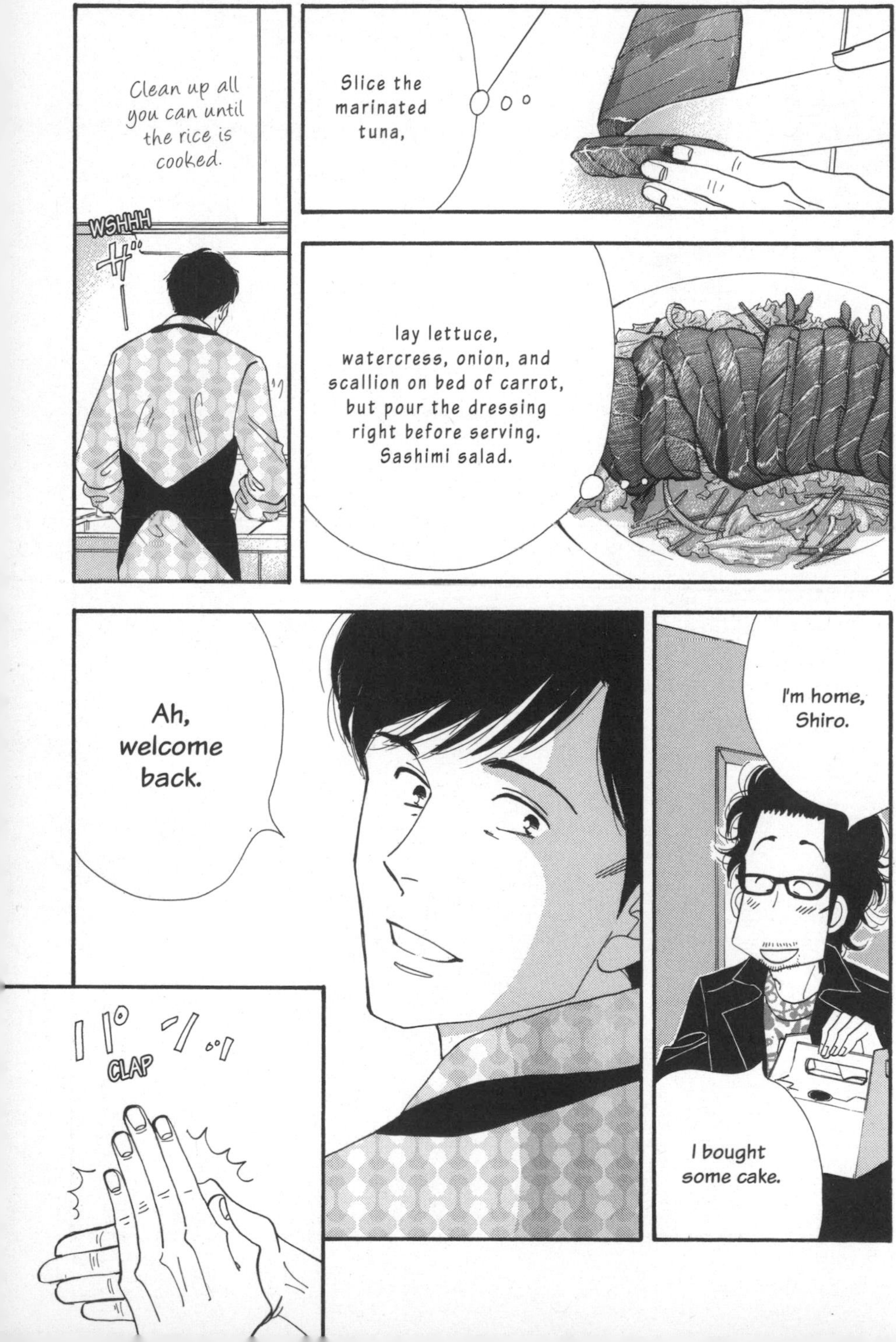
Slice the marinated tuna,
lay lettuce, watercress, onion, and scallion on bed of carrot, but pour the dressing right before serving. Sashimi salad.
Clean up all you can until the rice is cooked.
WSHHH
I'm home, Shiro.
I bought some cake.
Ah, welcome back.
CLAP

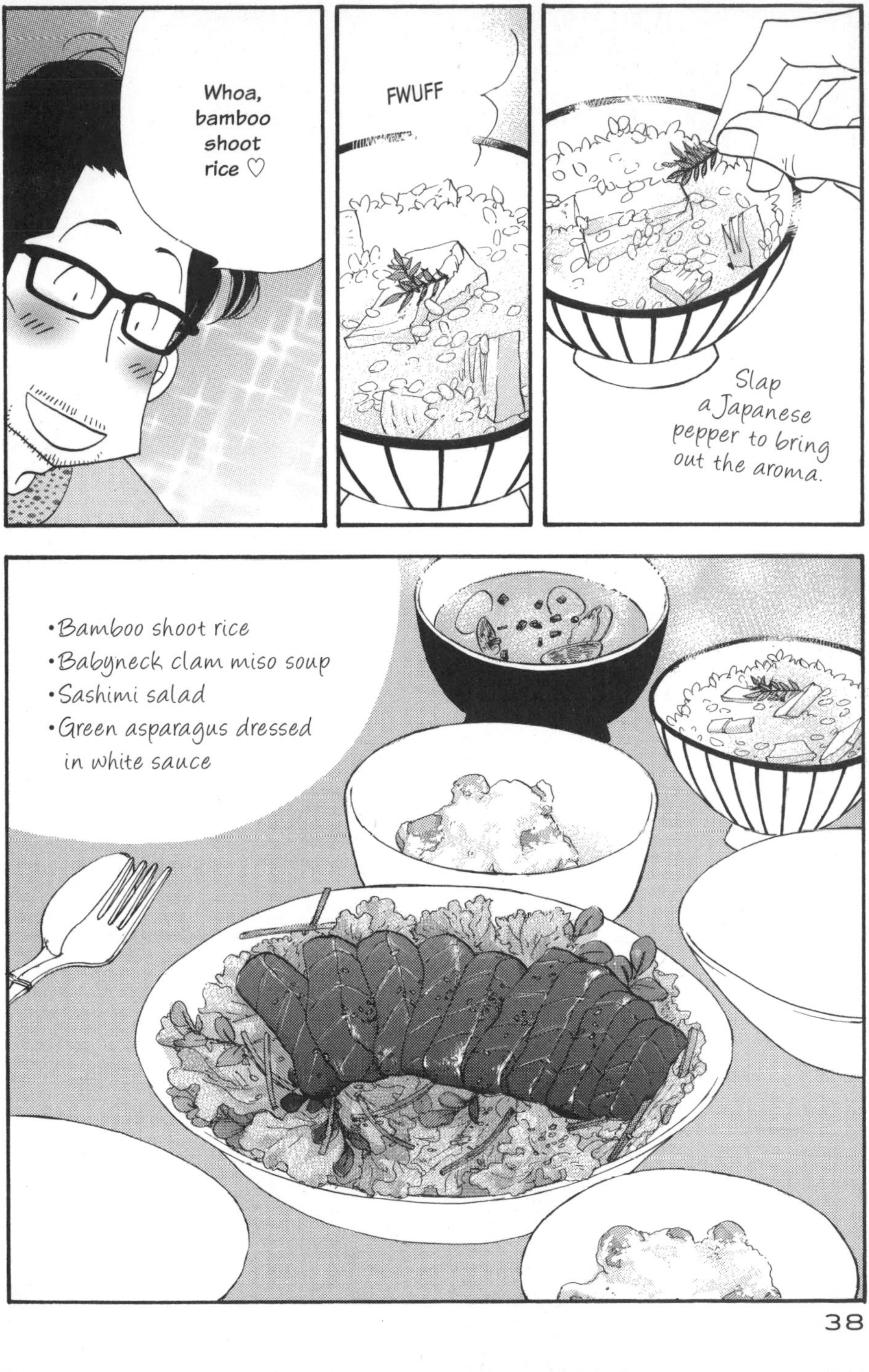
Slap a Japanese pepper to bring out the aroma.
FWUFF
Whoa, bamboo shoot rice ♡
•Bamboo shoot rice
•Babyneck clam miso soup
•Sashimi salad
•Green asparagus dressed in white sauce

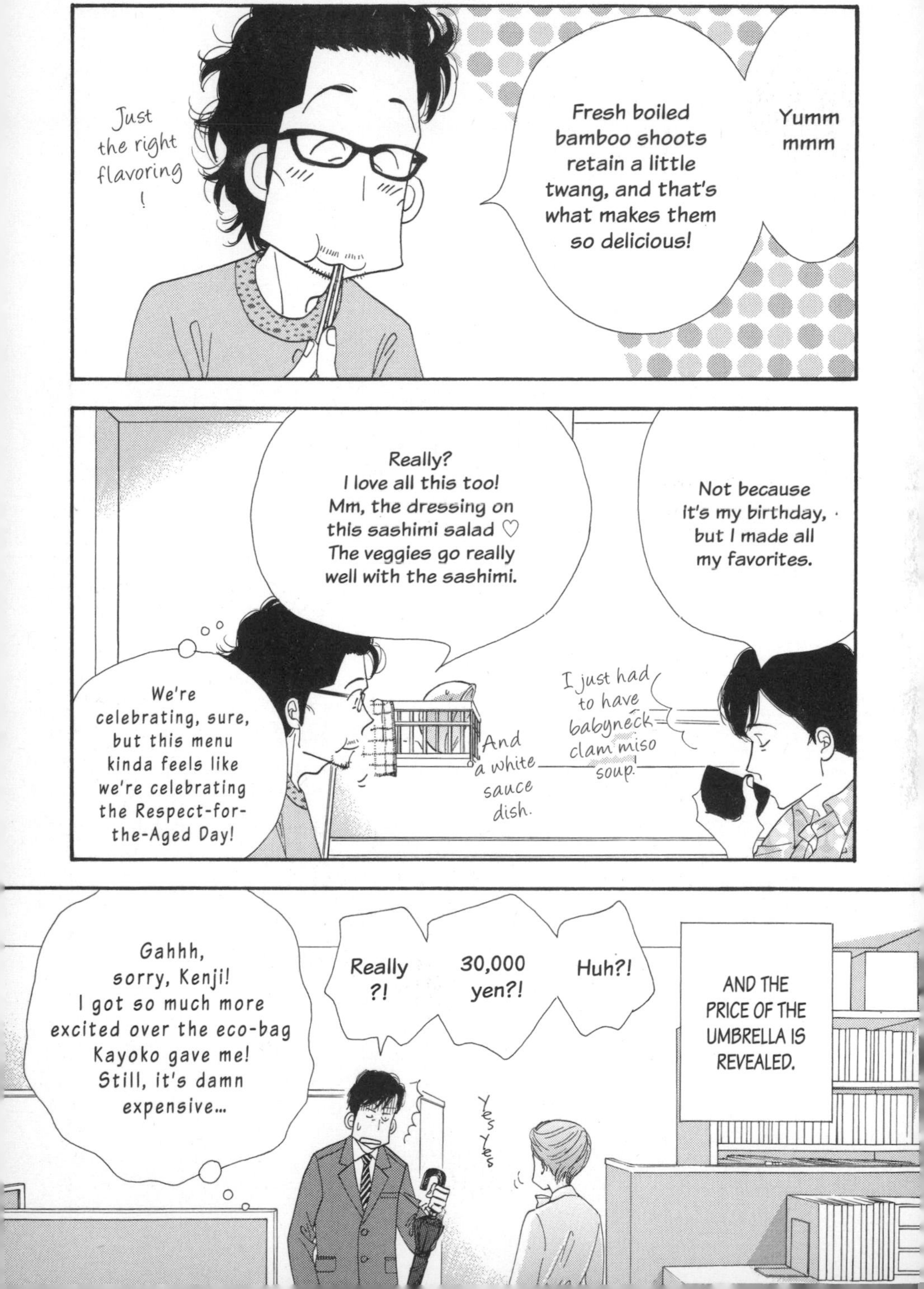
Yumm mmm
Fresh boiled bamboo shoots retain a little twang, and that's what makes them so delicious!
Just the right flavoring!
Not because it's my birthday, but I made all my favorites.
I just had to have babyneck clam miso soup.
And a white sauce dish.
Really? I love all this too! Mm, the dressing on this sashimi salad ♡ The veggies go really well with the sashimi.
We're celebrating, sure, but this menu kinda feels like we're celebrating the Respect-for-the-Aged Day!
AND THE PRICE OF THE UMBRELLA IS REVEALED.
Huh?!
30,000 yen?!
Really ?!
Yes Yes
Gahhh, sorry, Kenji! I got so much more excited over the eco-bag Kayoko gave me! Still, it's damn expensive...

Tuna or bonito is recommended
for the **sashimi salad.**
You could use light soy sauce
for the dressing, and if you don't
mind it looking brown, you could
use white-meat fish too.

カ

KAANN..GG
キィーン

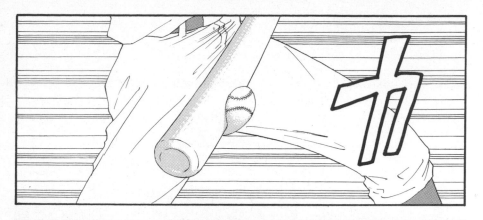

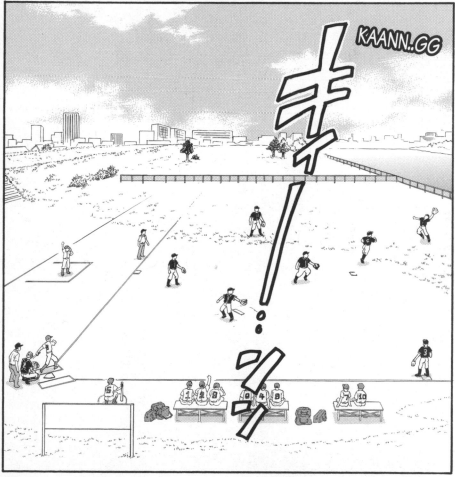

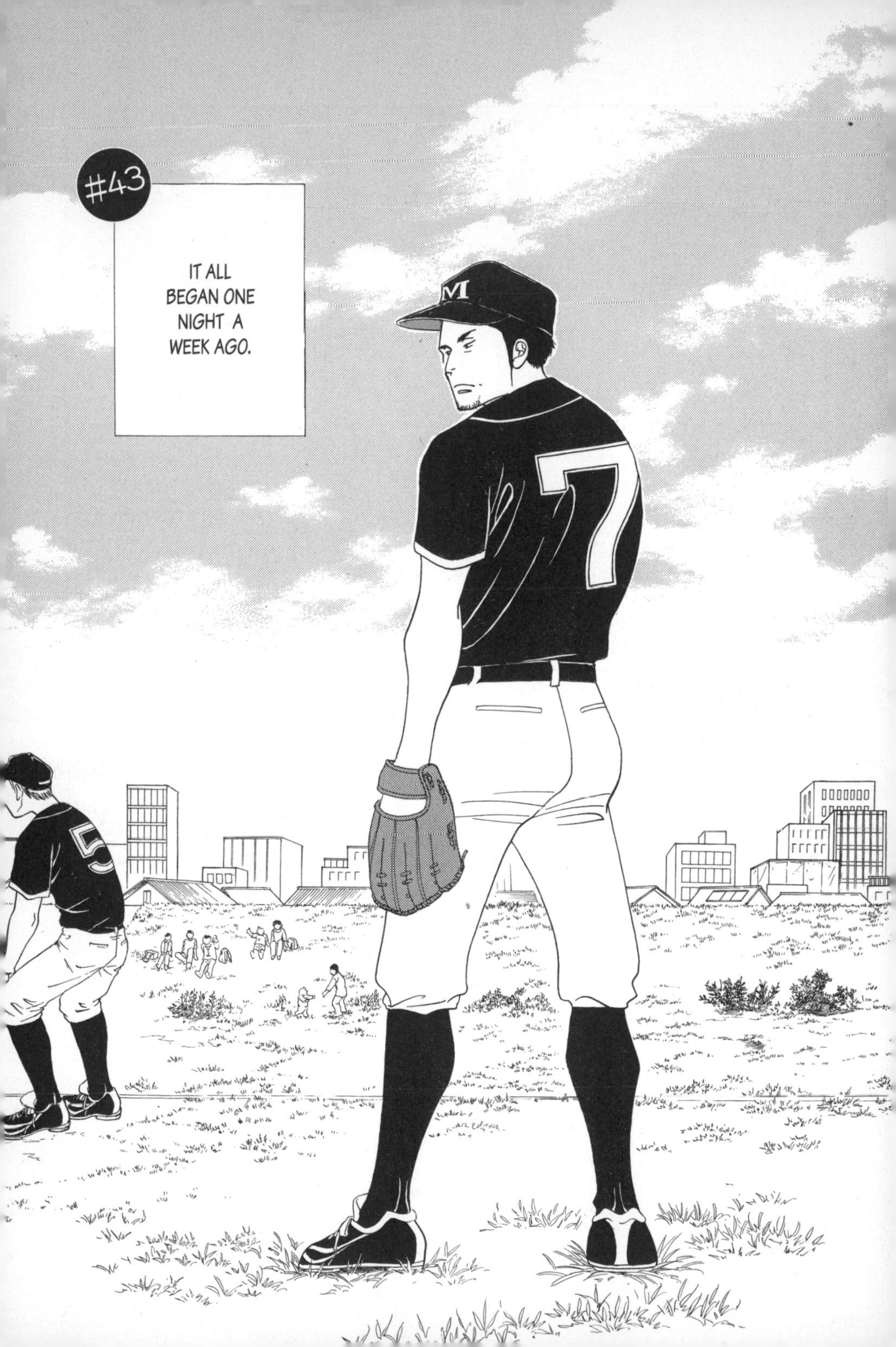
#43
IT ALL BEGAN ONE NIGHT A WEEK AGO.

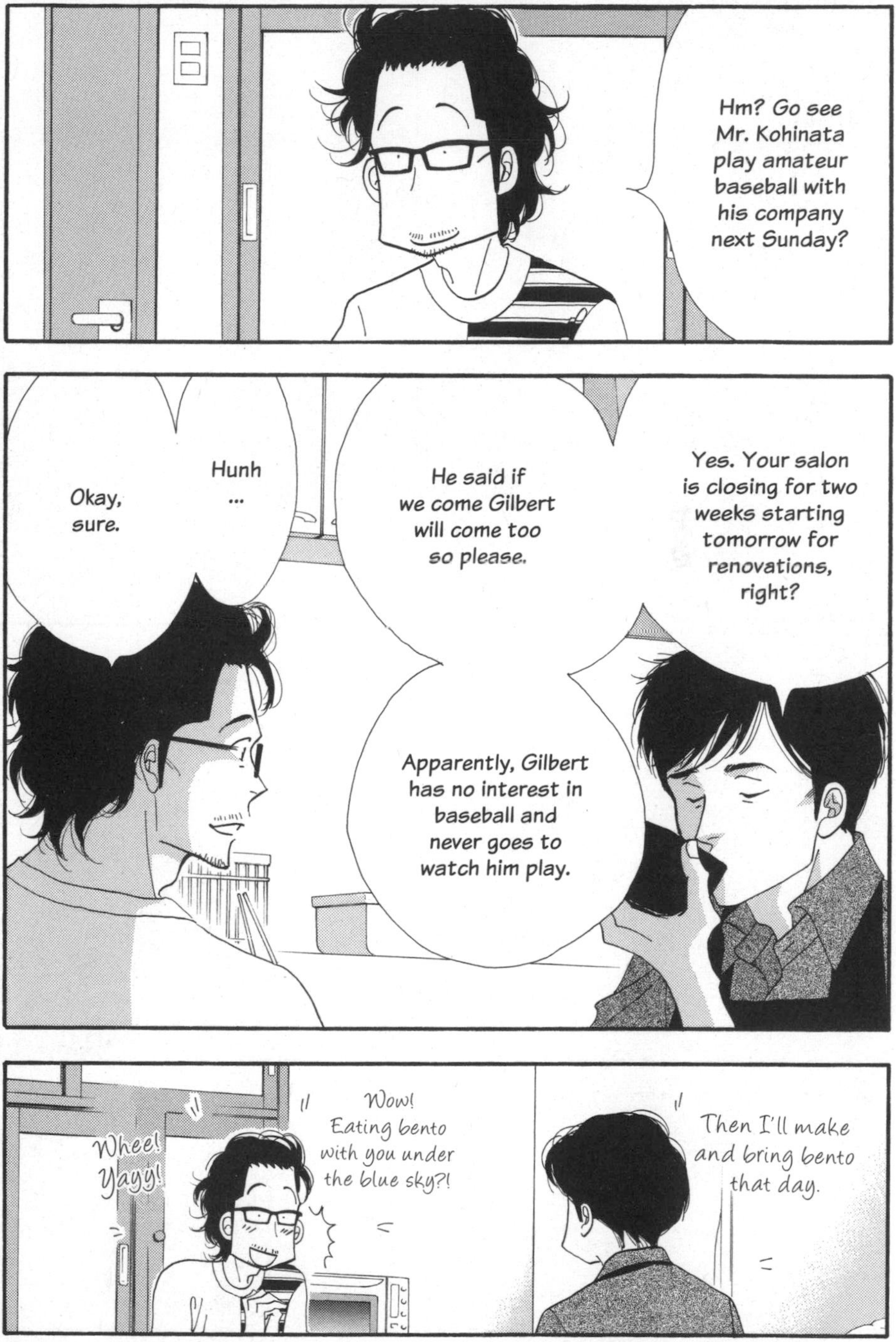
Hm? Go see Mr. Kohinata play amateur baseball with his company next Sunday?
Yes. Your salon is closing for two weeks starting tomorrow for renovations, right?
He said if we come Gilbert will come too so please.
Apparently, Gilbert has no interest in baseball and never goes to watch him play.
Hunh ...
Okay, sure.
Then I'll make and bring bento that day.
Wow! Eating bento with you under the blue sky?!
Whee! Yayy!

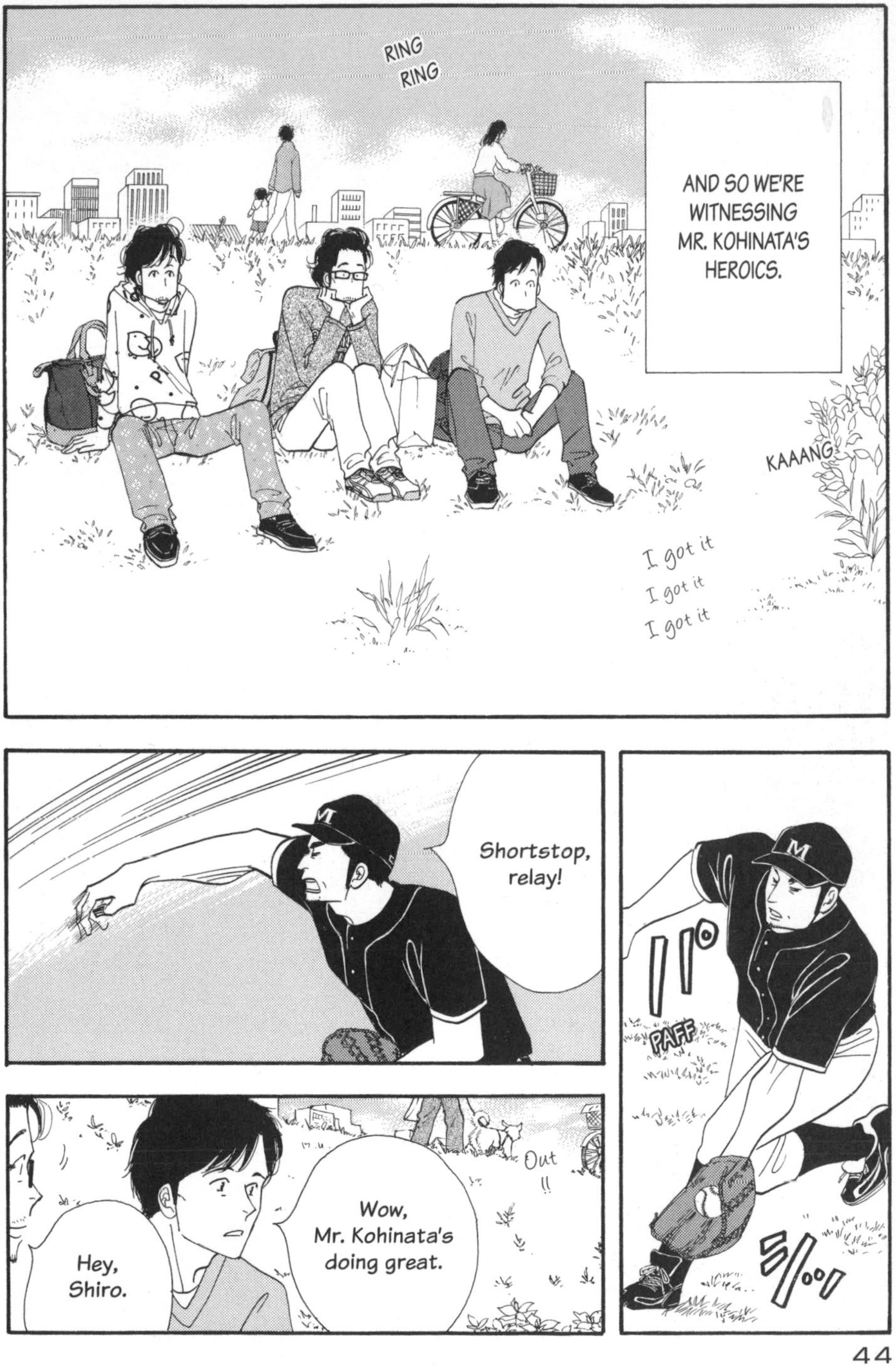
AND SO WE'RE WITNESSING MR. KOHINATA'S HEROICS.
RING RING
KAAANG
I got it
I got it
I got it
PAFF
Shortstop, relay!
Out !!
Wow, Mr. Kohinata's doing great.
Hey, Shiro.

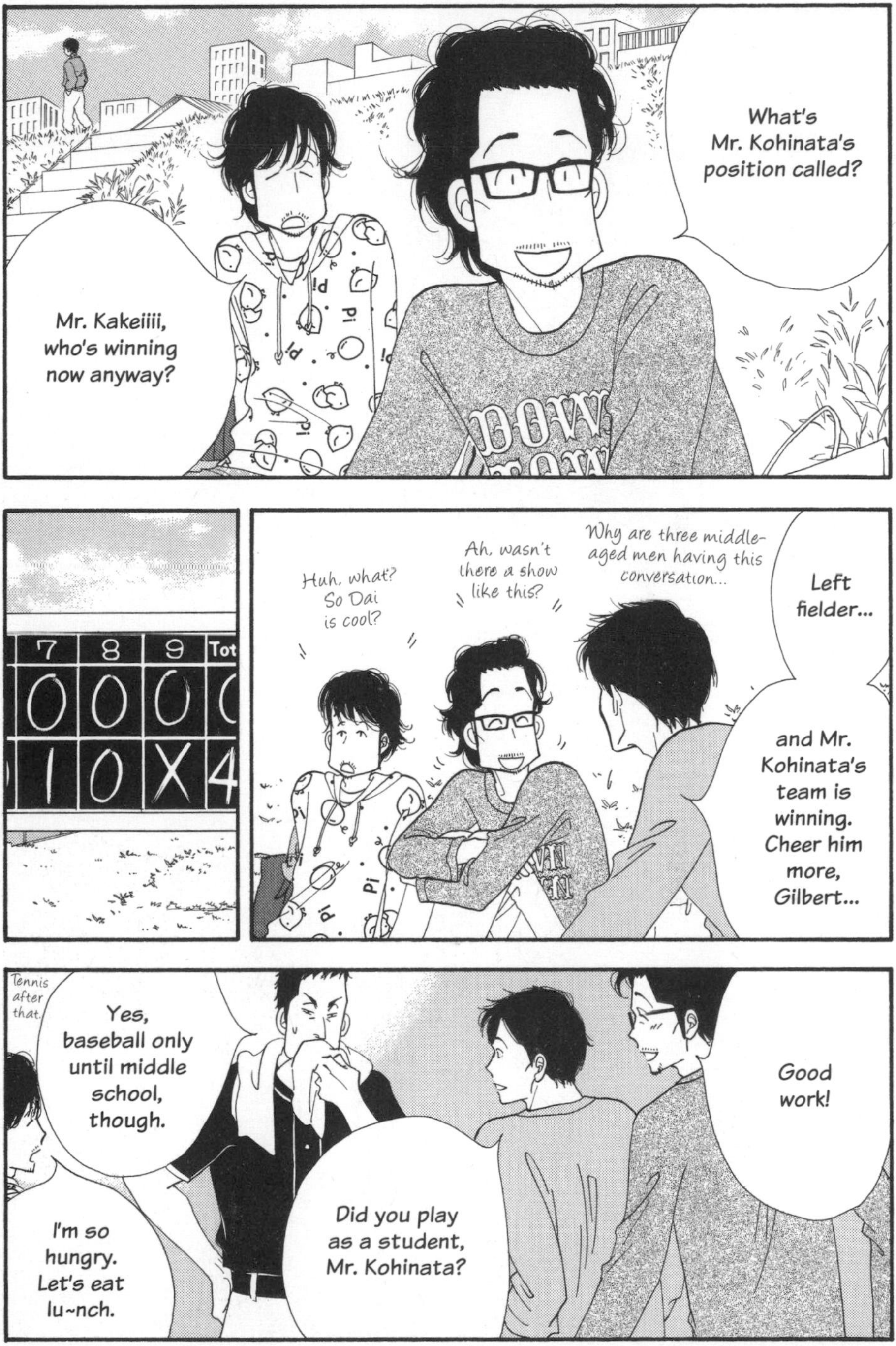
What's Mr. Kohinata's position called?
Mr. Kakeiiii, who's winning now anyway?
Left fielder...
and Mr. Kohinata's team is winning. Cheer him more, Gilbert...
Why are three middle-aged men having this conversation...
Ah, wasn't there a show like this?
Huh, what? So Dai is cool?
7 8 9 Tot
Good work!
Did you play as a student, Mr. Kohinata?
Yes, baseball only until middle school, though.
Tennis after that.
I'm so hungry. Let's eat lu~nch.

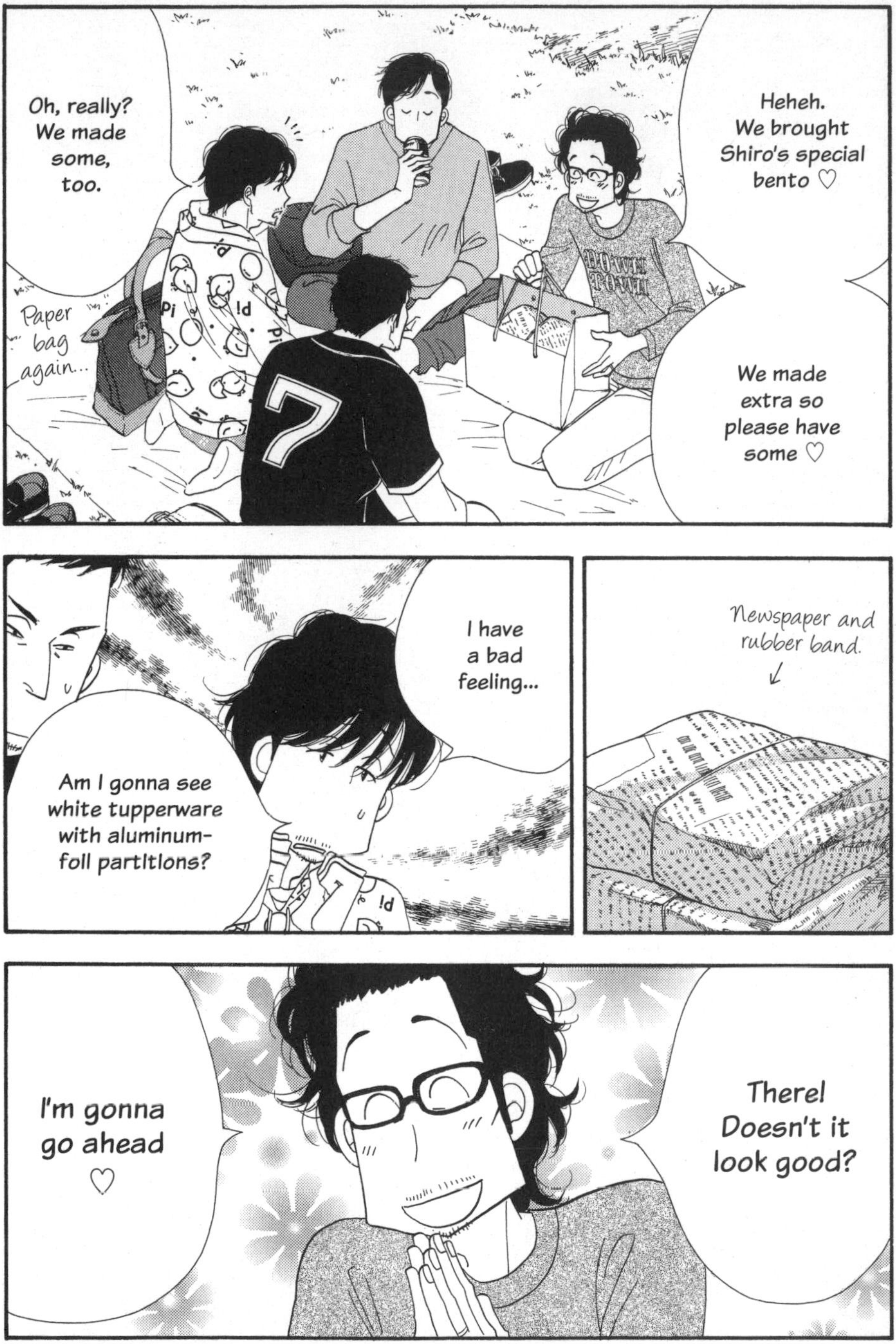
Heheh. We brought Shiro's special bento ♡
We made extra so please have some ♡
Oh, really? We made some, too.
Paper bag again...
Newspaper and rubber band.
I have a bad feeling...
Am I gonna see white tupperware with aluminum-foil partitions?
There! Doesn't it look good?
I'm gonna go ahead ♡

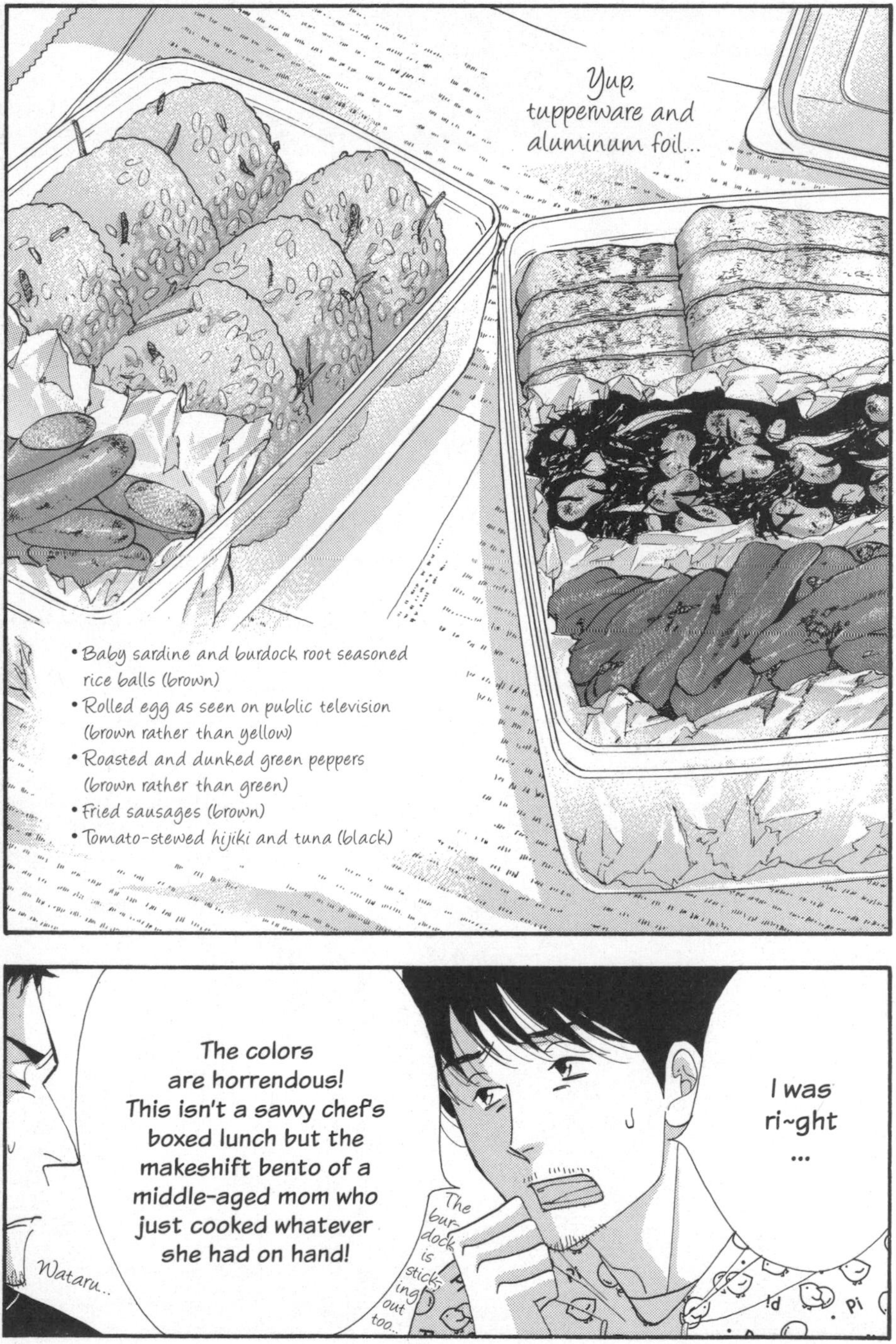
Yup, tupperware and aluminum foil...
• Baby sardine and burdock root seasoned rice balls (brown)
• Rolled egg as seen on public television (brown rather than yellow)
• Roasted and dunked green peppers (brown rather than green)
• Fried sausages (brown)
• Tomato-stewed hijiki and tuna (black)
I was ri~ght ...
The colors are horrendous! This isn't a savvy chef's boxed lunch but the makeshift bento of a middle-aged mom who just cooked whatever she had on hand!
The burdock is sticking out too...
Wataru..

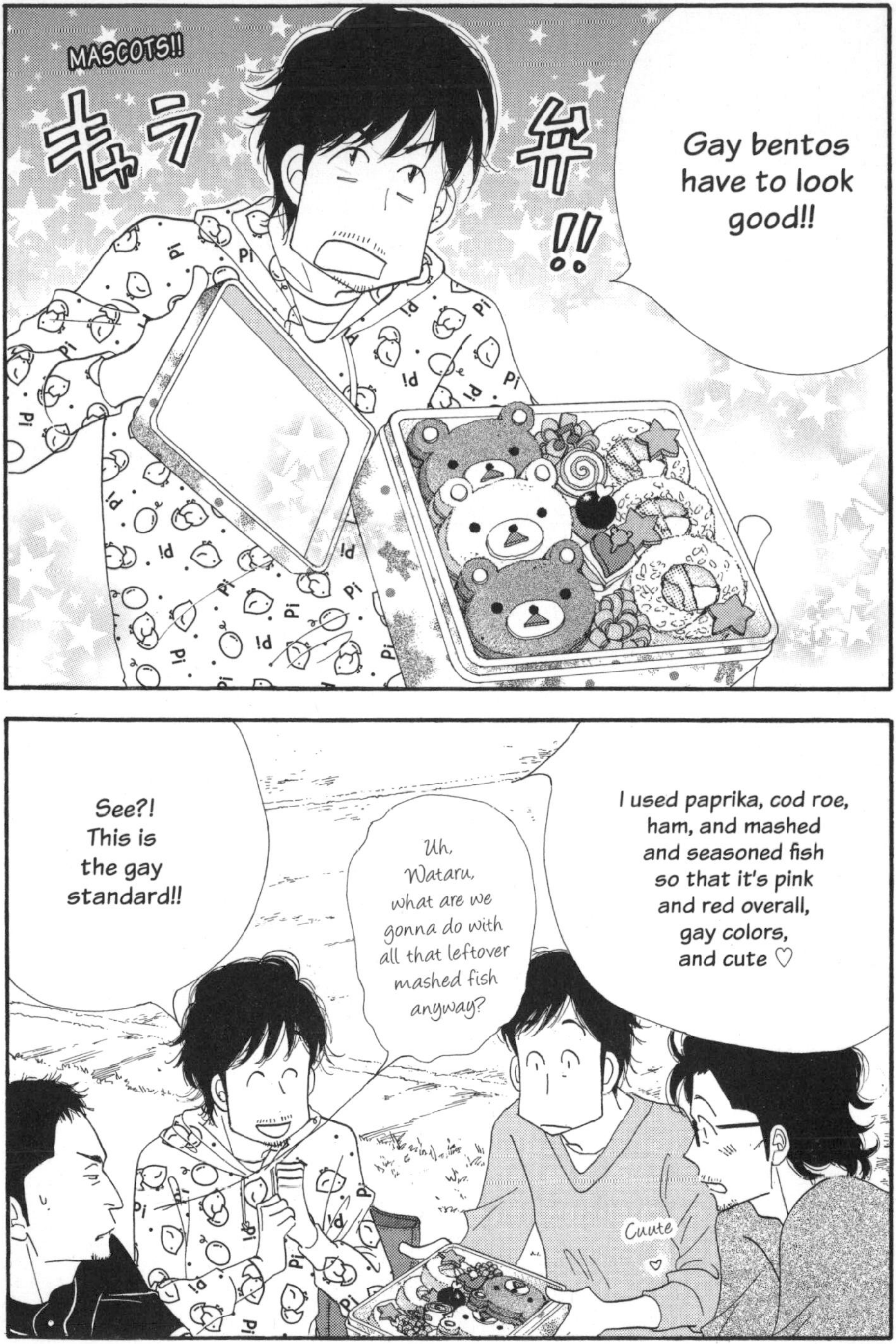
MASCOTS!!
キャラ弁!!
Gay bentos have to look good!!
I used paprika, cod roe, ham, and mashed and seasoned fish so that it's pink and red overall, gay colors, and cute ♡
See?! This is the gay standard!!
Uh, Wataru, what are we gonna do with all that leftover mashed fish anyway?
Cuute ♡

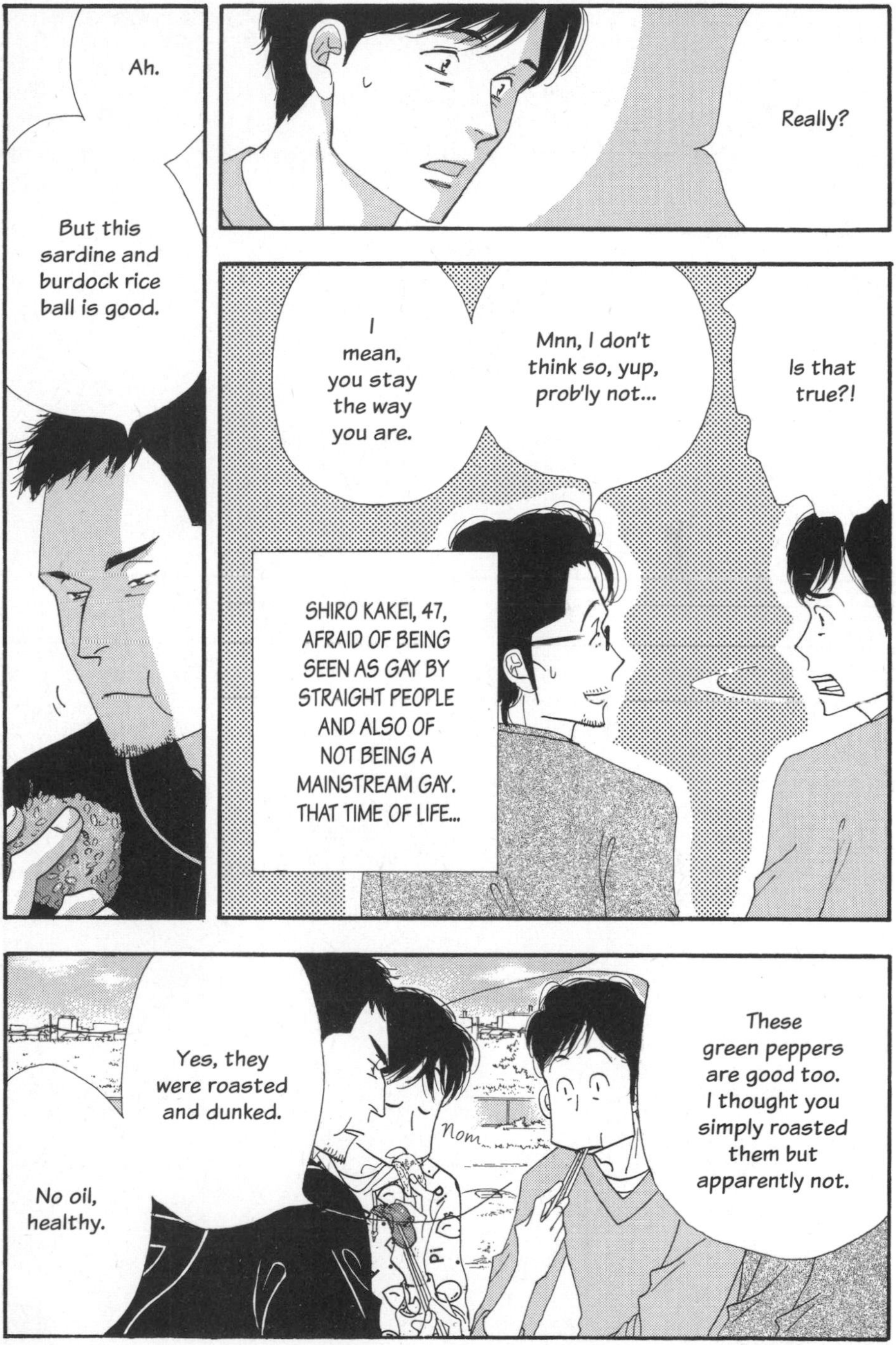
Really?
Is that true?!
Mnn, I don't think so, yup, prob'ly not...
I mean, you stay the way you are.
SHIRO KAKEI, 47, AFRAID OF BEING SEEN AS GAY BY STRAIGHT PEOPLE AND ALSO OF NOT BEING A MAINSTREAM GAY. THAT TIME OF LIFE...
Ah.
But this sardine and burdock rice ball is good.
These green peppers are good too. I thought you simply roasted them but apparently not.
Nom
Yes, they were roasted and dunked.
No oil, healthy.

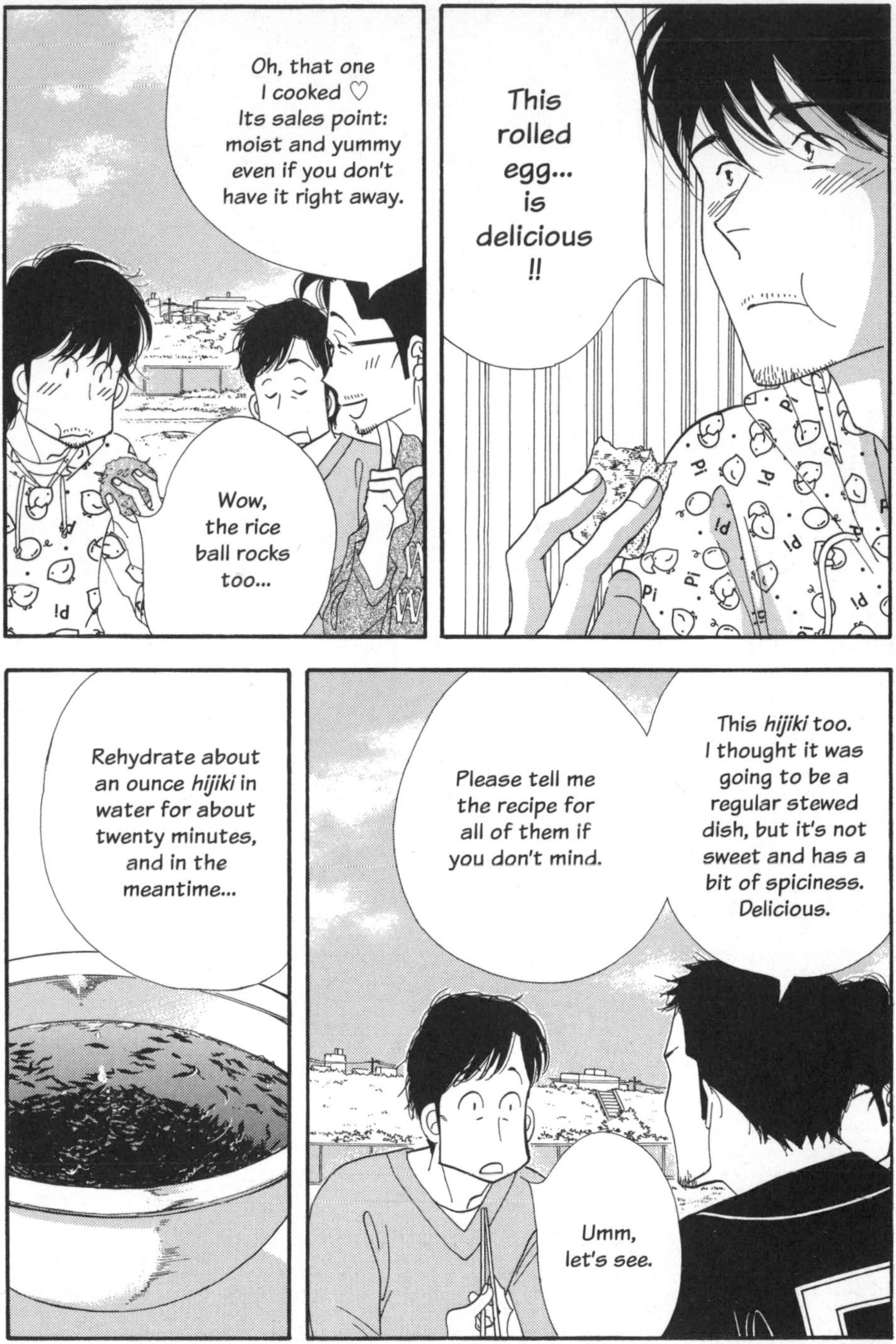
This rolled egg... is delicious !!
Oh, that one I cooked ♡ Its sales point: moist and yummy even if you don't have it right away.
Wow, the rice ball rocks too...
This *hijiki* too. I thought it was going to be a regular stewed dish, but it's not sweet and has a bit of spiciness. Delicious.
Please tell me the recipe for all of them if you don't mind.
Umm, let's see.
Rehydrate about an ounce *hijiki* in water for about twenty minutes, and in the meantime...

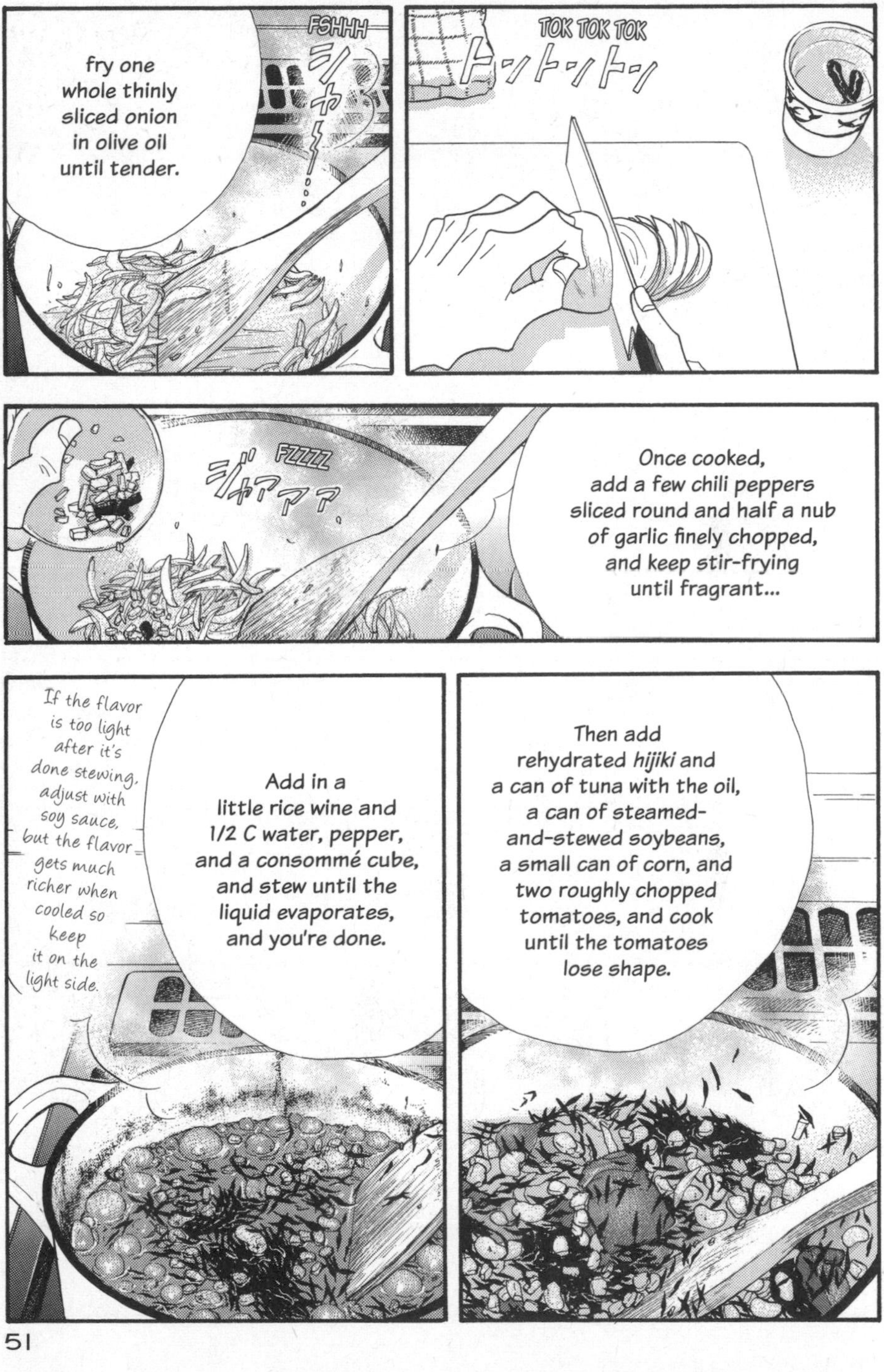
TOK TOK TOK
FSHHH
fry one whole thinly sliced onion in olive oil until tender.
FZZZZ
Once cooked, add a few chili peppers sliced round and half a nub of garlic finely chopped, and keep stir-frying until fragrant...
Then add rehydrated *hijiki* and a can of tuna with the oil, a can of steamed-and-stewed soybeans, a small can of corn, and two roughly chopped tomatoes, and cook until the tomatoes lose shape.
Add in a little rice wine and 1/2 C water, pepper, and a consommé cube, and stew until the liquid evaporates, and you're done.
If the flavor is too light after it's done stewing, adjust with soy sauce, but the flavor gets much richer when cooled so keep it on the light side.

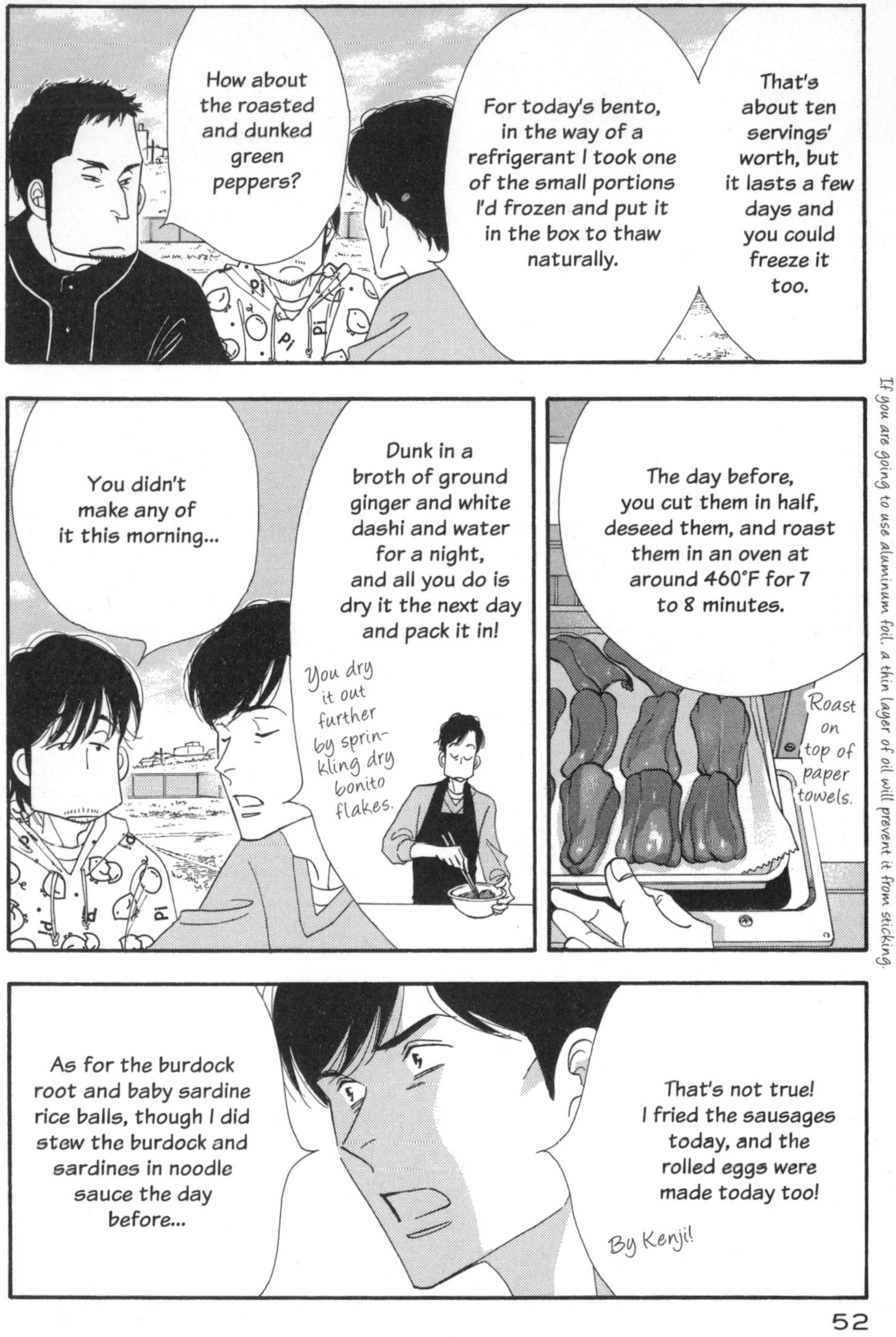
That's about ten servings' worth, but it lasts a few days and you could freeze it too.
For today's bento, in the way of a refrigerant I took one of the small portions I'd frozen and put it in the box to thaw naturally.
How about the roasted and dunked green peppers?
If you are going to use aluminum foil, a thin layer of oil will prevent it from sticking.
The day before, you cut them in half, deseed them, and roast them in an oven at around 460°F for 7 to 8 minutes.
Roast on top of paper towels.
Dunk in a broth of ground ginger and white dashi and water for a night, and all you do is dry it the next day and pack it in!
You dry it out further by sprin-kling dry bonito flakes.
You didn't make any of it this morning...
That's not true! I fried the sausages today, and the rolled eggs were made today too!
By Kenji!
As for the burdock root and baby sardine rice balls, though I did stew the burdock and sardines in noodle sauce the day before...

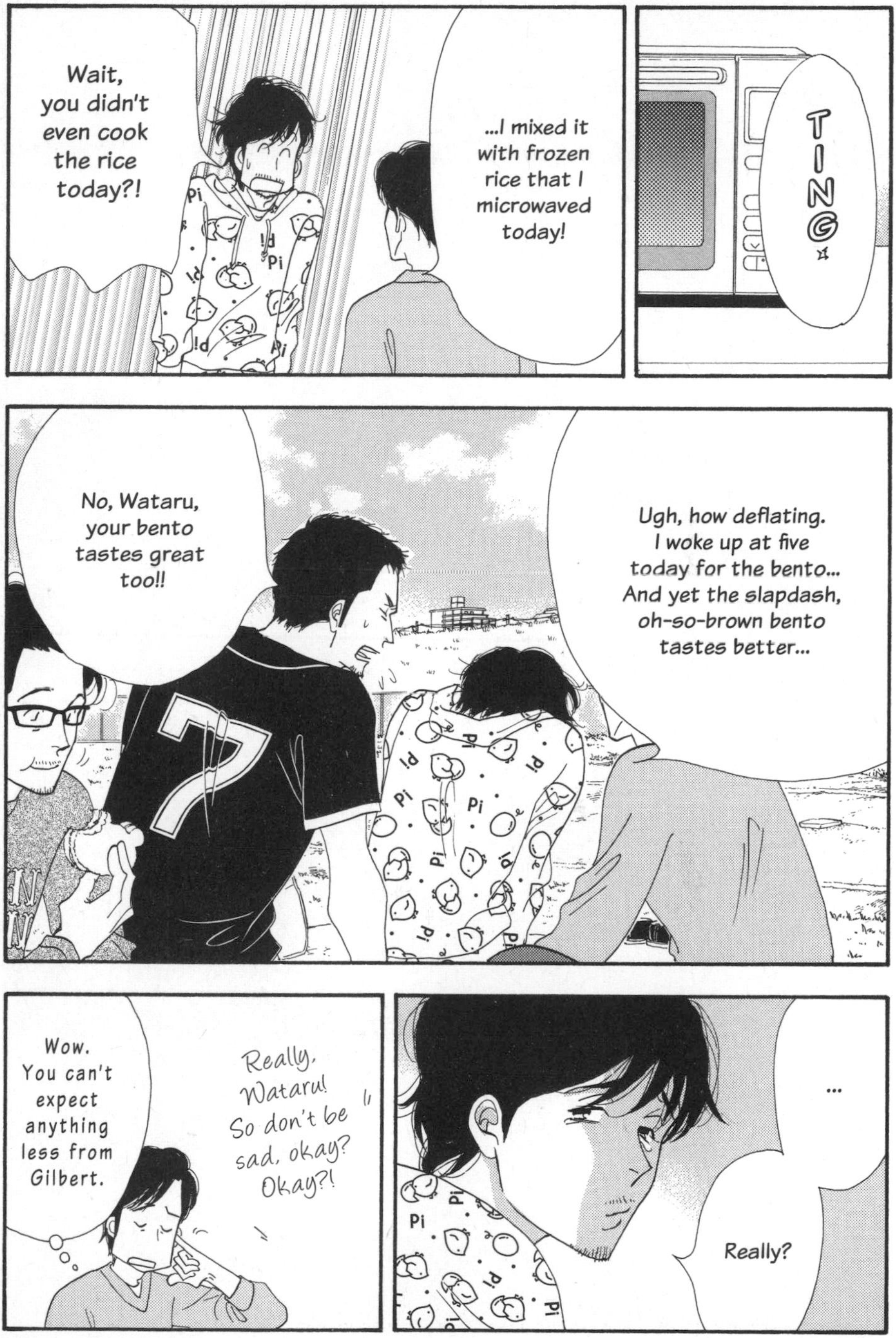
TING
Wait, you didn't even cook the rice today?!
...I mixed it with frozen rice that I microwaved today!
Ugh, how deflating. I woke up at five today for the bento... And yet the slapdash, oh-so-brown bento tastes better...
No, Wataru, your bento tastes great too!!
...
Really?
Really, Wataru! So don't be sad, okay? Okay?!
Wow. You can't expect anything less from Gilbert.

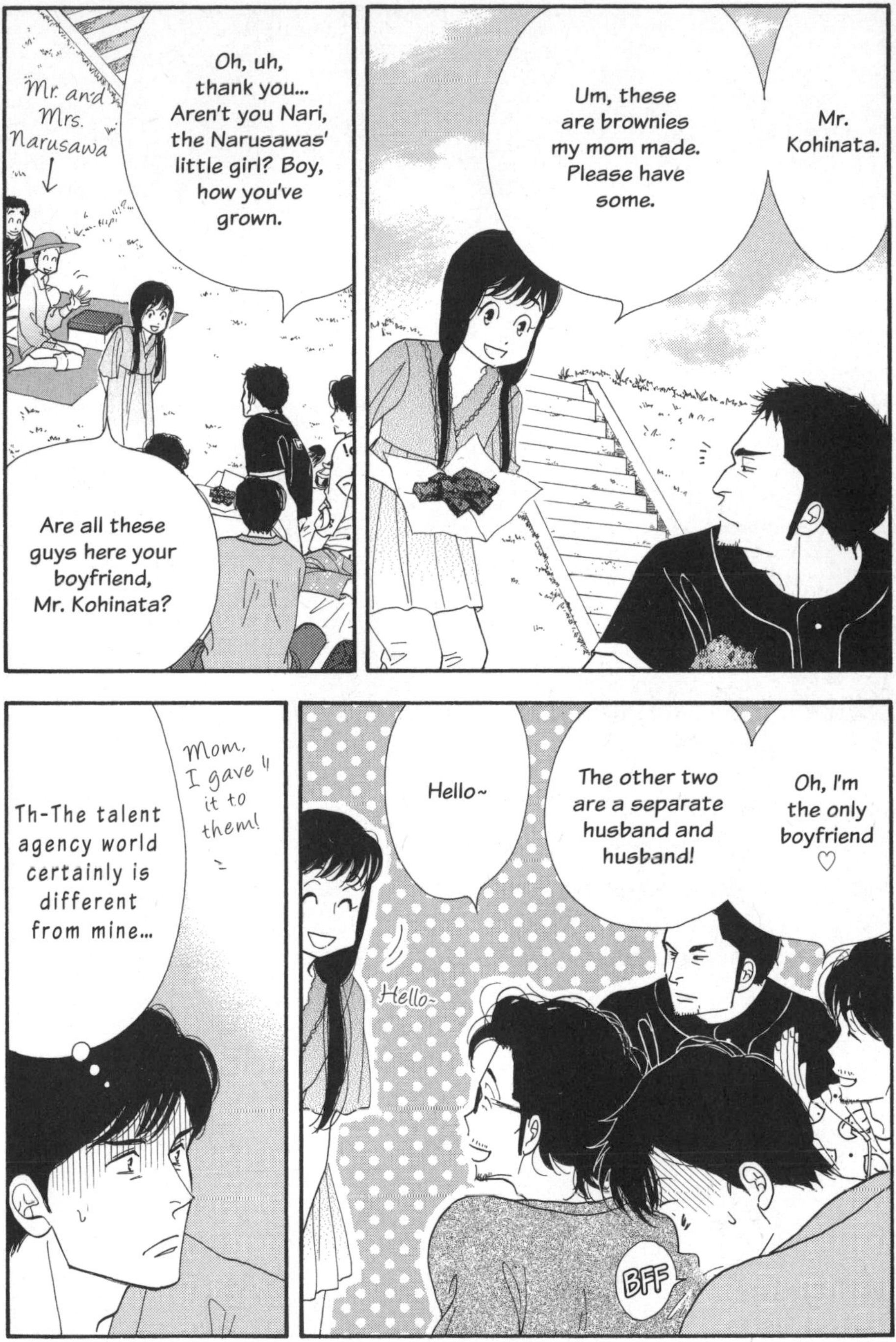
Mr. Kohinata.
Um, these are brownies my mom made. Please have some.
Oh, uh, thank you... Aren't you Nari, the Narusawas' little girl? Boy, how you've grown.
Mr. and Mrs. Narusawa
Are all these guys here your boyfriend, Mr. Kohinata?
Oh, I'm the only boyfriend ♡
The other two are a separate husband and husband!
Hello~
Hello~
BFF
Mom, I gave it to them!
Th-The talent agency world certainly is different from mine...

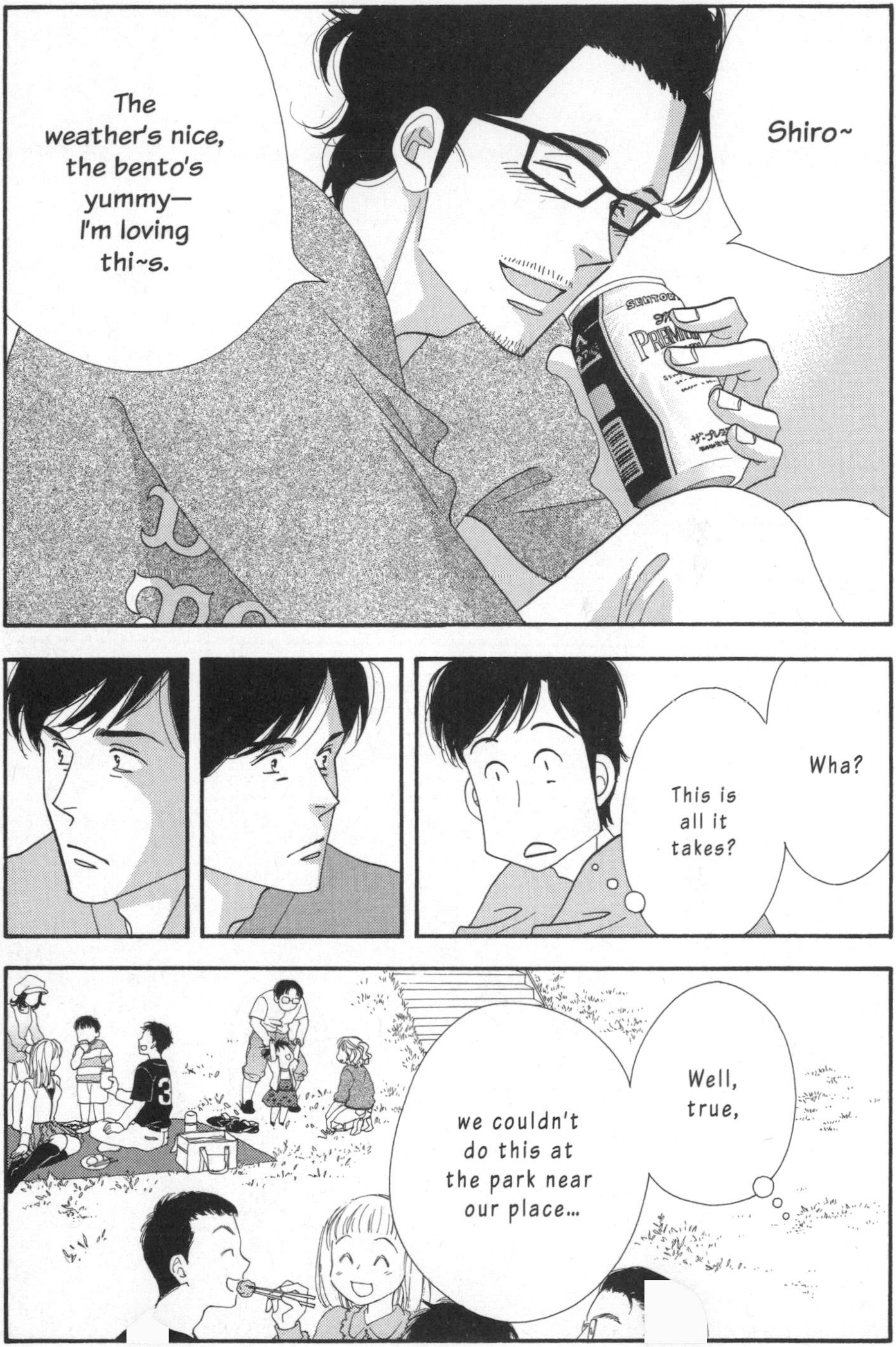
Shiro~
The weather's nice, the bento's yummy— I'm loving thi~s.
Wha?
This is all it takes?
Well, true,
we couldn't do this at the park near our place...

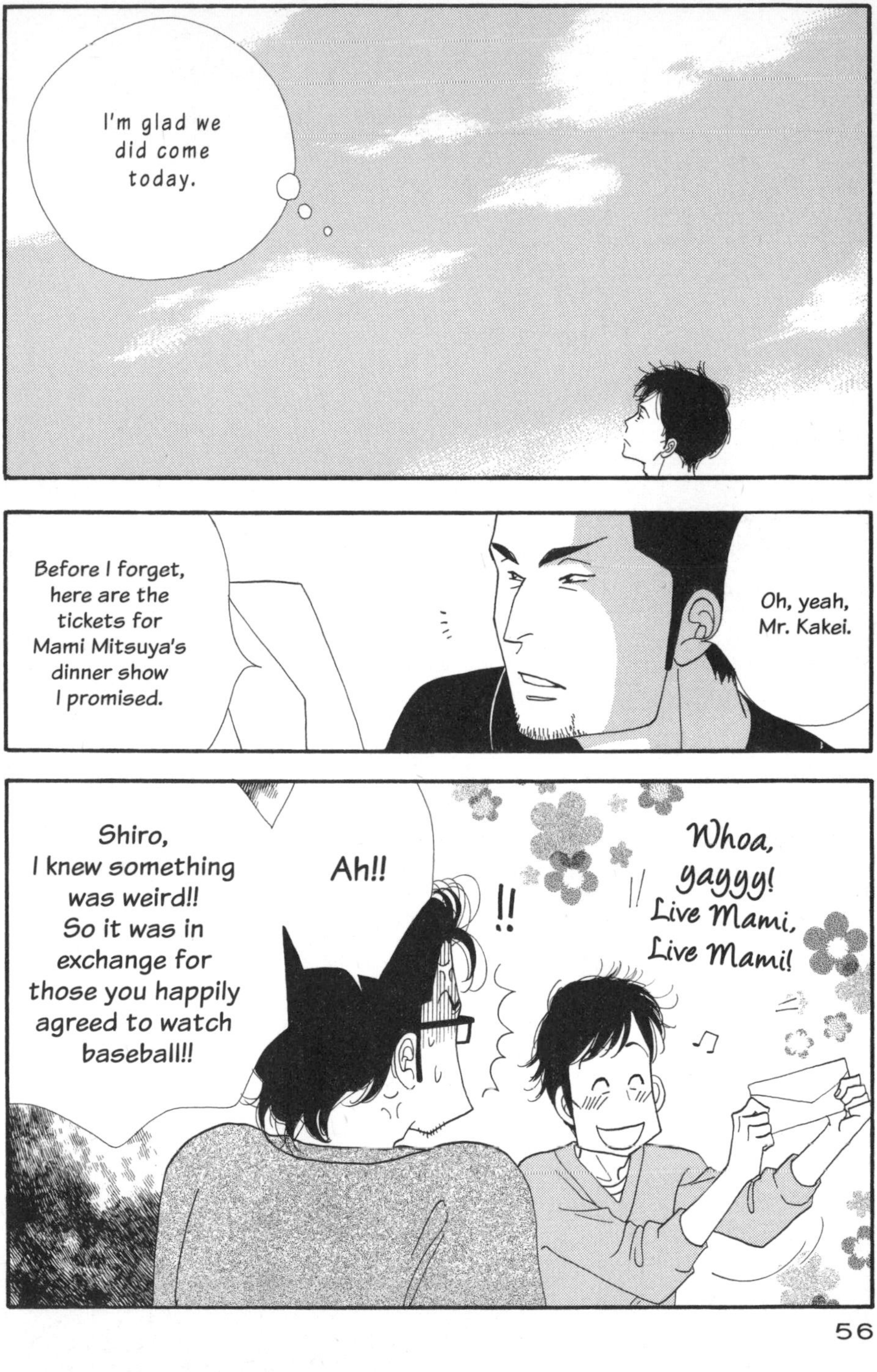
I'm glad we did come today.
Oh, yeah, Mr. Kakei.
Before I forget, here are the tickets for Mami Mitsuya's dinner show I promised.
Whoa, yayyy! Live Mami, Live Mami!
!!
Ah!!
Shiro, I knew something was weird!! So it was in exchange for those you happily agreed to watch baseball!!

The flavor won't be as good as when you cook it on the same day, but you can freeze the **rolled eggs** too. Wrap amounts for one bento separately, pack a portion in a box in the morning, and let it thaw naturally.

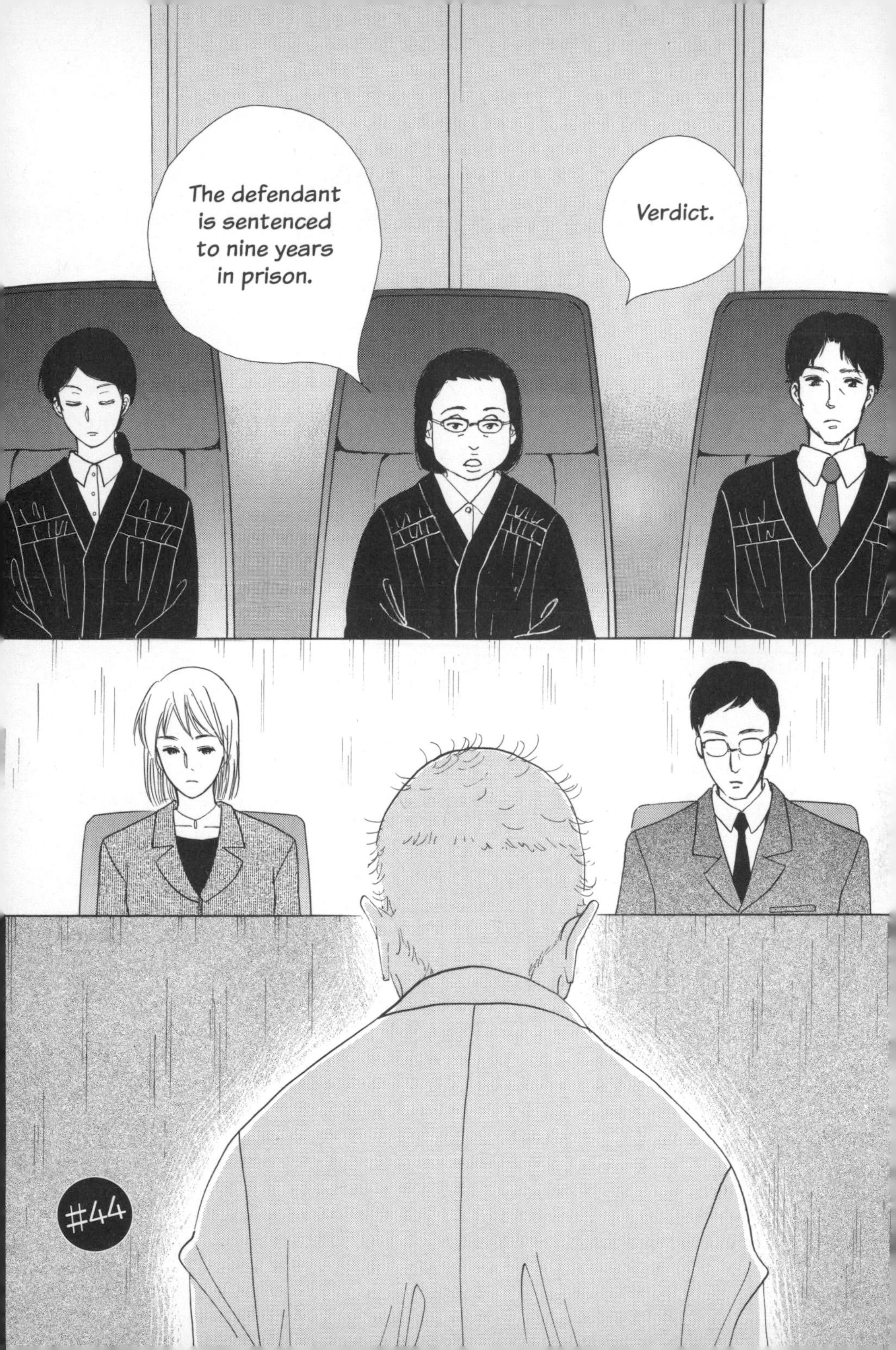
Verdict.
The defendant is sentenced to nine years in prison.
#44

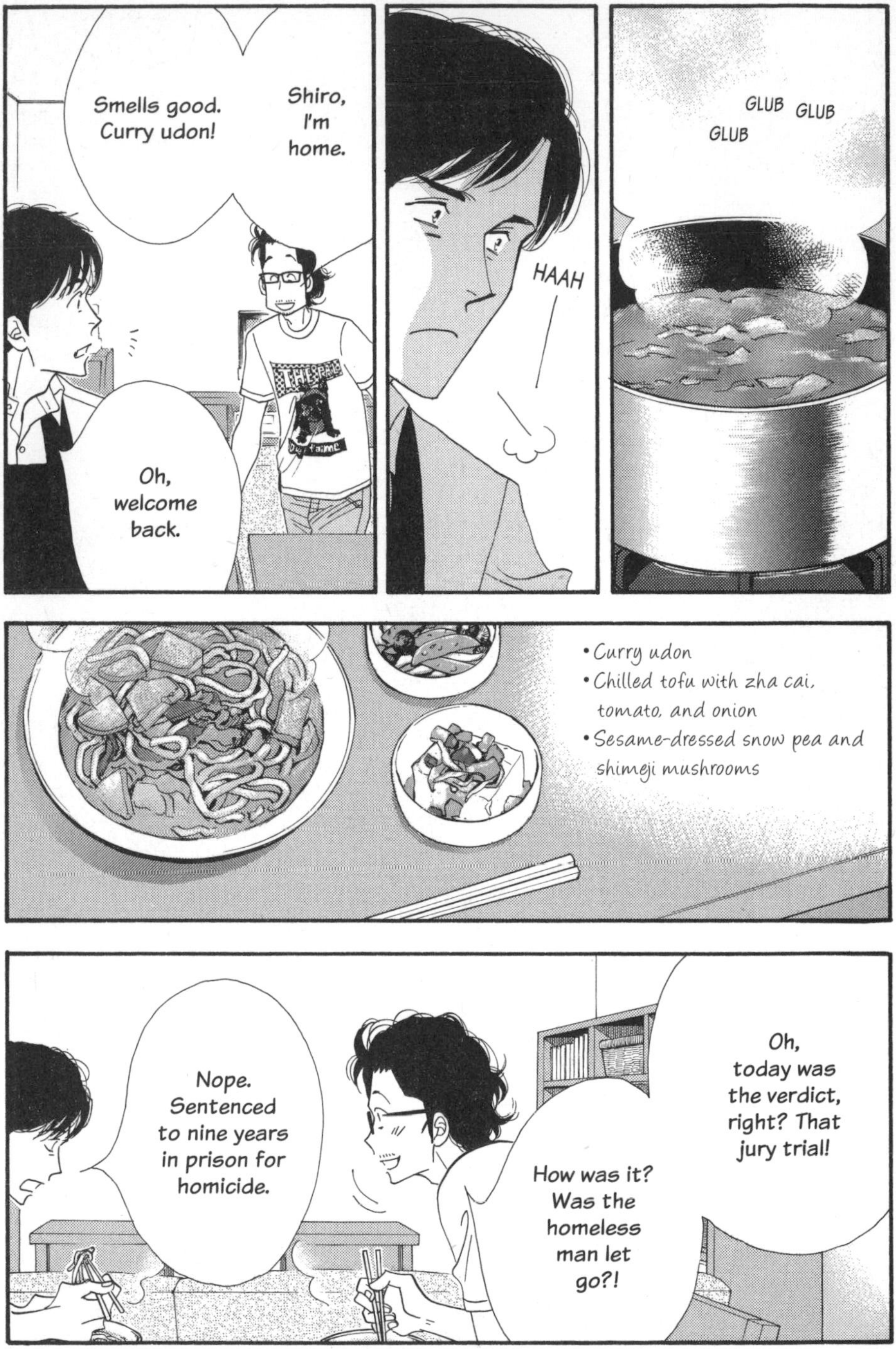

GLUB GLUB
GLUB
HAAH
Shiro, I'm home.
Smells good. Curry udon!
Oh, welcome back.
• Curry udon
• Chilled tofu with zha cai, tomato, and onion
• Sesame-dressed snow pea and shimeji mushrooms
Oh, today was the verdict, right? That jury trial!
How was it? Was the homeless man let go?!
Nope. Sentenced to nine years in prison for homicide.

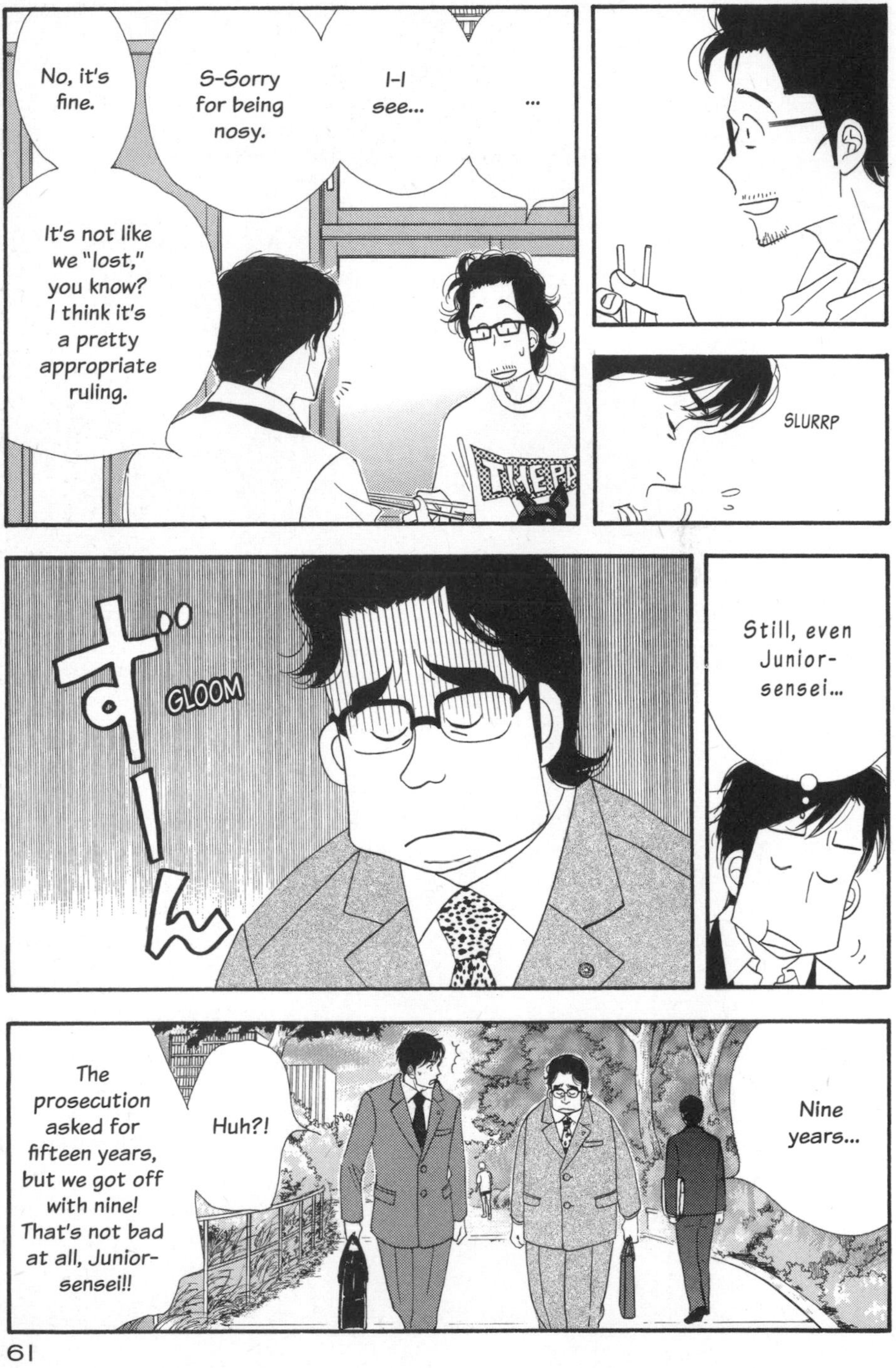
SLURRP
...
I-I see...
S-Sorry for being nosy.
No, it's fine.
It's not like we "lost," you know? I think it's a pretty appropriate ruling.
Still, even Junior-sensei...
ずーん
GLOOM
Nine years...
Huh?!
The prosecution asked for fifteen years, but we got off with nine! That's not bad at all, Junior-sensei!!

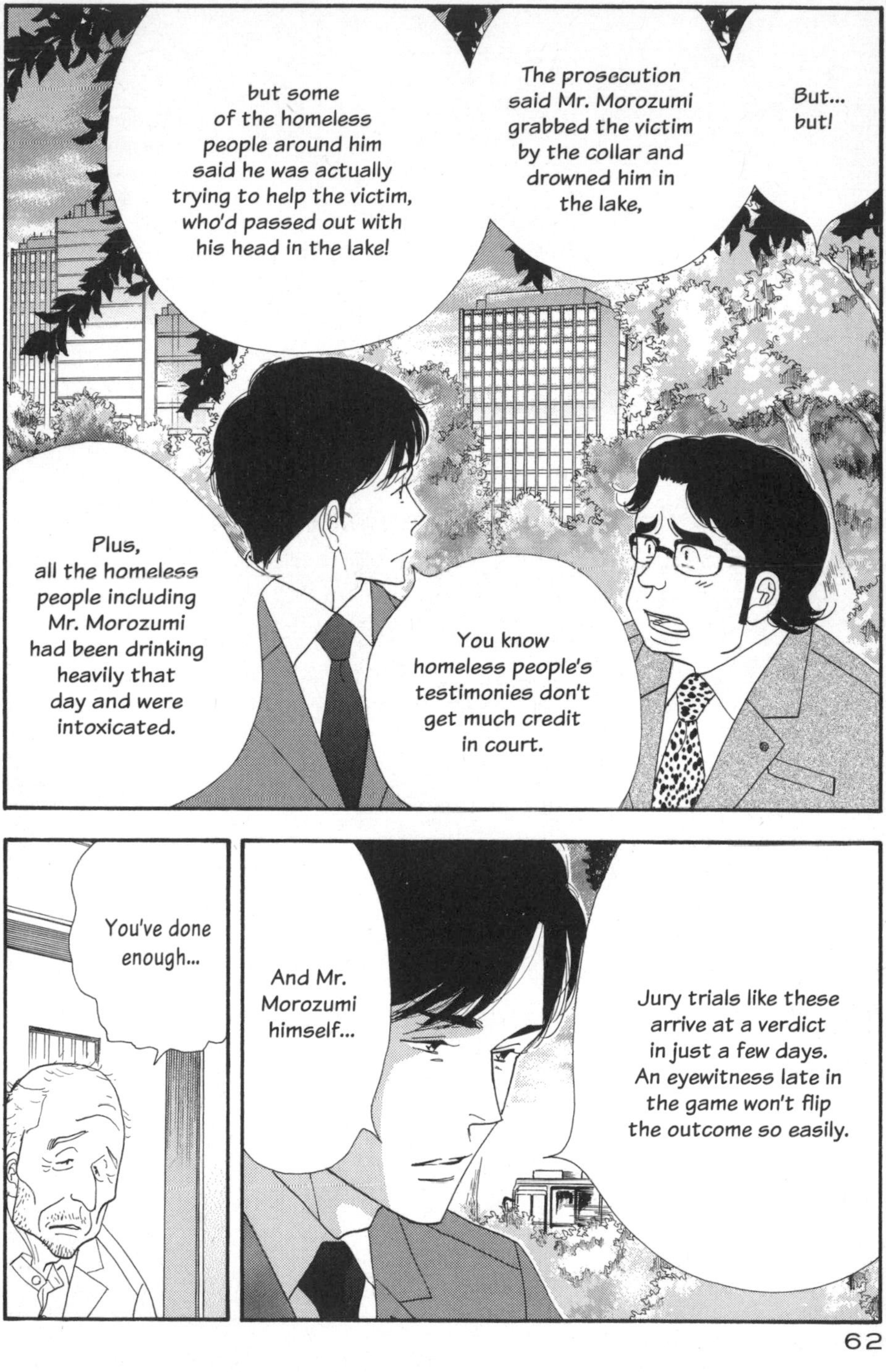
But... but!
The prosecution said Mr. Morozumi grabbed the victim by the collar and drowned him in the lake,
but some of the homeless people around him said he was actually trying to help the victim, who'd passed out with his head in the lake!
You know homeless people's testimonies don't get much credit in court.
Plus, all the homeless people including Mr. Morozumi had been drinking heavily that day and were intoxicated.
Jury trials like these arrive at a verdict in just a few days. An eyewitness late in the game won't flip the outcome so easily.
And Mr. Morozumi himself...
You've done enough...

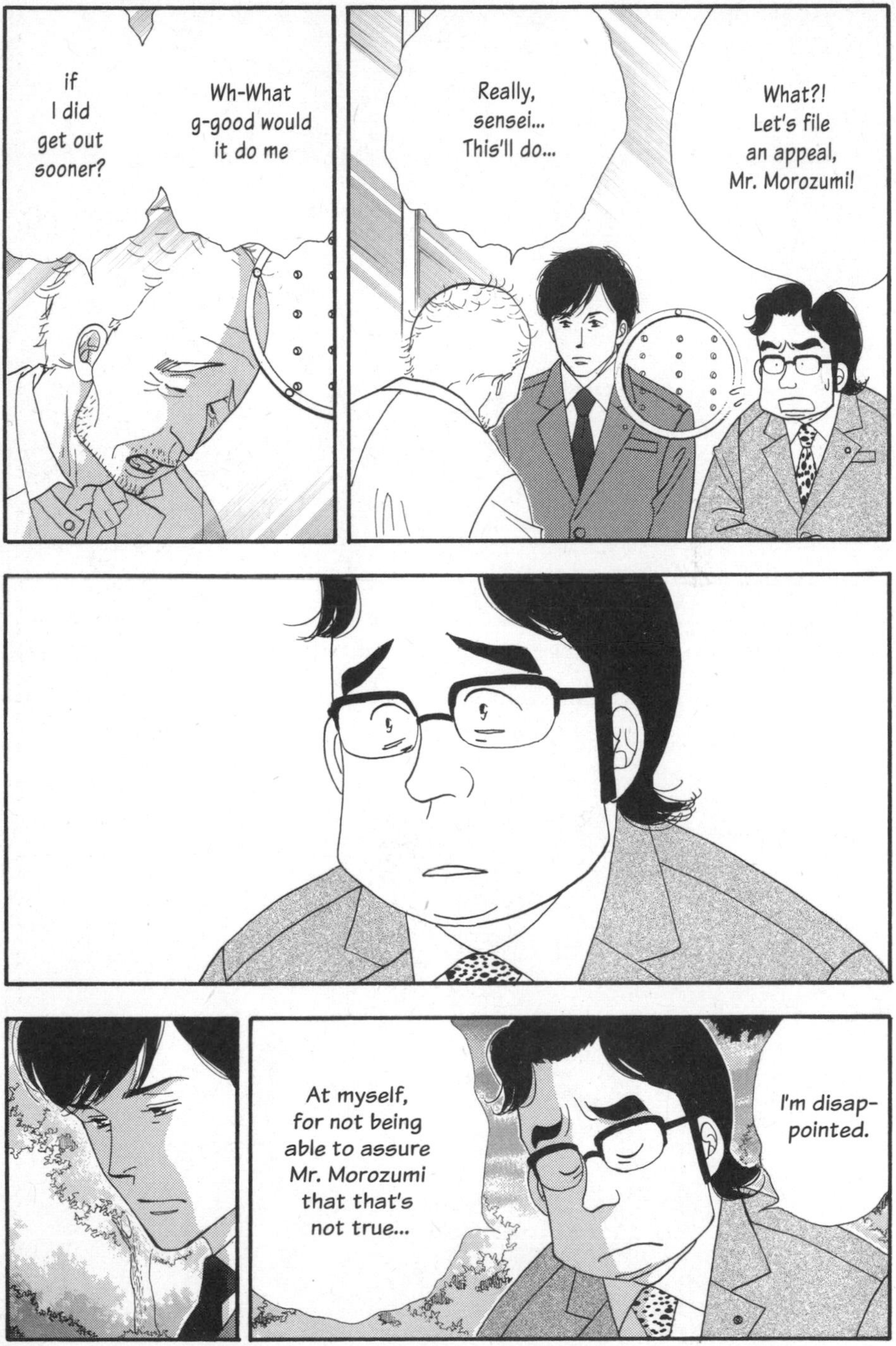
What?! Let's file an appeal, Mr. Morozumi!
Really, sensei... This'll do...
Wh-What g-good would it do me
if I did get out sooner?
I'm disap-pointed.
At myself, for not being able to assure Mr. Morozumi that that's not true...

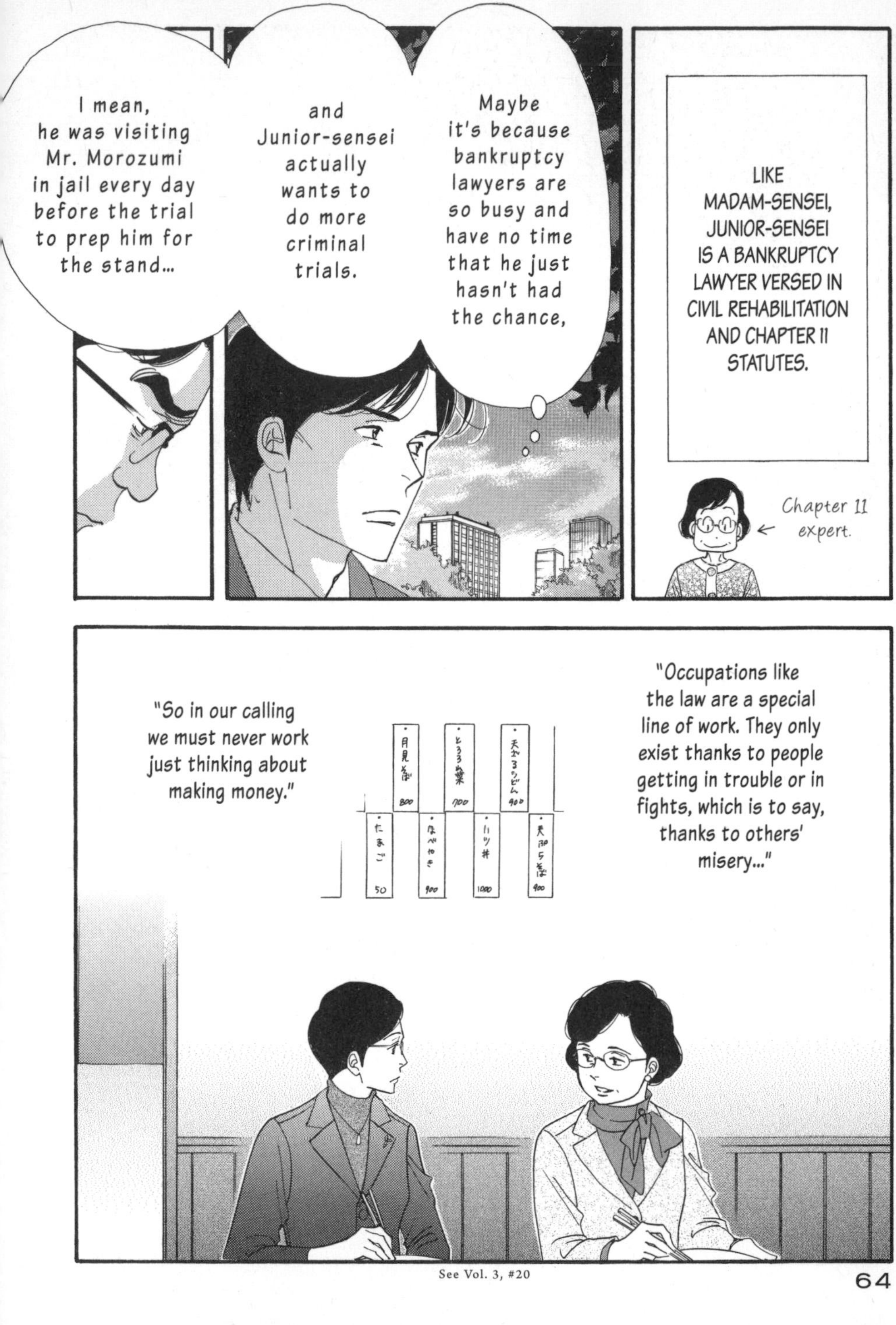
LIKE MADAM-SENSEI, JUNIOR-SENSEI IS A BANKRUPTCY LAWYER VERSED IN CIVIL REHABILITATION AND CHAPTER 11 STATUTES.
Chapter 11 expert.
Maybe it's because bankruptcy lawyers are so busy and have no time that he just hasn't had the chance,
and Junior-sensei actually wants to do more criminal trials.
I mean, he was visiting Mr. Morozumi in jail every day before the trial to prep him for the stand...
"Occupations like the law are a special line of work. They only exist thanks to people getting in trouble or in fights, which is to say, thanks to others' misery..."
"So in our calling we must never work just thinking about making money."

See Vol. 3, #20

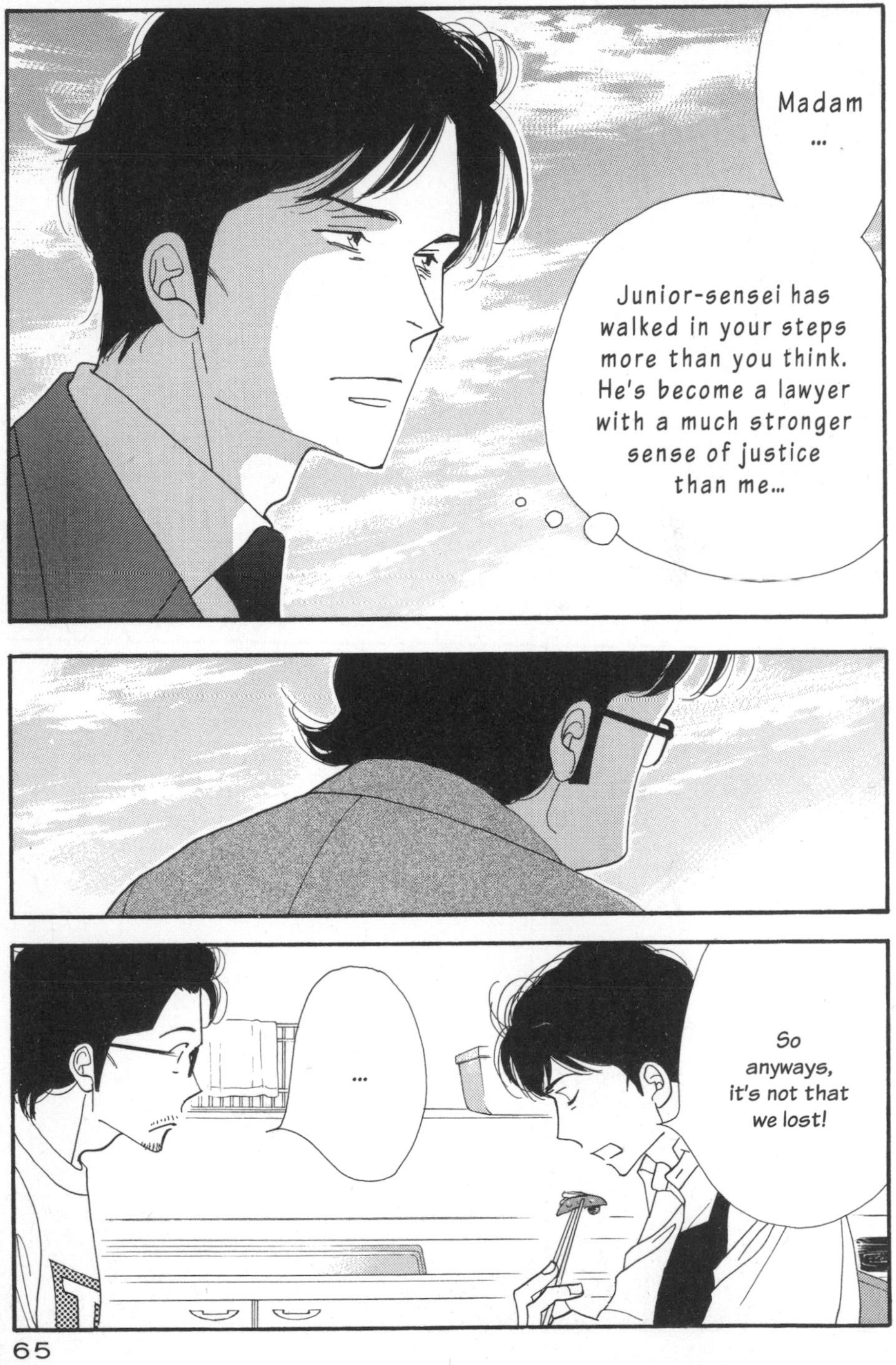

Madam ...
Junior-sensei has walked in your steps more than you think. He's become a lawyer with a much stronger sense of justice than me...
So anyways, it's not that we lost!
...

ZZZ
ZZZ
ZZZ

WHSHHH

FSHH

I'm gonna cook breakfast!!

All right!!

Urrrrr!!

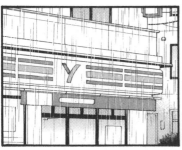

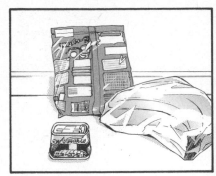

rustle
rustle
rustle
TOK
TOK
First, slice one banana on the bias. So it won't change color, and to add tartness, pour a little lemon juice on it.
Ladle some yogurt and honey on top, and we have one dish!!
TOK
TOK
Next, thinly slice a quarter onion and sprinkle on half a teaspoon salt to soften it.

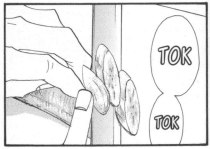

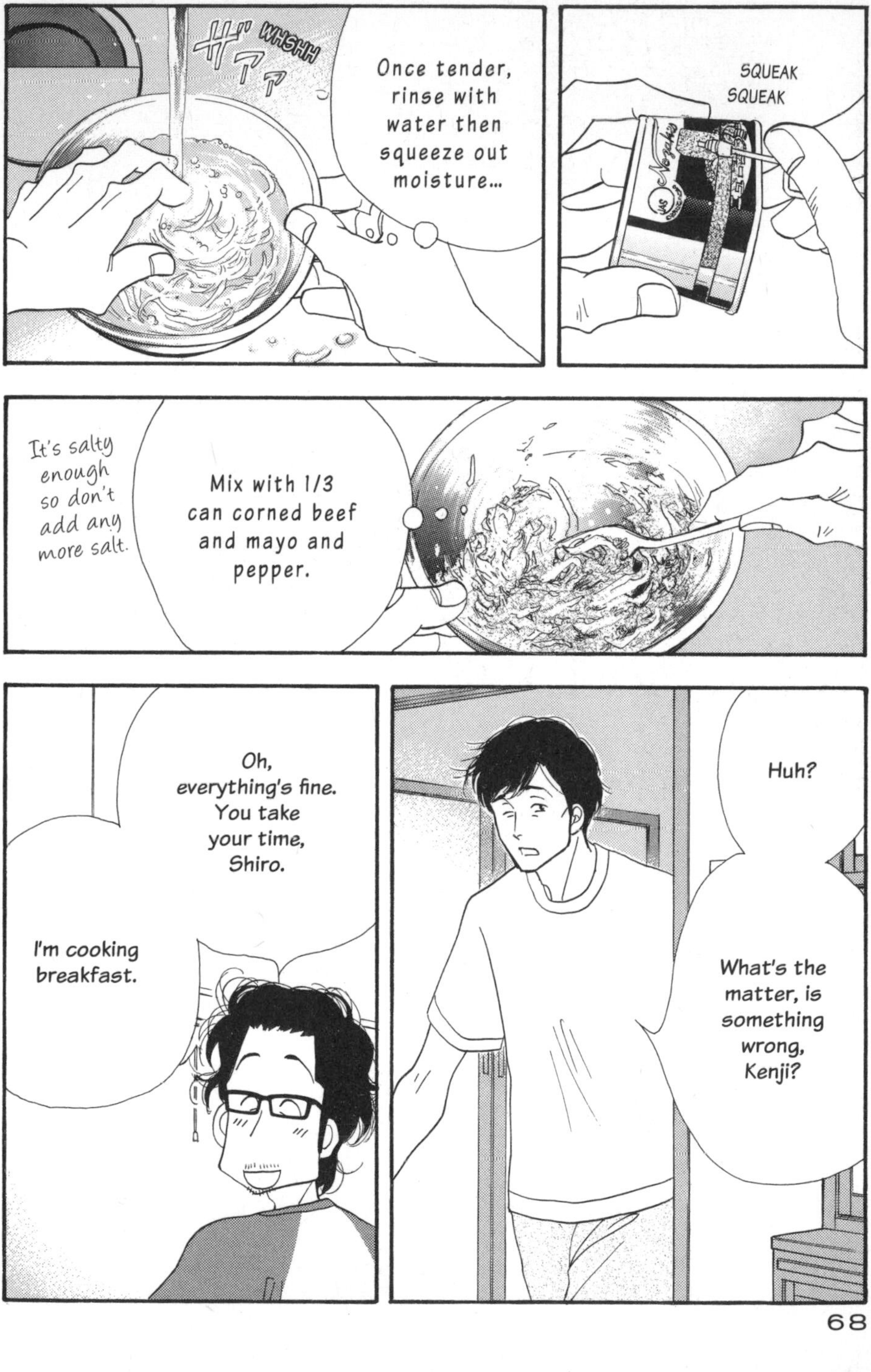
SQUEAK
SQUEAK
Once tender, rinse with water then squeeze out moisture...
ザァァ
WHSHH
Mix with 1/3 can corned beef and mayo and pepper.
It's salty enough so don't add any more salt.
Huh?
What's the matter, is something wrong, Kenji?
Oh, everything's fine. You take your time, Shiro.
I'm cooking breakfast.

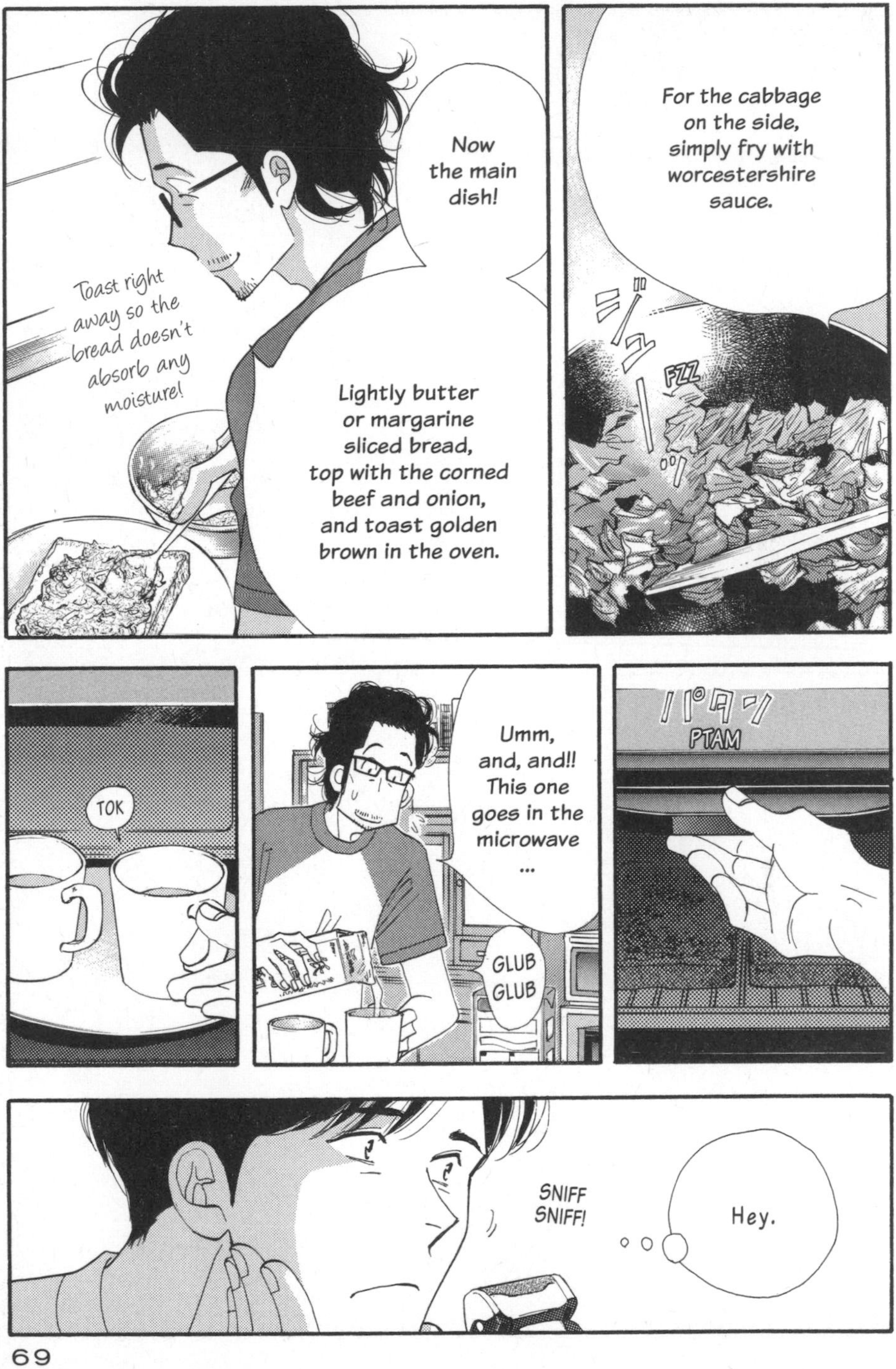

Now the main dish!
Lightly butter or margarine sliced bread, top with the corned beef and onion, and toast golden brown in the oven.
Toast right away so the bread doesn't absorb any moisture!
For the cabbage on the side, simply fry with worcestershire sauce.
FZZ
TOK
Umm, and, and!! This one goes in the microwave ...
GLUB GLUB
PTAM
SNIFF SNIFF!
Hey.

Kenji! Something smells really good.

Heheh. It's ready ♡

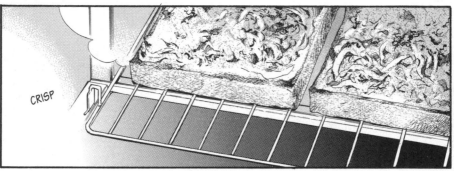

CRISP

- Corned beef and onion toast
- Worcestershire fried cabbage
- Banana yogurt
- Kenji au lait

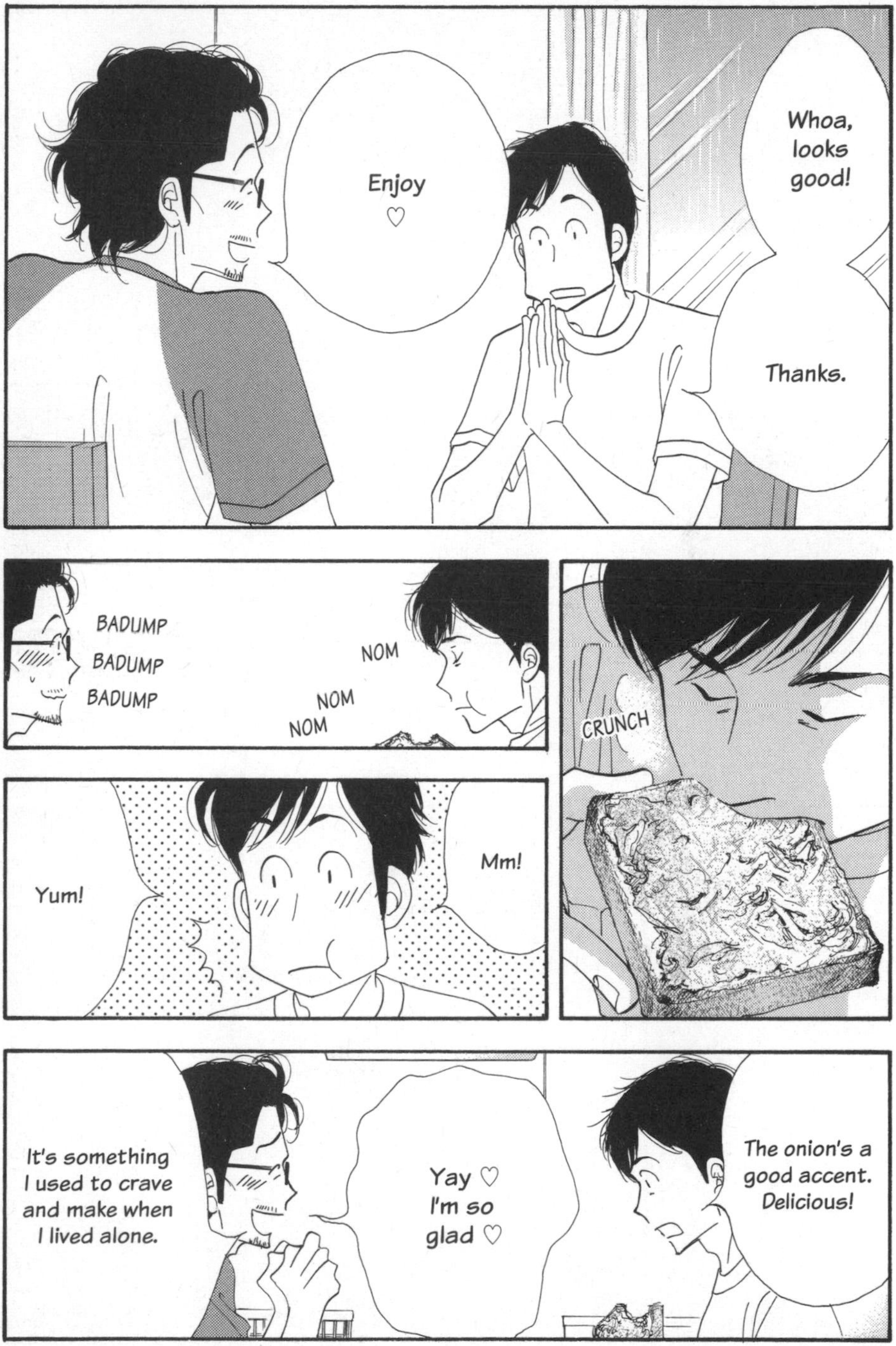

Whoa, looks good!
Thanks.
Enjoy ♡
CRUNCH
NOM
NOM
NOM
BADUMP
BADUMP
BADUMP
Mm!
Yum!
The onion's a good accent. Delicious!
Yay ♡ I'm so glad ♡
It's something I used to crave and make when I lived alone.

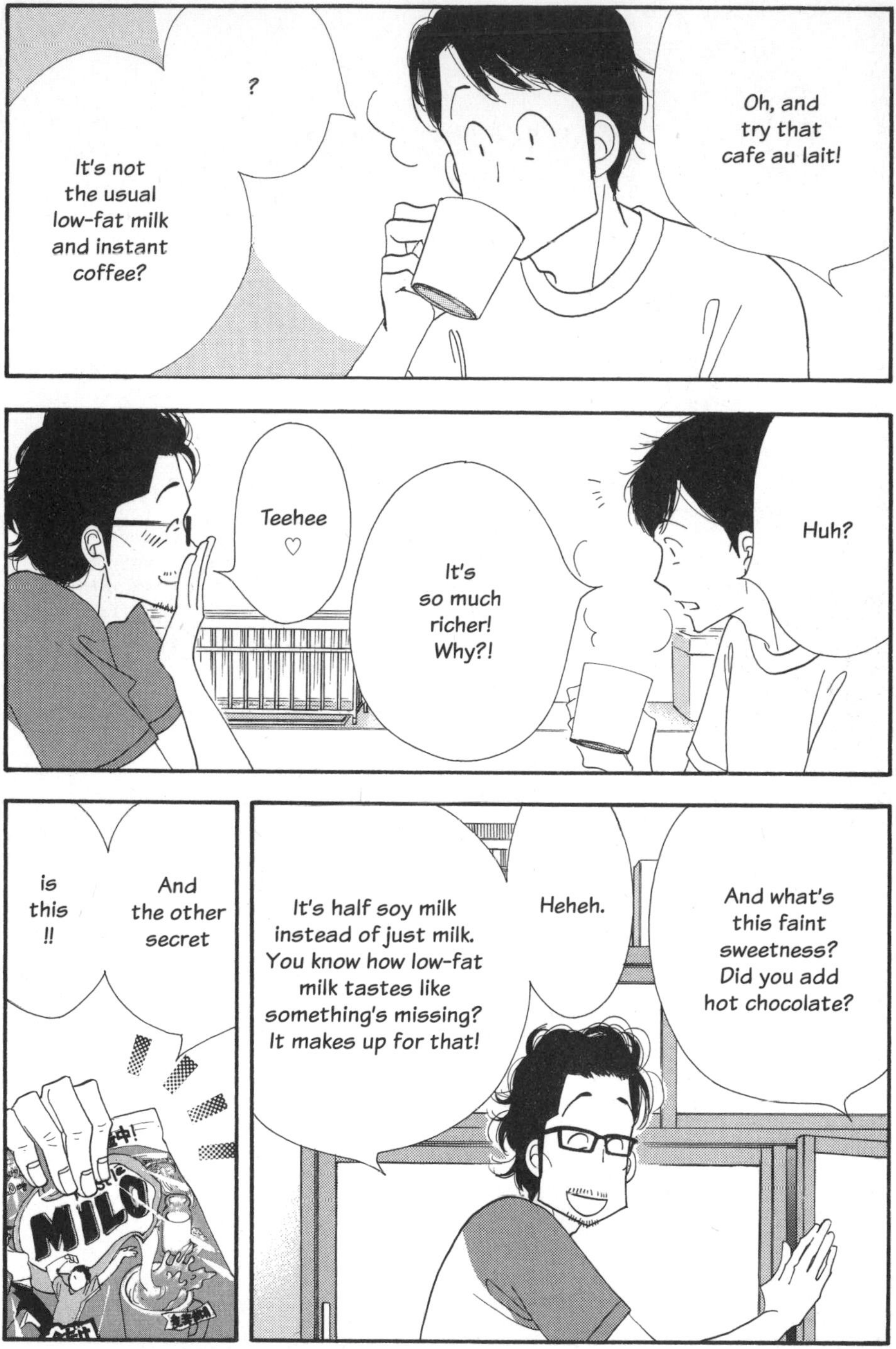
Oh, and try that cafe au lait!
?
It's not the usual low-fat milk and instant coffee?
Huh?
It's so much richer! Why?!
Teehee ♡
And what's this faint sweetness? Did you add hot chocolate?
Heheh.
It's half soy milk instead of just milk. You know how low-fat milk tastes like something's missing? It makes up for that!
And the other secret
is this !!
MILO

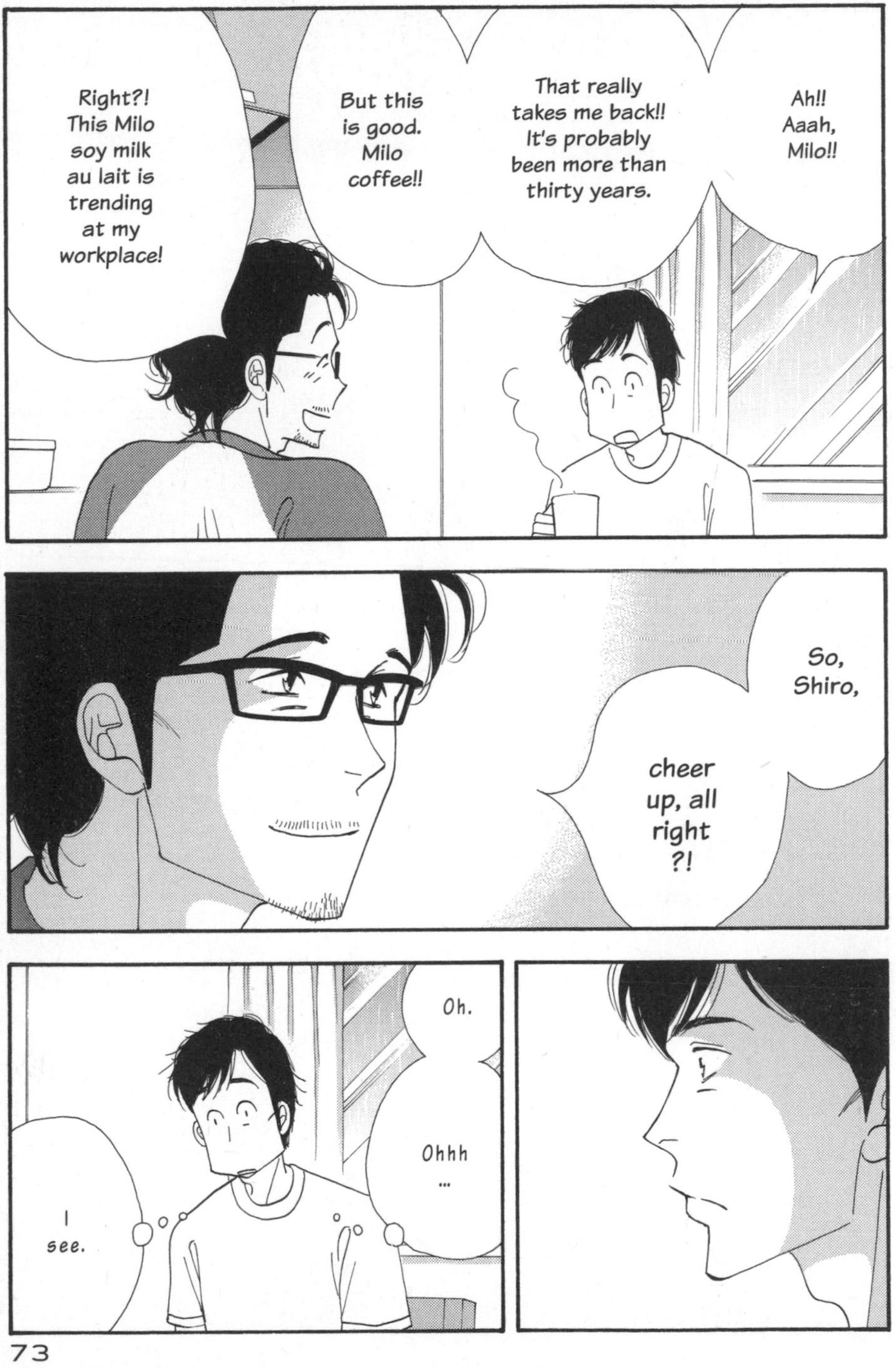
Ah!! Aaah, Milo!!
That really takes me back!! It's probably been more than thirty years.
But this is good. Milo coffee!!
Right?! This Milo soy milk au lait is trending at my workplace!
So, Shiro,
cheer up, all right ?!
Oh.
Ohhh ...
I see.

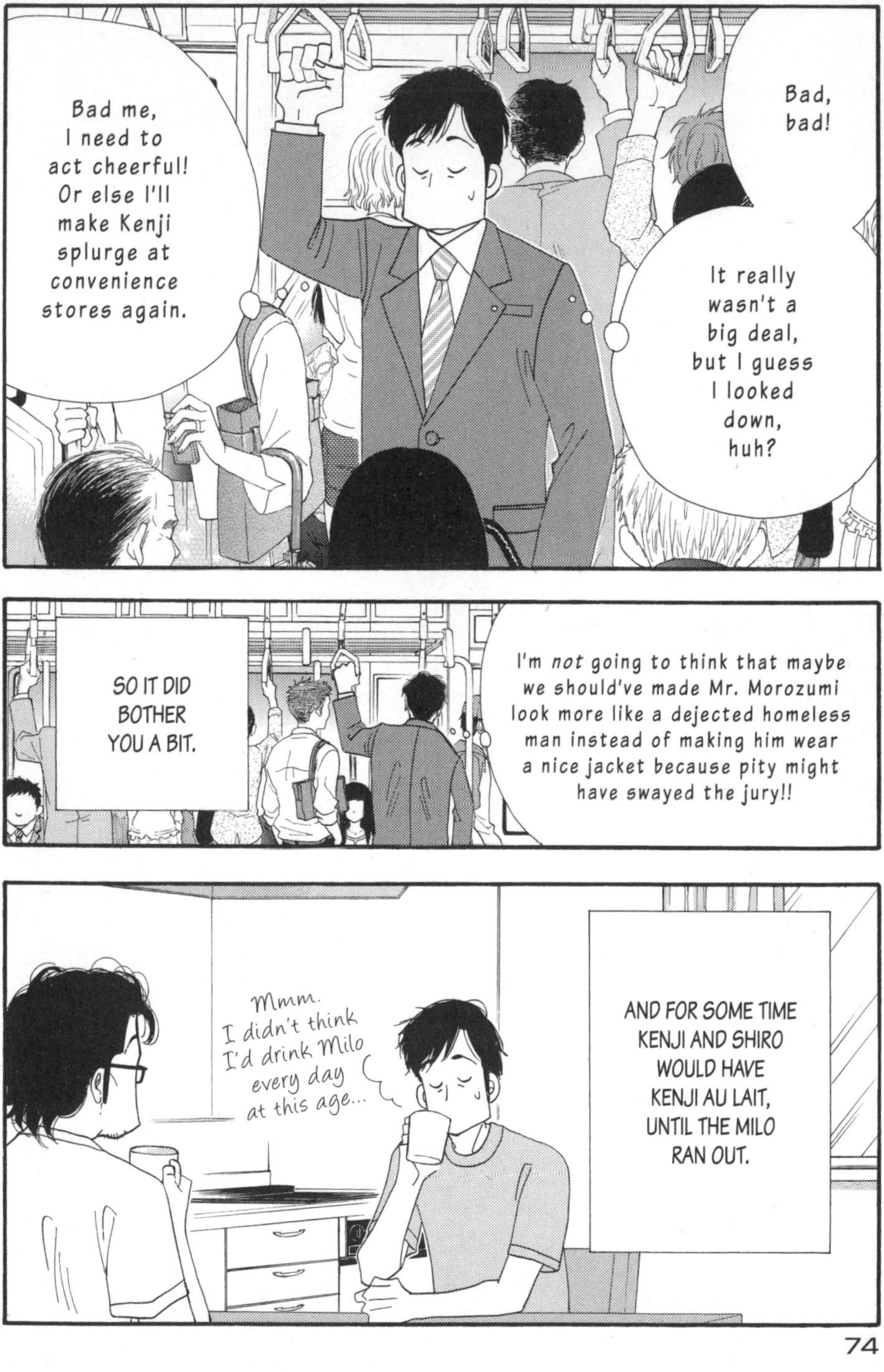
Bad, bad!
It really wasn't a big deal, but I guess I looked down, huh?
Bad me, I need to act cheerful! Or else I'll make Kenji splurge at convenience stores again.
I'm *not* going to think that maybe we should've made Mr. Morozumi look more like a dejected homeless man instead of making him wear a nice jacket because pity might have swayed the jury!!
SO IT DID BOTHER YOU A BIT.
AND FOR SOME TIME KENJI AND SHIRO WOULD HAVE KENJI AU LAIT, UNTIL THE MILO RAN OUT.
Mmm. I didn't think I'd drink Milo every day at this age...

The **curry udon** in the beginning is a root vegetable curry udon. Fry carrots, pork, daikon, burdock root, and *konnyaku* in that order, and serve in water, noodle sauce, Japanese dashi powder, and curry roux. Top with small round sliced scallion.

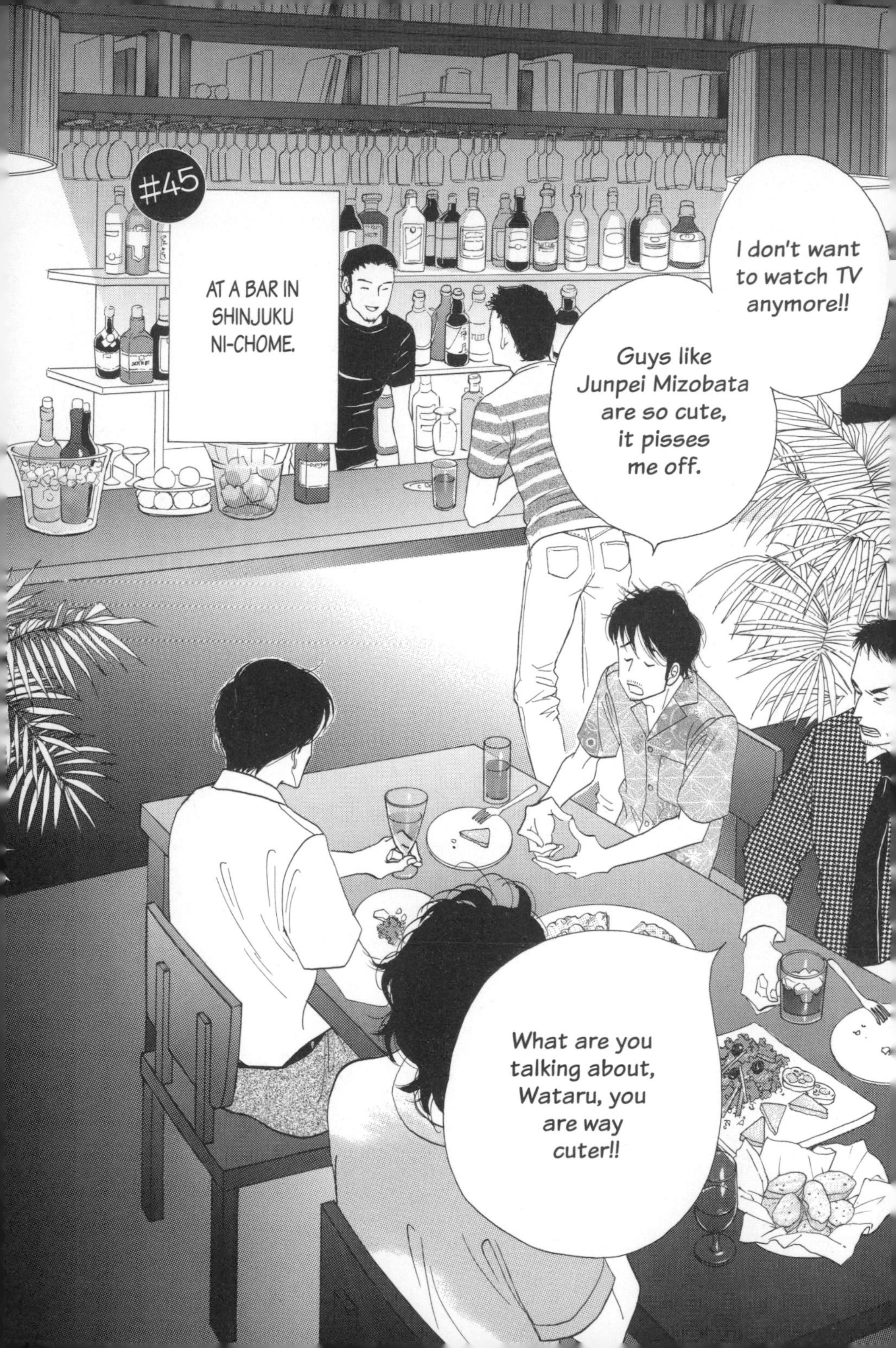
#45
AT A BAR IN SHINJUKU NI-CHOME.
I don't want to watch TV anymore!!
Guys like Junpei Mizobata are so cute, it pisses me off.
What are you talking about, Wataru, you are way cuter!!

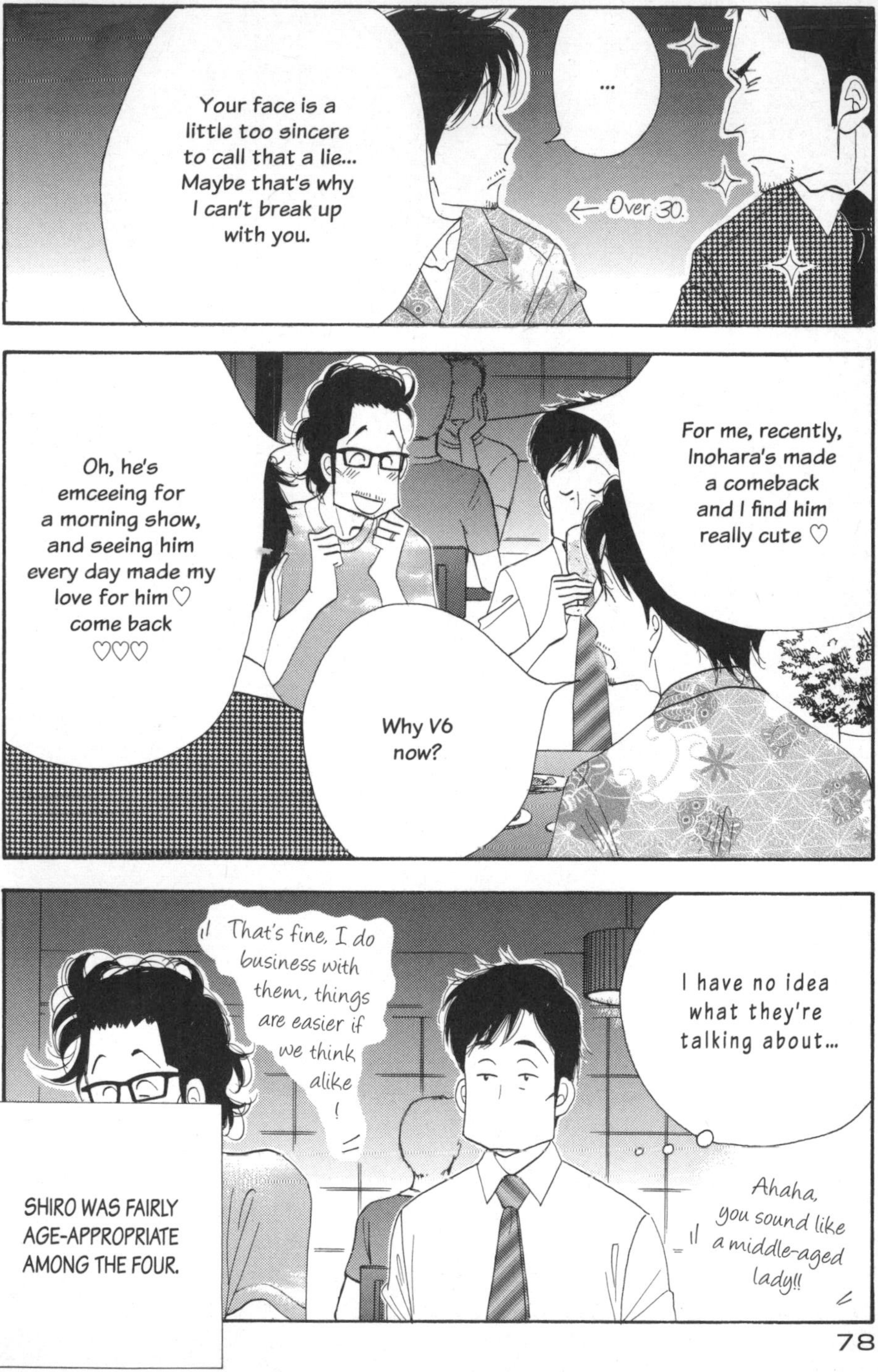
...
Your face is a little too sincere to call that a lie... Maybe that's why I can't break up with you.
← Over 30.
For me, recently, Inohara's made a comeback and I find him really cute ♡
Oh, he's emceeing for a morning show, and seeing him every day made my love for him ♡ come back ♡♡♡
Why V6 now?
I have no idea what they're talking about...
Ahaha, you sound like a middle-aged lady!!
That's fine, I do business with them, things are easier if we think alike!
SHIRO WAS FAIRLY AGE-APPROPRIATE AMONG THE FOUR.

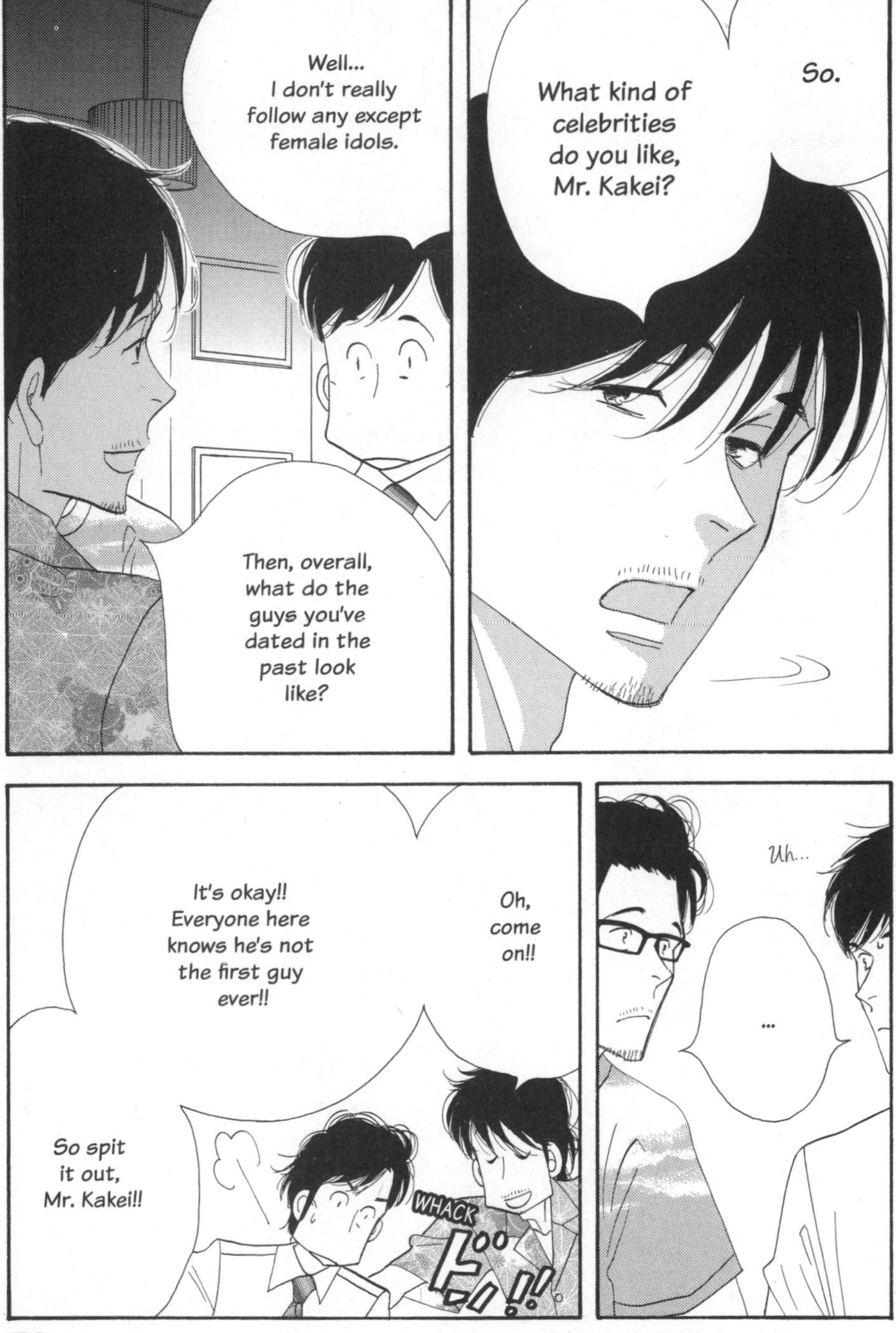
So.
What kind of celebrities do you like, Mr. Kakei?
Well... I don't really follow any except female idols.
Then, overall, what do the guys you've dated in the past look like?
Uh...
...
Oh, come on!!
It's okay!! Everyone here knows he's not the first guy ever!!
So spit it out, Mr. Kakei!!
WHACK

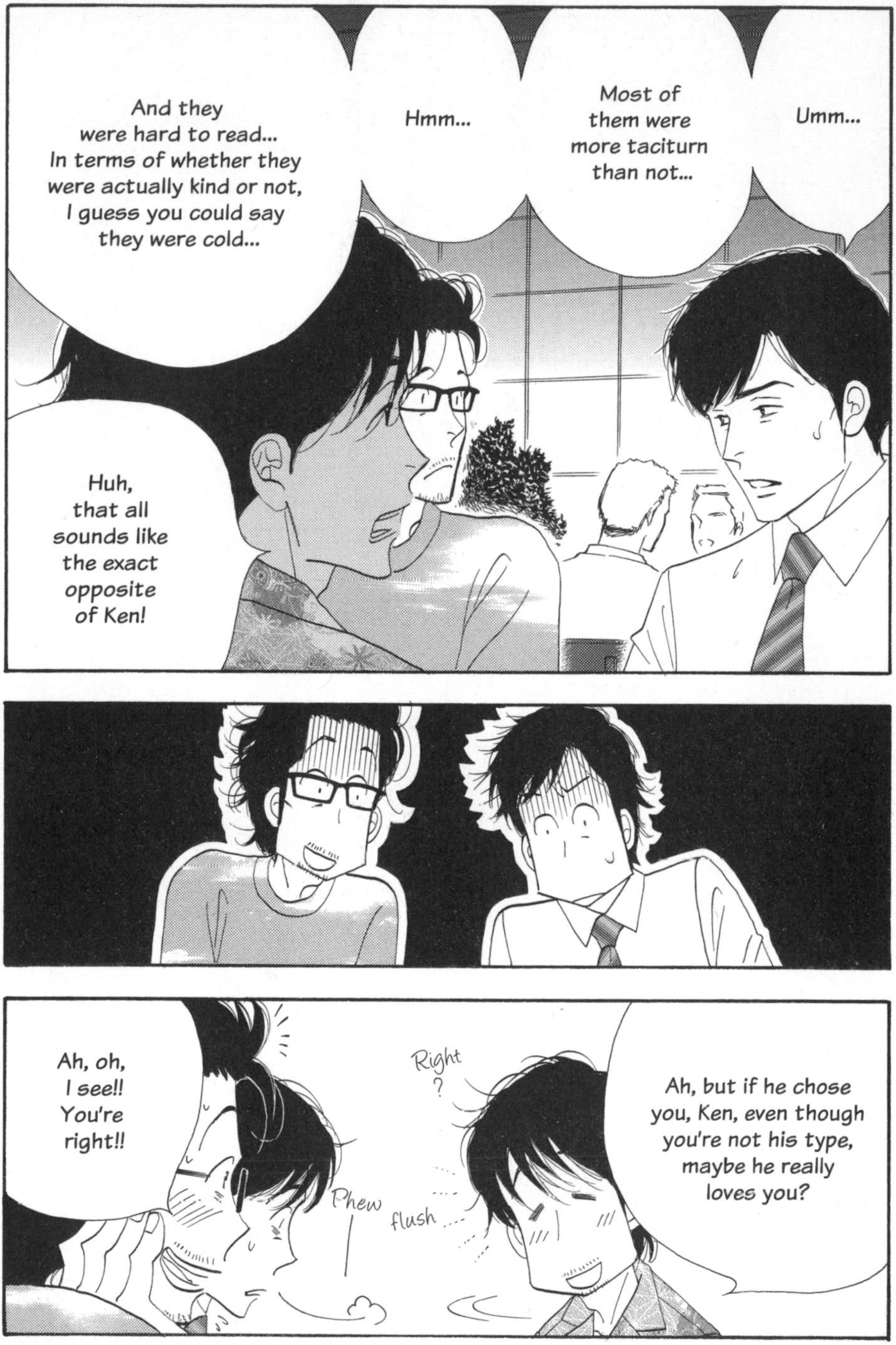
Umm...
Most of them were more taciturn than not...
Hmm...
And they were hard to read... In terms of whether they were actually kind or not, I guess you could say they were cold...
Huh, that all sounds like the exact opposite of Ken!
Ah, but if he chose you, Ken, even though you're not his type, maybe he really loves you?
Right?
flush
Phew
Ah, oh, I see!! You're right!!

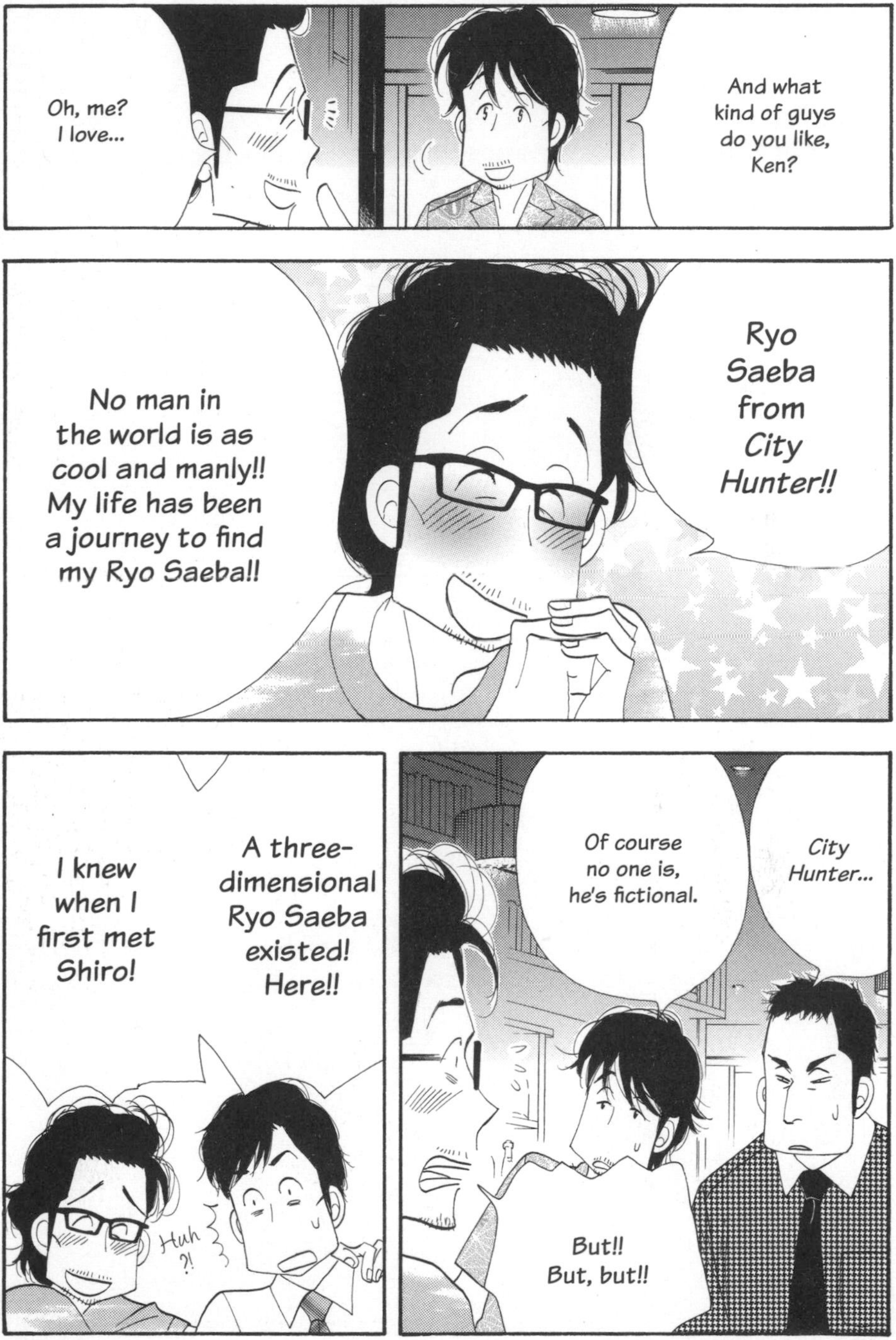
And what kind of guys do you like, Ken?
Oh, me? I love...
Ryo Saeba from City Hunter!!
No man in the world is as cool and manly!! My life has been a journey to find my Ryo Saeba!!
City Hunter...
Of course no one is, he's fictional.
But!! But, but!!
A three-dimensional Ryo Saeba existed! Here!!
I knew when I first met Shiro!
Huh ?!

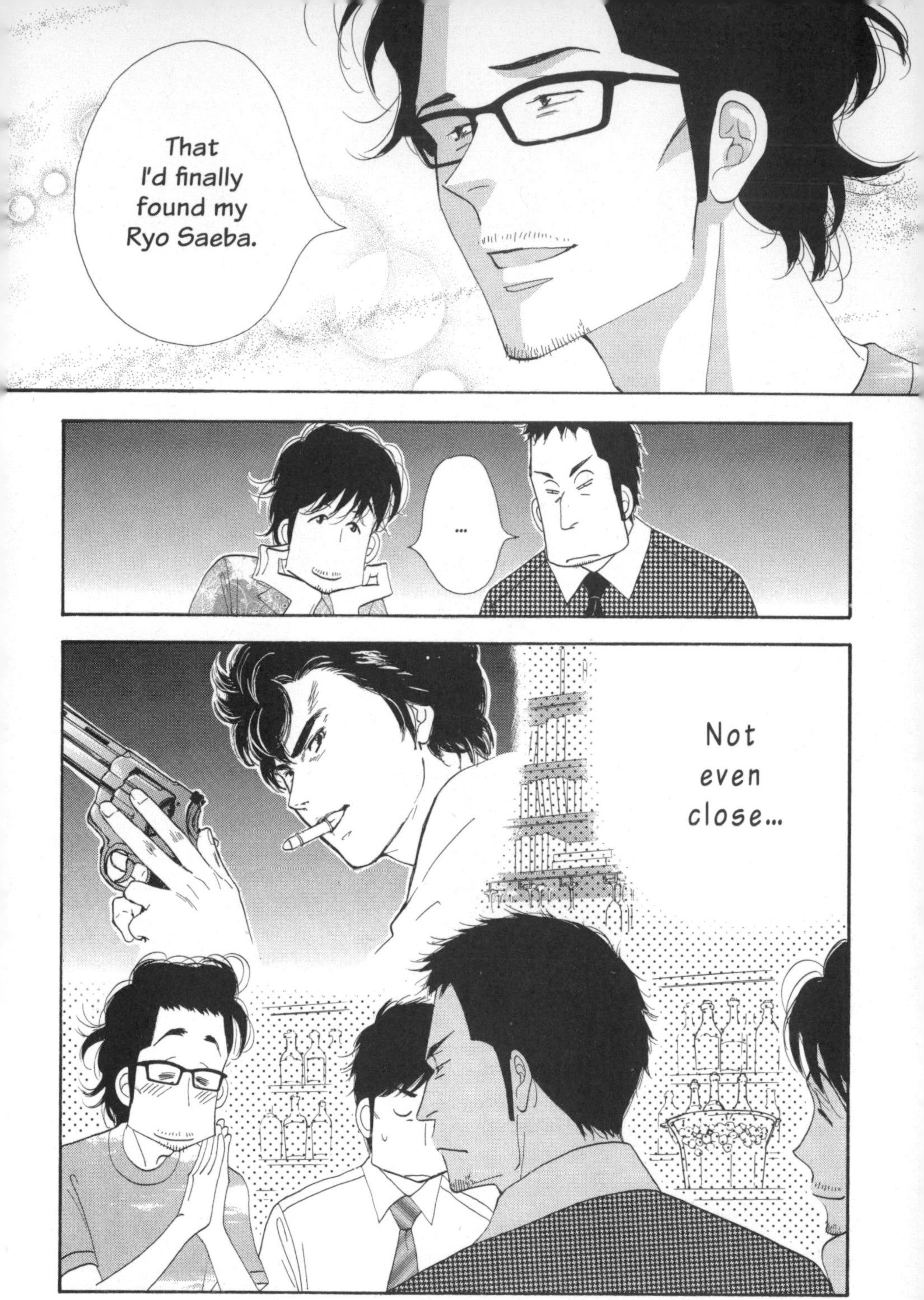
That I'd finally found my Ryo Saeba.
...
Not even close...

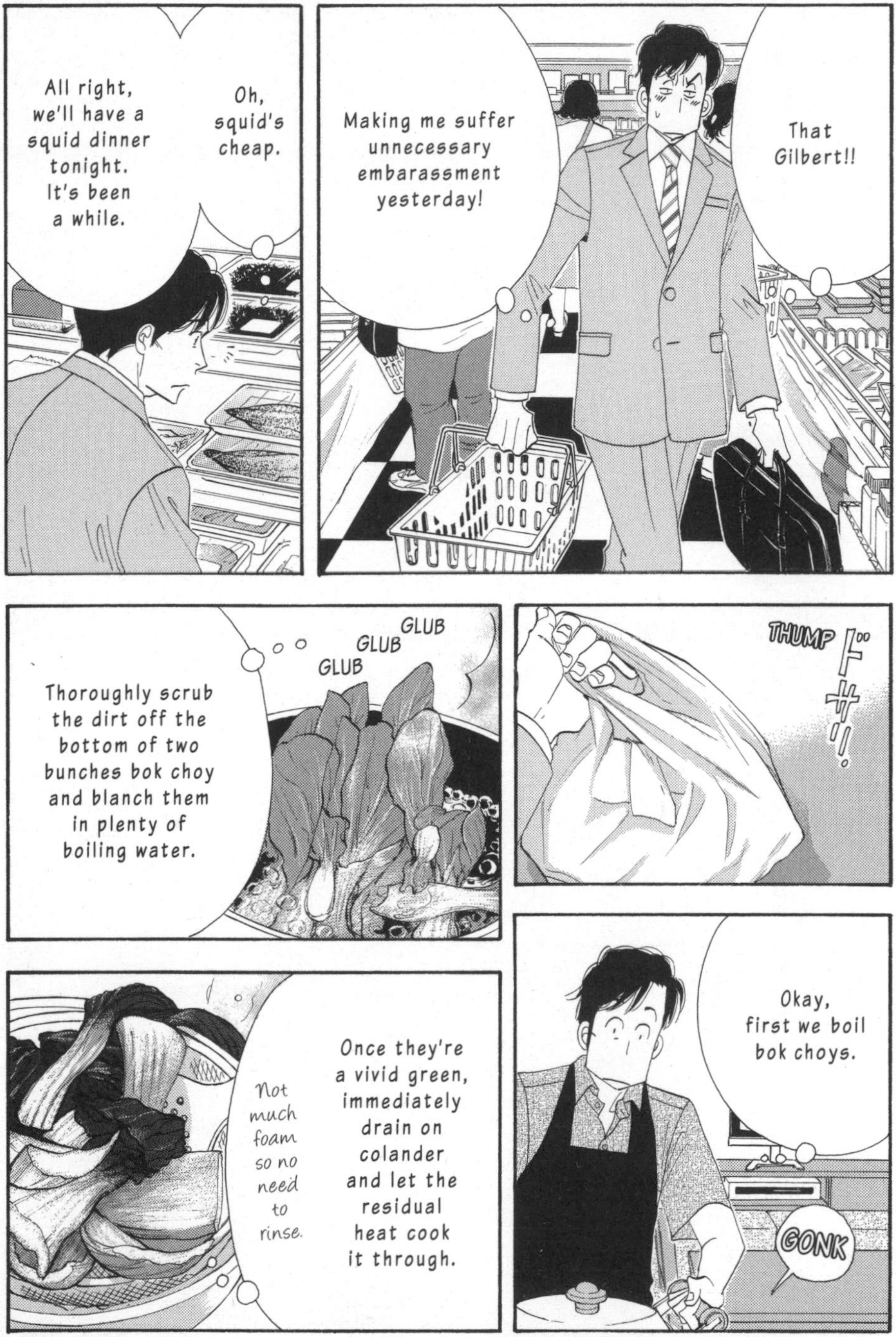
That Gilbert!!
Making me suffer unnecessary embarassment yesterday!
Oh, squid's cheap.
All right, we'll have a squid dinner tonight. It's been a while.
THUMP
ドサッ!!
Okay, first we boil bok choys.
GONK
Thoroughly scrub the dirt off the bottom of two bunches bok choy and blanch them in plenty of boiling water.
GLUB
GLUB
GLUB
Once they're a vivid green, immediately drain on colander and let the residual heat cook it through.
Not much foam so no need to rinse.

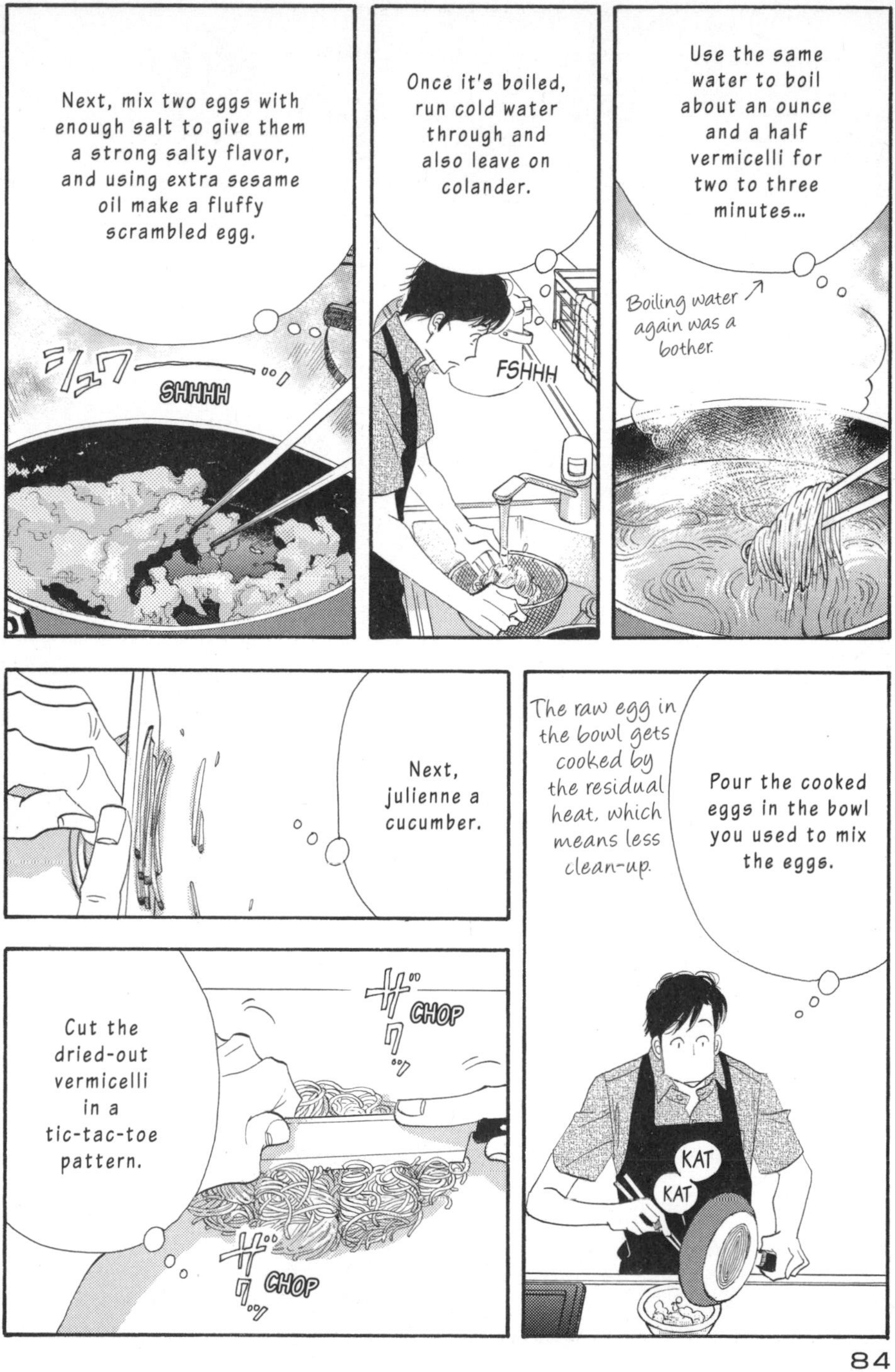

Use the same water to boil about an ounce and a half vermicelli for two to three minutes...
Boiling water again was a bother.
Once it's boiled, run cold water through and also leave on colander.
FSHHH
Next, mix two eggs with enough salt to give them a strong salty flavor, and using extra sesame oil make a fluffy scrambled egg.
SHHHH
Pour the cooked eggs in the bowl you used to mix the eggs.
The raw egg in the bowl gets cooked by the residual heat, which means less clean-up.
KAT
KAT
Next, julienne a cucumber.
CHOP
Cut the dried-out vermicelli in a tic-tac-toe pattern.
CHOP

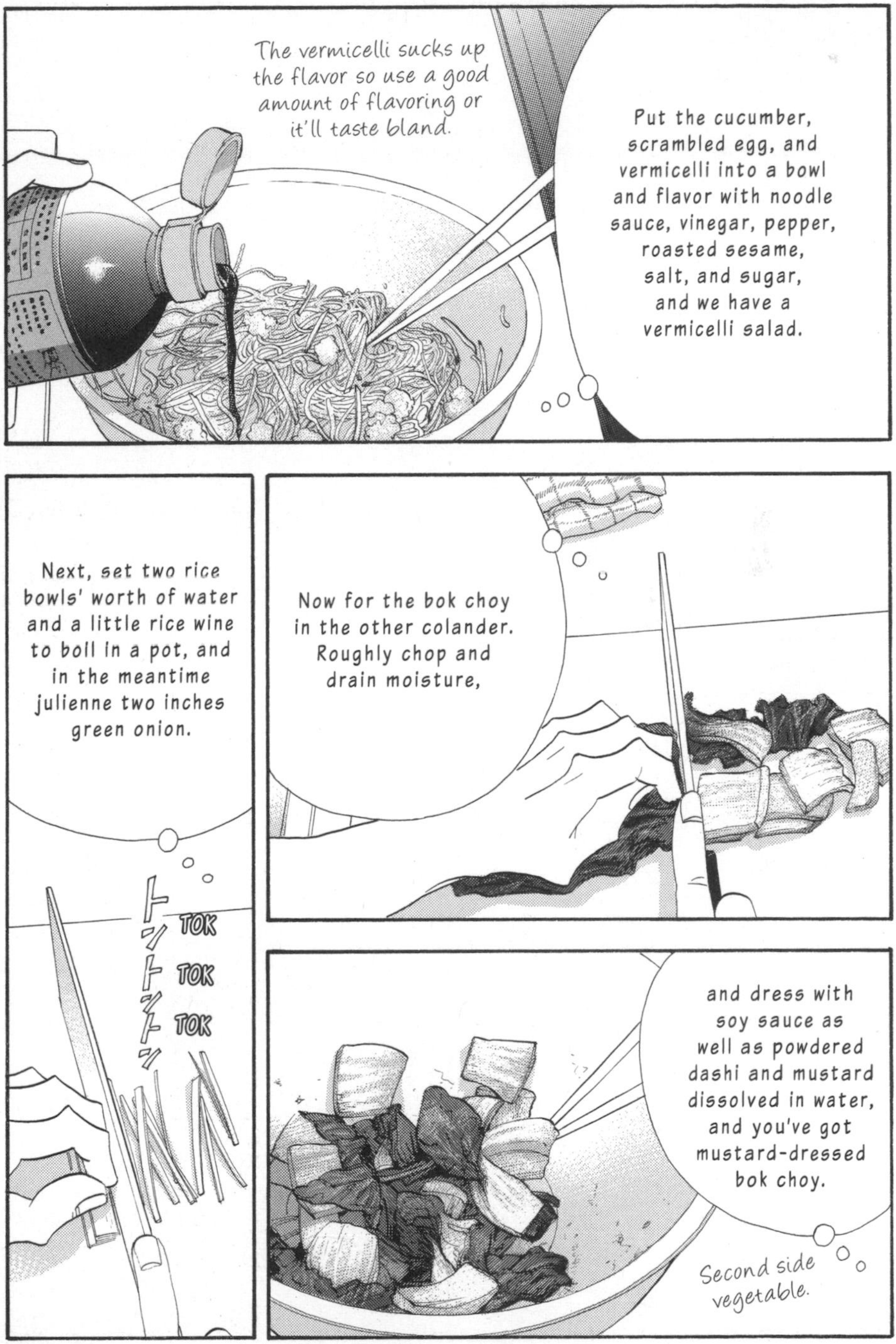

Put the cucumber, scrambled egg, and vermicelli into a bowl and flavor with noodle sauce, vinegar, pepper, roasted sesame, salt, and sugar, and we have a vermicelli salad.
The vermicelli sucks up the flavor so use a good amount of flavoring or it'll taste bland.
Now for the bok choy in the other colander. Roughly chop and drain moisture,
and dress with soy sauce as well as powdered dashi and mustard dissolved in water, and you've got mustard-dressed bok choy.
Second side vegetable.
Next, set two rice bowls' worth of water and a little rice wine to boil in a pot, and in the meantime julienne two inches green onion.
トントントン
TOK
TOK
TOK

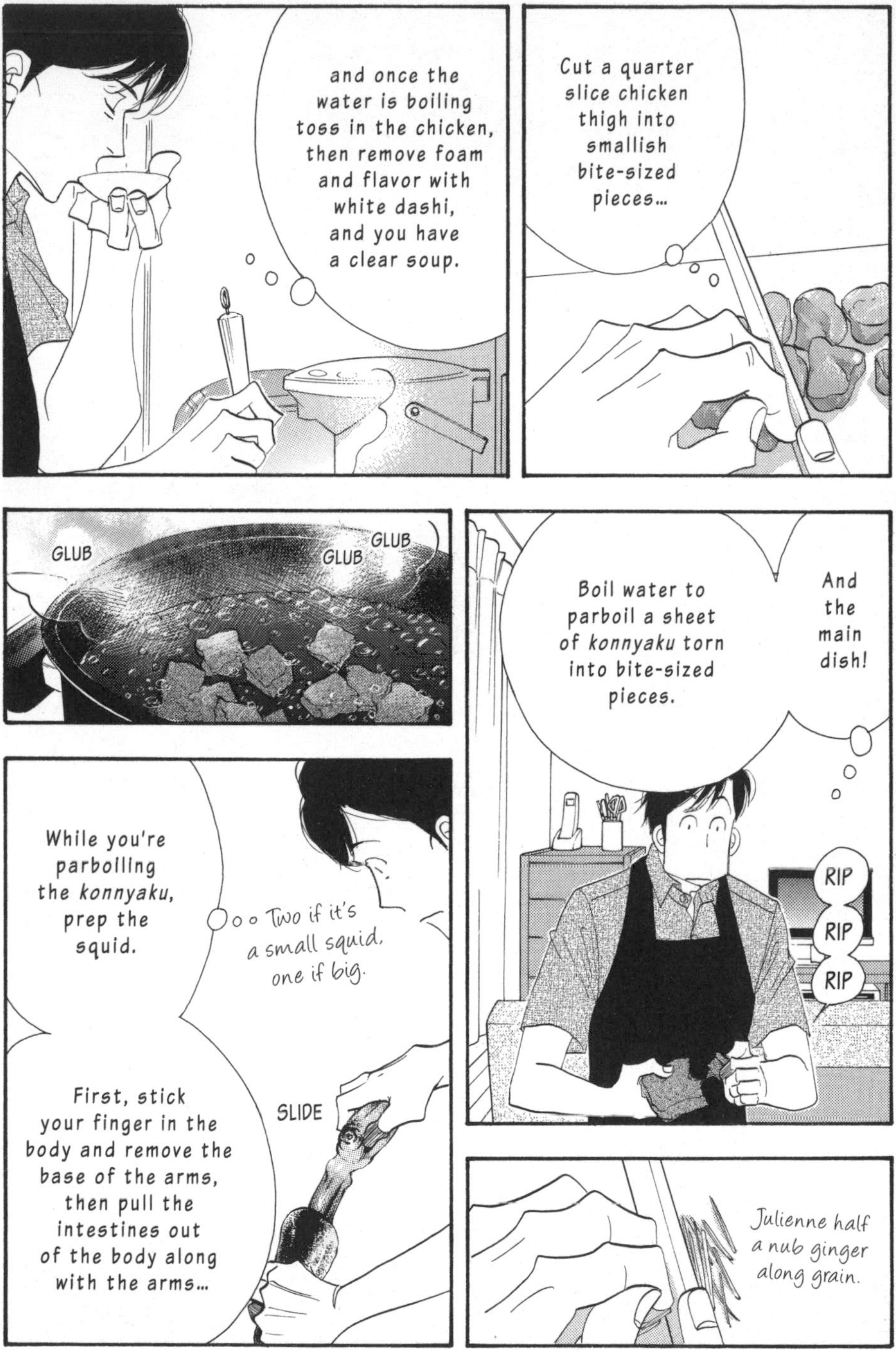
Cut a quarter slice chicken thigh into smallish bite-sized pieces...
and once the water is boiling toss in the chicken, then remove foam and flavor with white dashi, and you have a clear soup.
And the main dish!
Boil water to parboil a sheet of konnyaku torn into bite-sized pieces.
RIP
RIP
RIP
GLUB
GLUB
GLUB
While you're parboiling the konnyaku, prep the squid.
Two if it's a small squid, one if big.
SLIDE
First, stick your finger in the body and remove the base of the arms, then pull the intestines out of the body along with the arms...
Julienne half a nub ginger along grain.

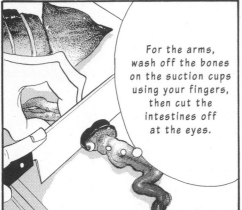

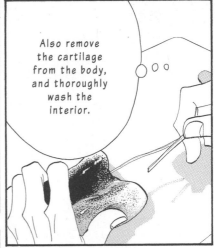

Also remove the cartilage from the body, and thoroughly wash the interior.
For the arms, wash off the bones on the suction cups using your fingers, then cut the intestines off at the eyes.
Cut body into half-inch rings.
The beak is tough so take that off too, and cut the arms into chunks of two to three each.
Now drain the parboiled *konnyaku* in a colander and rinse well.
ZWSH
Mix the flavoring beforehand:
Dissolve approximately 1 Tbsp miso in 2 Tbsp mirin and 1/2 Tbsp rice wine.

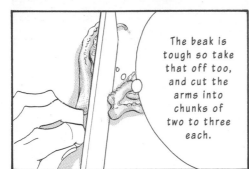

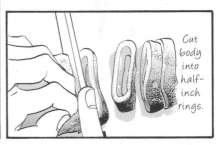

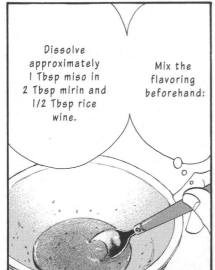

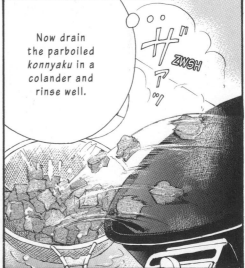

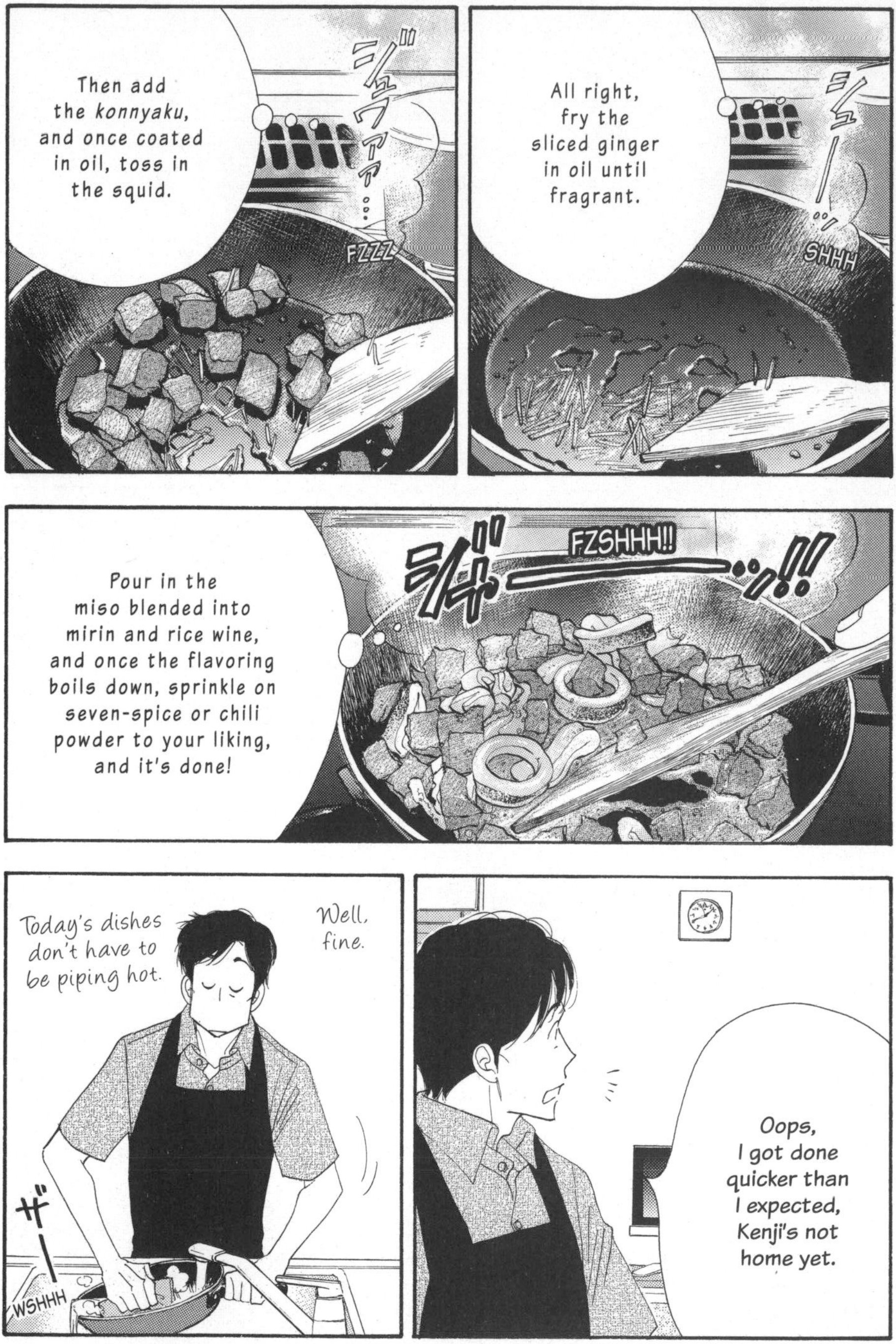
All right, fry the sliced ginger in oil until fragrant.
SHHH
Then add the *konnyaku*, and once coated in oil, toss in the squid.
FZZZ
FZSHHH!!
Pour in the miso blended into mirin and rice wine, and once the flavoring boils down, sprinkle on seven-spice or chili powder to your liking, and it's done!
Oops, I got done quicker than I expected, Kenji's not home yet.
Today's dishes don't have to be piping hot.
Well, fine.
WSHHH

Welcome back

I'm ho-me

- Miso-fried squid and konnyaku
- Vermicelli, egg, and cucumber salad
- Mustard-dressed bok choy
- Clear soup with green onions and chicken

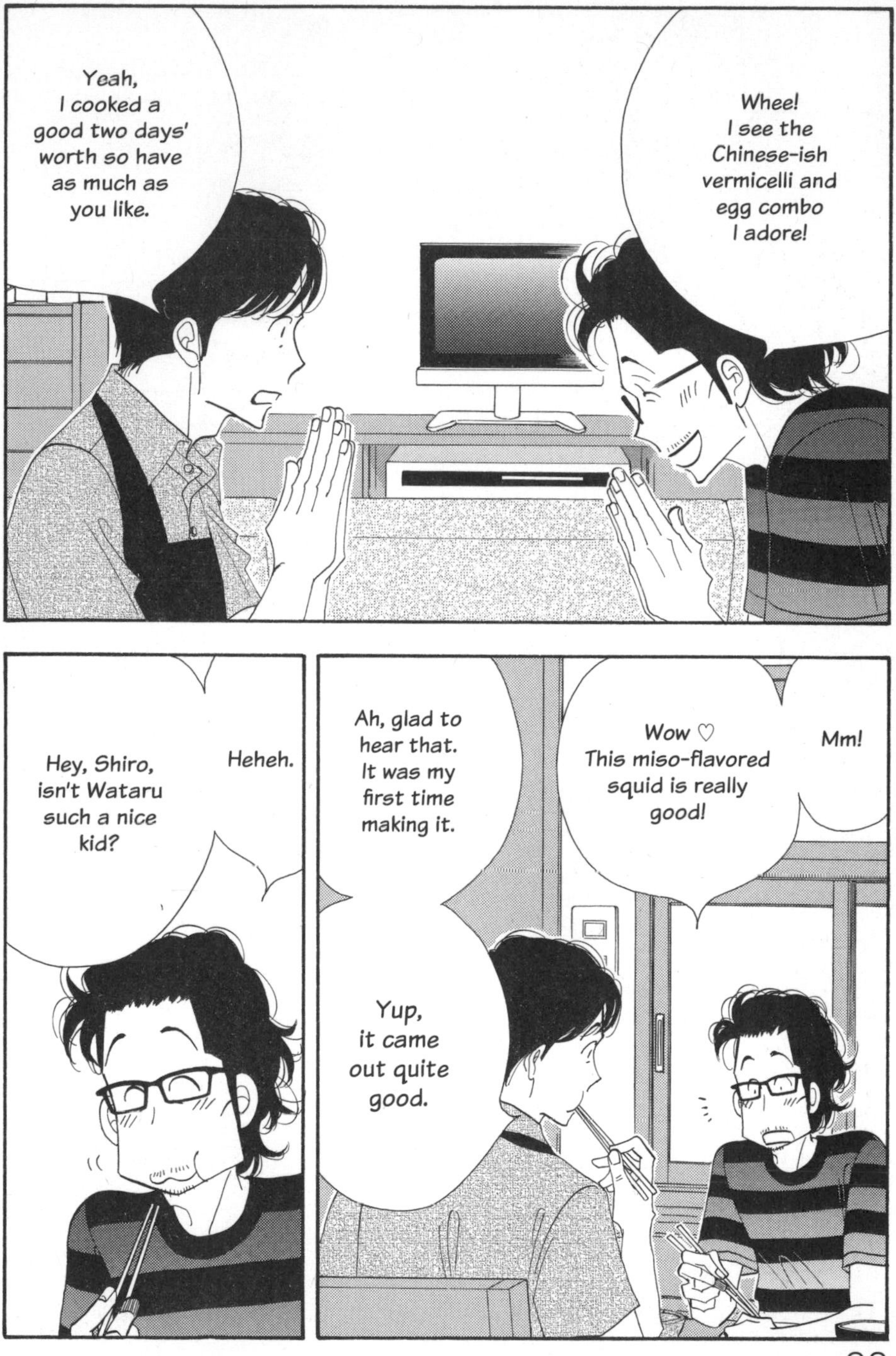
Whee! I see the Chinese-ish vermicelli and egg combo I adore!
Yeah, I cooked a good two days' worth so have as much as you like.
Mm!
Wow ♡ This miso-flavored squid is really good!
Ah, glad to hear that. It was my first time making it.
Yup, it came out quite good.
Heheh.
Hey, Shiro, isn't Wataru such a nice kid?

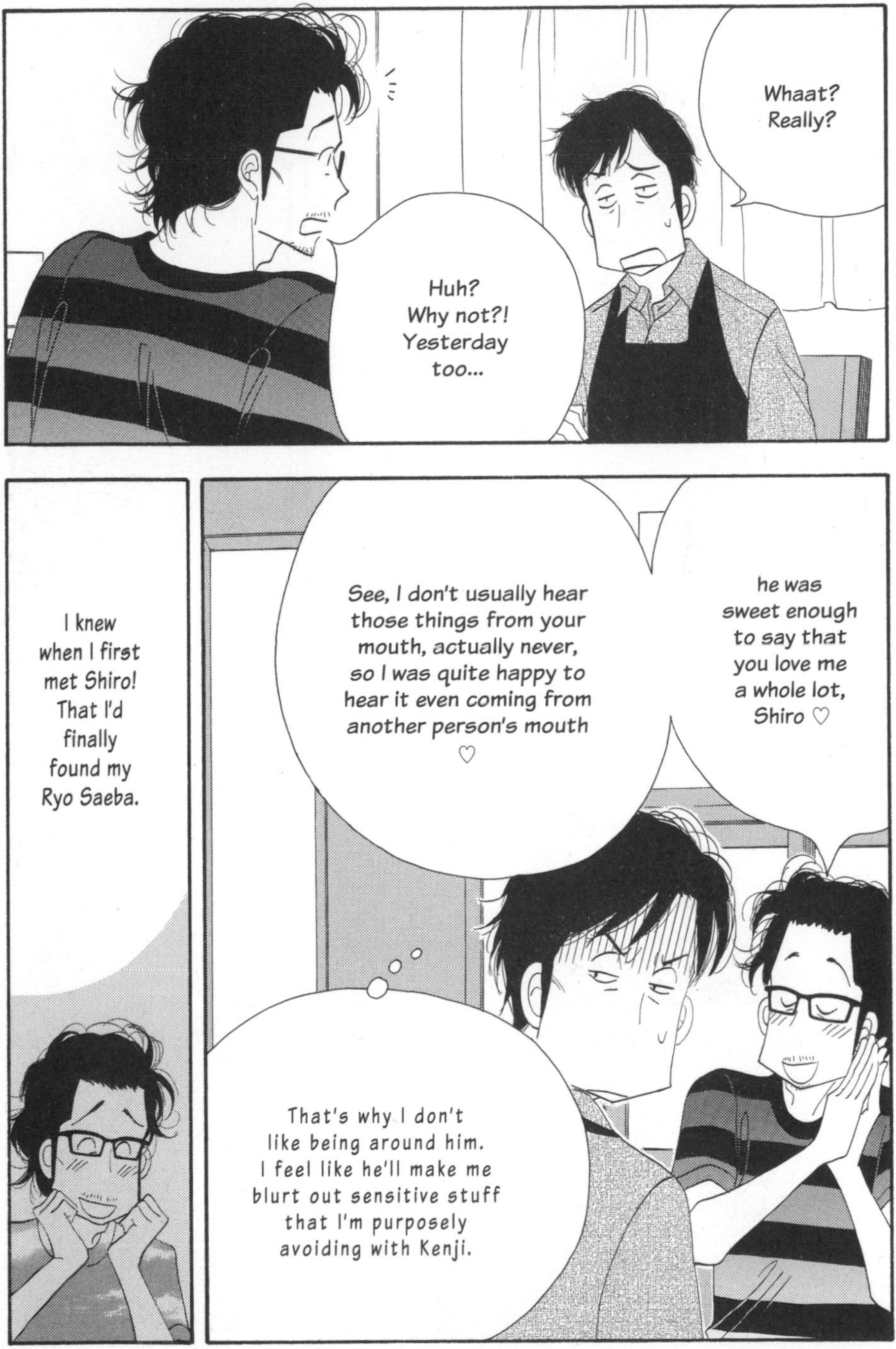
Whaat? Really?
Huh? Why not?! Yesterday too...
he was sweet enough to say that you love me a whole lot, Shiro ♡
See, I don't usually hear those things from your mouth, actually never, so I was quite happy to hear it even coming from another person's mouth ♡
That's why I don't like being around him. I feel like he'll make me blurt out sensitive stuff that I'm purposely avoiding with Kenji.
I knew when I first met Shiro! That I'd finally found my Ryo Saeba.

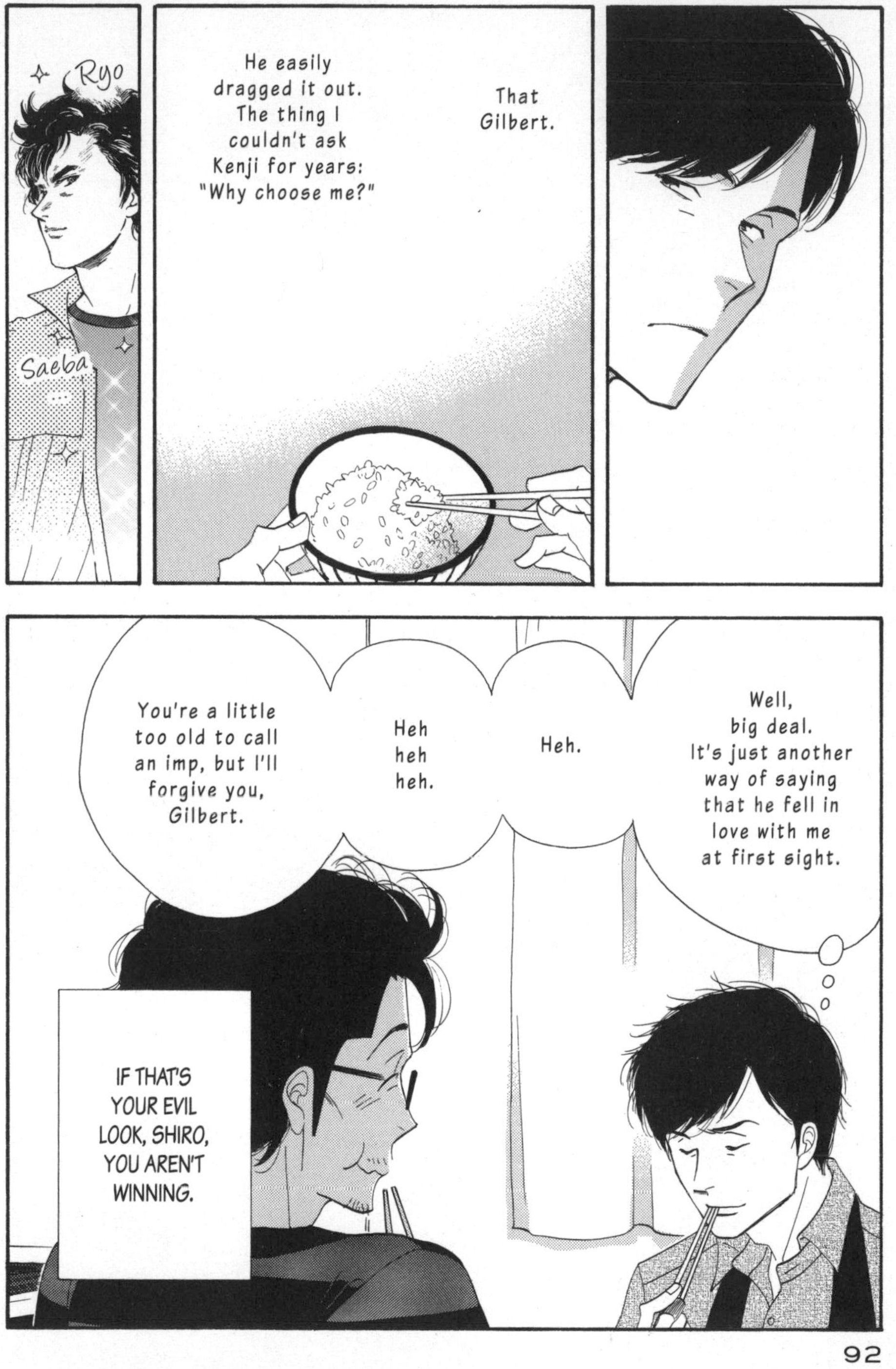

That Gilbert.
He easily dragged it out. The thing I couldn't ask Kenji for years: "Why choose me?"
Ryo
Saeba
...
Well, big deal. It's just another way of saying that he fell in love with me at first sight.
Heh.
Heh heh heh.
You're a little too old to call an imp, but I'll forgive you, Gilbert.
IF THAT'S YOUR EVIL LOOK, SHIRO, YOU AREN'T WINNING.

Squids become tough when you heat them too much, so the key is to fry them quick.

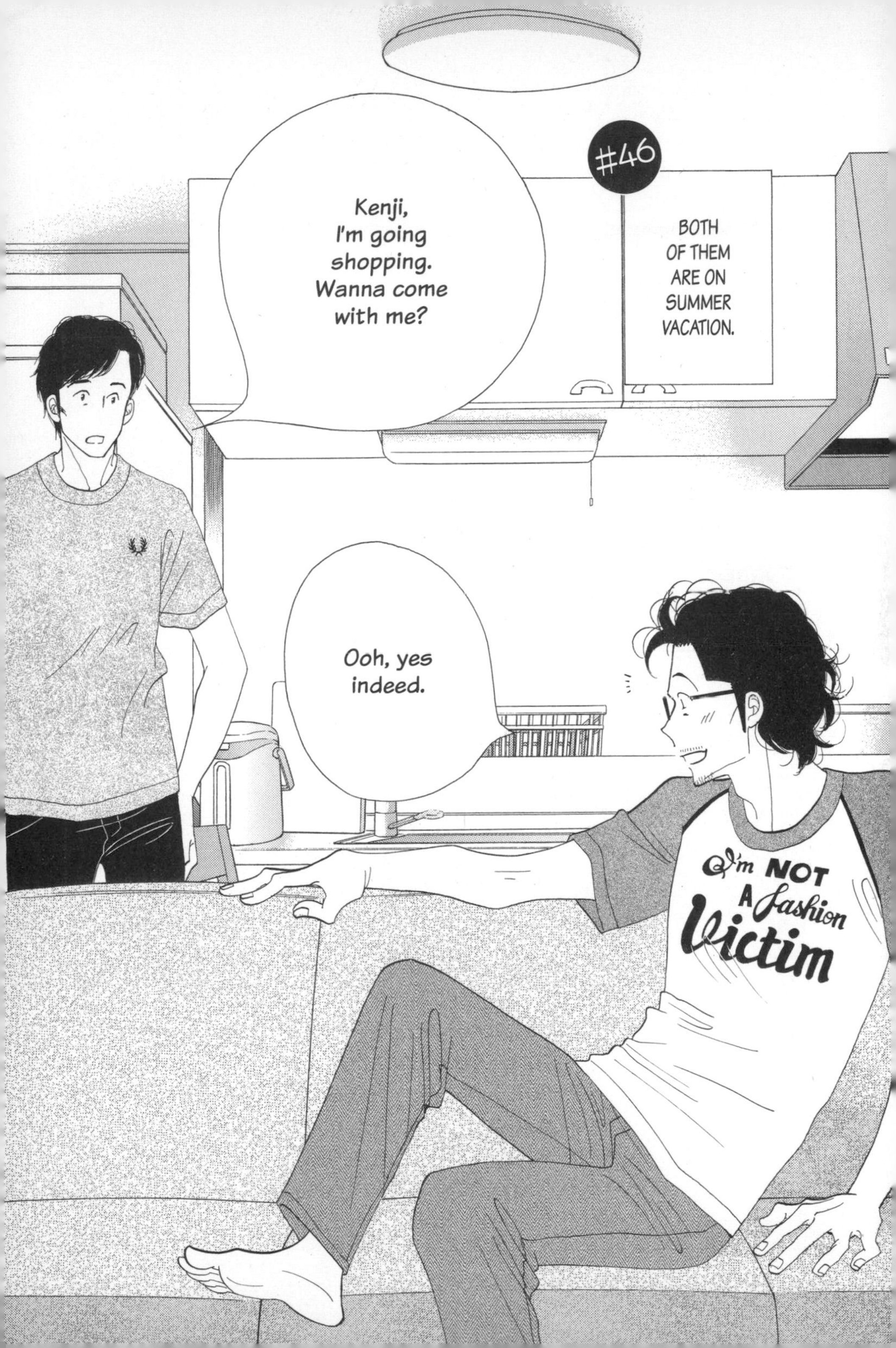
#46
BOTH OF THEM ARE ON SUMMER VACATION.
Kenji, I'm going shopping. Wanna come with me?
Ooh, yes indeed.
I'm NOT A fashion Victim

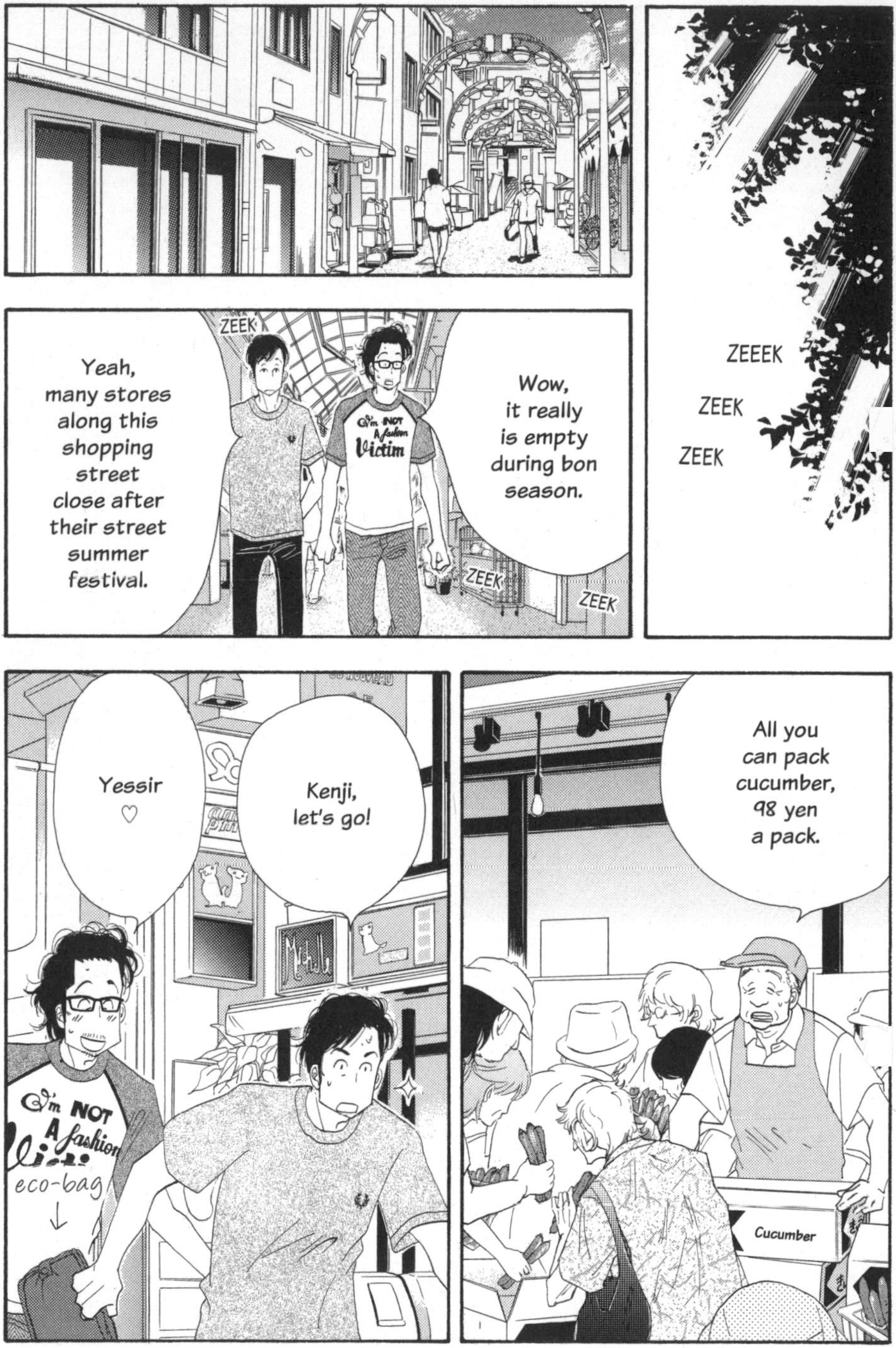
ZEEEK
ZEEK
ZEEK
ZEEK
Wow, it really is empty during bon season.
I'm NOT A fashion Victim
Yeah, many stores along this shopping street close after their street summer festival.
ZEEK
ZEEK
All you can pack cucumber, 98 yen a pack.
Cucumber
Kenji, let's go!
Yessir ♡
I'm NOT A fashion
eco-bag
↓

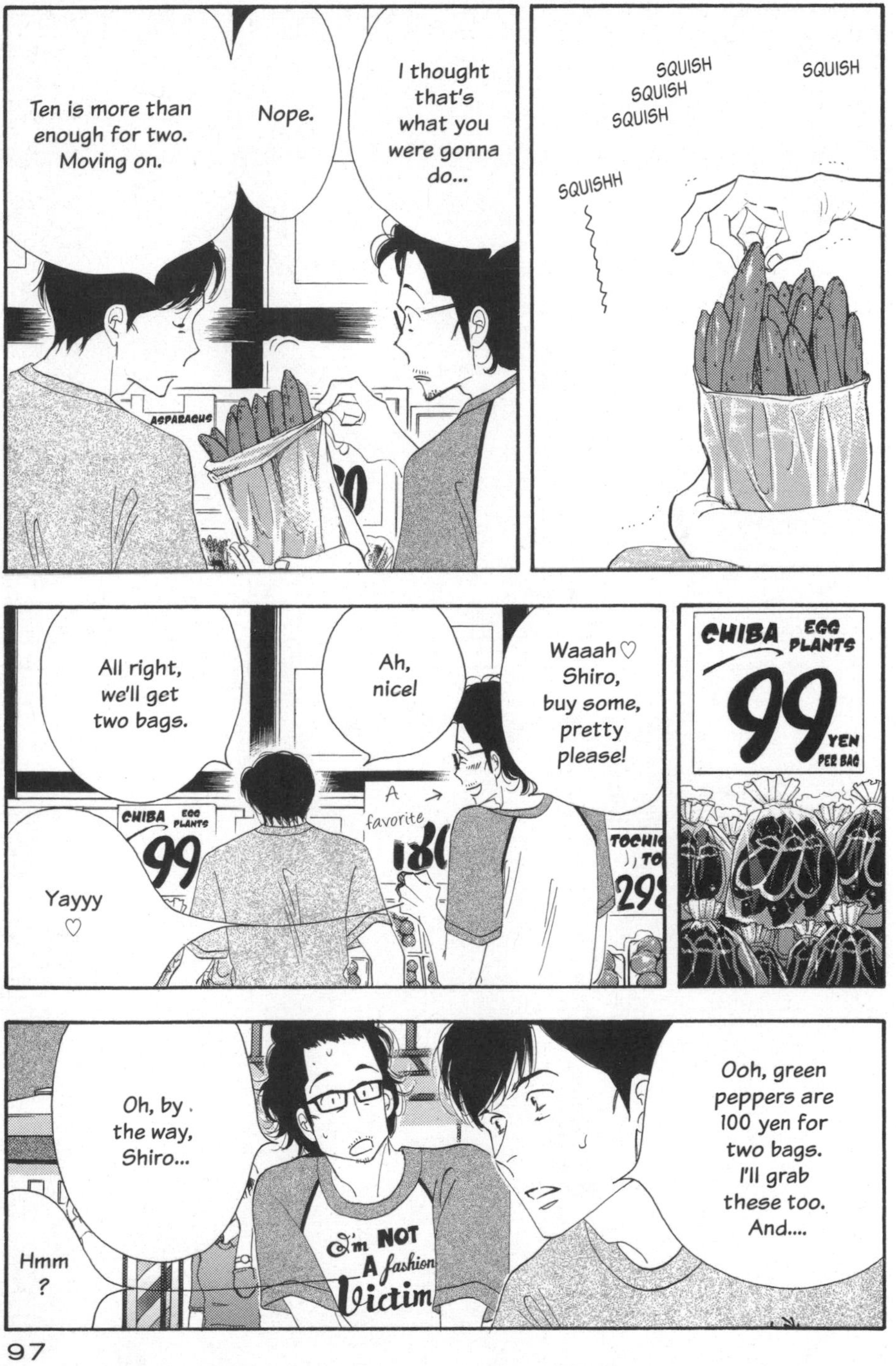
SQUISH
SQUISH
SQUISH
SQUISH
SQUISHH
I thought that's what you were gonna do...
Nope.
Ten is more than enough for two. Moving on.
ASPARAGUS
CHIBA EGG PLANTS
99 YEN PER BAG
Waaah♡ Shiro, buy some, pretty please!
Ah, nice!
All right, we'll get two bags.
A favorite →
CHIBA EGG PLANTS
99
Yayyy ♡
Ooh, green peppers are 100 yen for two bags. I'll grab these too. And....
Oh, by the way, Shiro...
I'm NOT A fashion Victim
Hmm ?

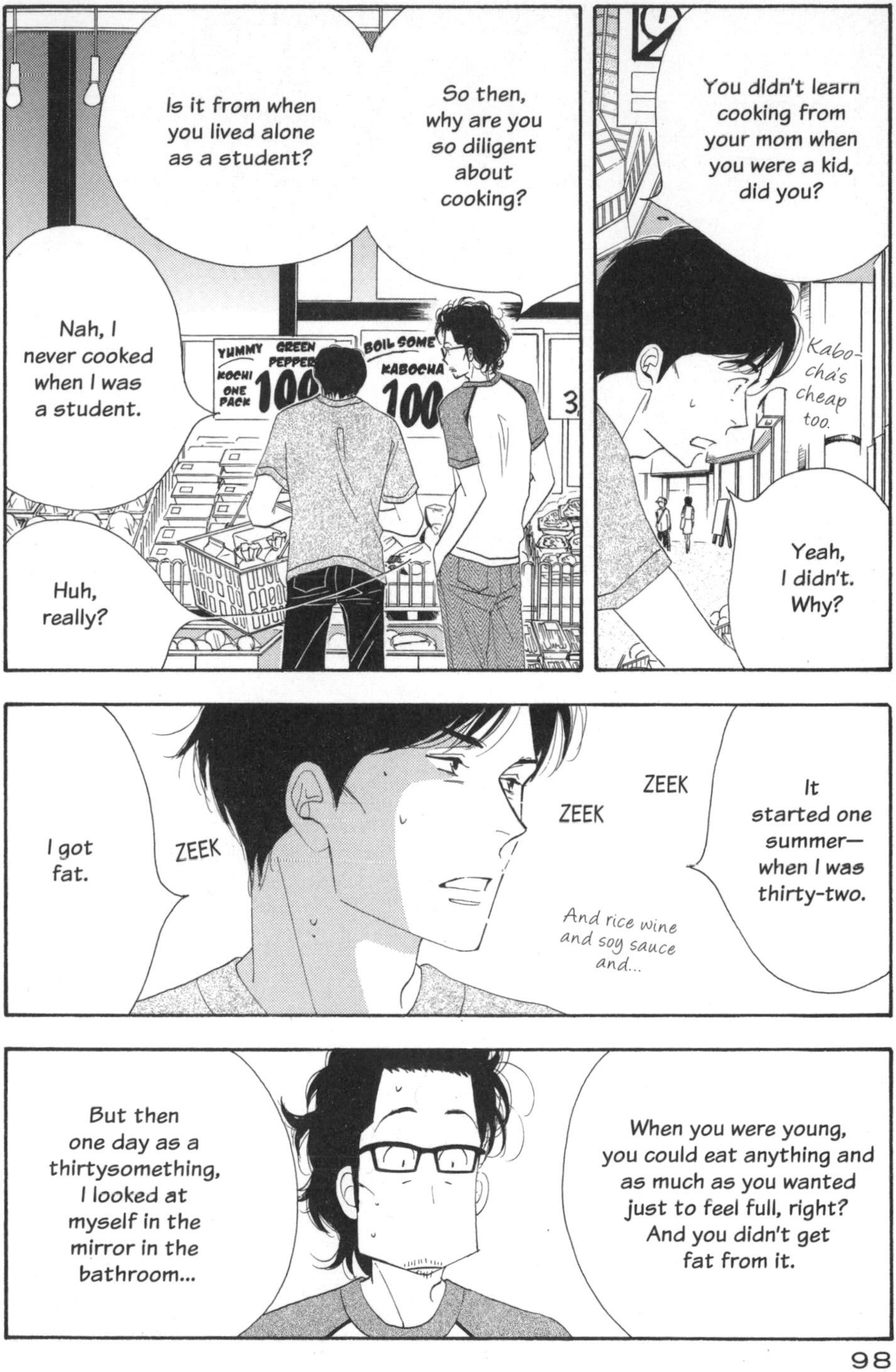
You didn't learn cooking from your mom when you were a kid, did you?
Kabocha's cheap too.
Yeah, I didn't. Why?
So then, why are you so diligent about cooking?
Is it from when you lived alone as a student?
BOIL SOME KABOCHA 100
YUMMY GREEN PEPPER KOCHI ONE PACK 100
Nah, I never cooked when I was a student.
Huh, really?
It started one summer— when I was thirty-two.
ZEEK
ZEEK
And rice wine and soy sauce and...
ZEEK
I got fat.
When you were young, you could eat anything and as much as you wanted just to feel full, right? And you didn't get fat from it.
But then one day as a thirtysomething, I looked at myself in the mirror in the bathroom...

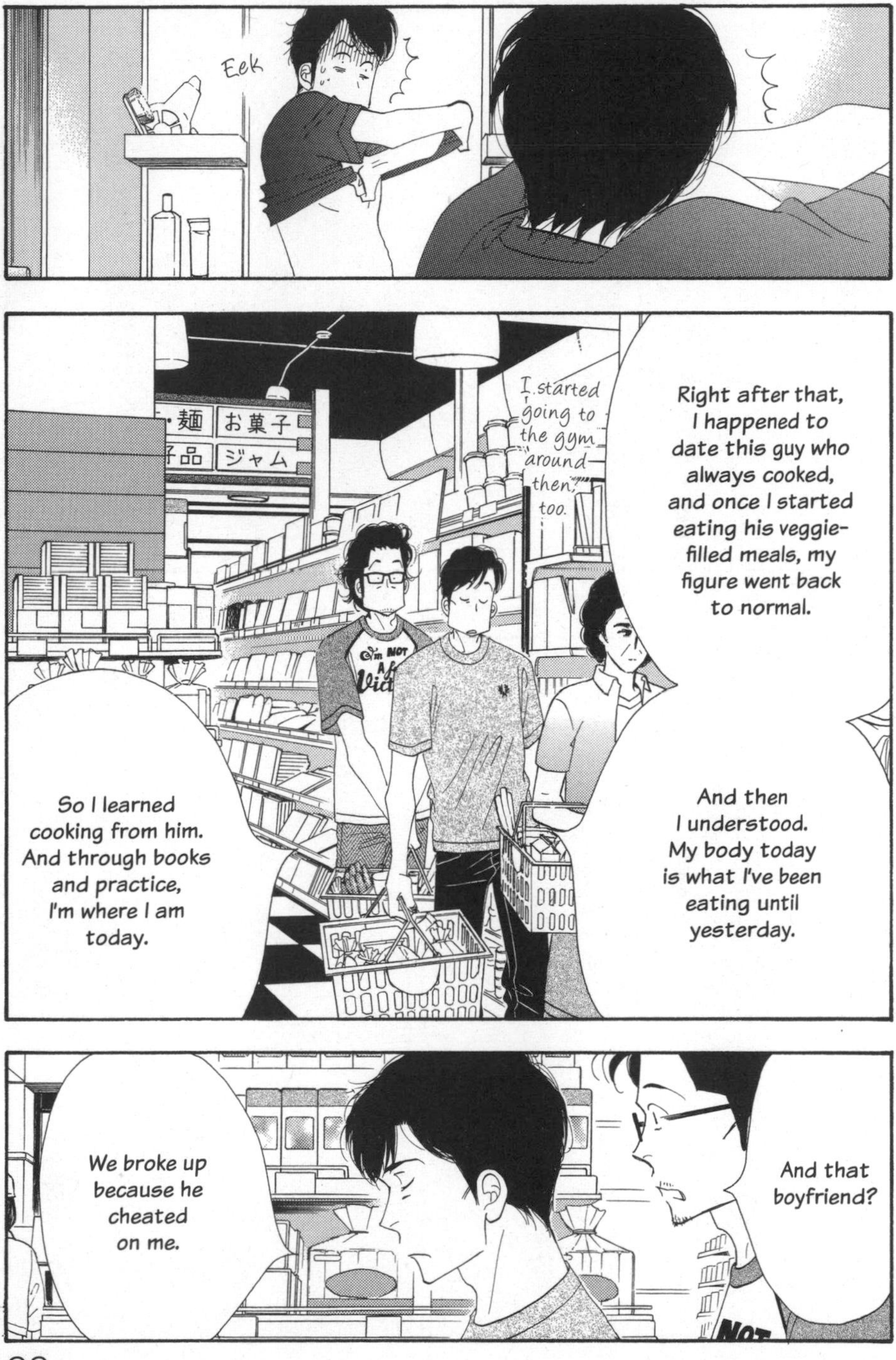
Eek
お菓子
ジャム
Right after that, I happened to date this guy who always cooked, and once I started eating his veggie-filled meals, my figure went back to normal.
I started going to the gym around then, too.
And then I understood. My body today is what I've been eating until yesterday.
So I learned cooking from him. And through books and practice, I'm where I am today.
And that boyfriend?
We broke up because he cheated on me.

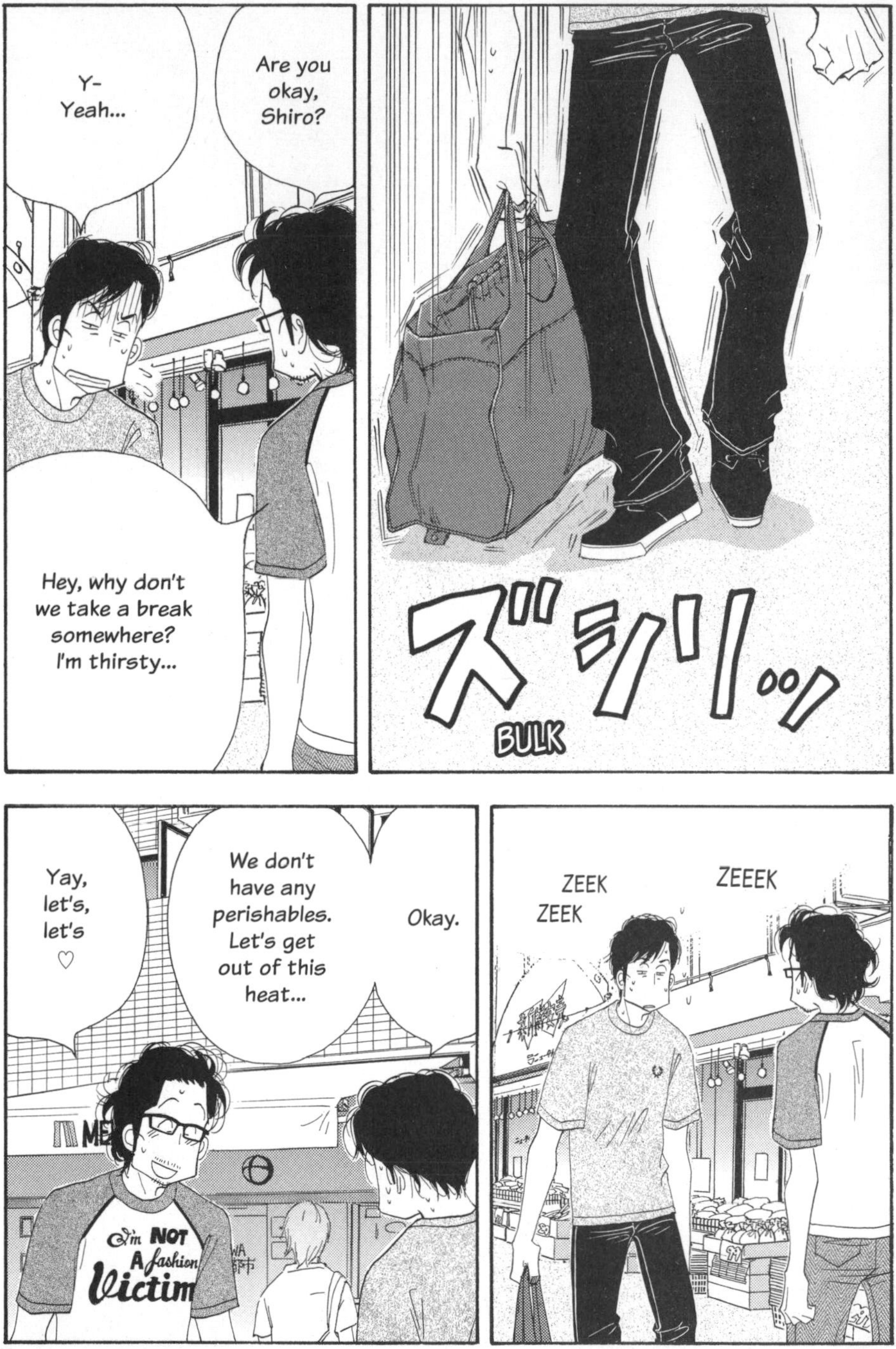
ズシリッ
BULK
Are you okay, Shiro?
Y- Yeah...
Hey, why don't we take a break somewhere? I'm thirsty...
ZEEEK
ZEEK
ZEEK
Okay.
We don't have any perishables. Let's get out of this heat...
Yay, let's, let's ♡
I'm NOT A fashion Victim

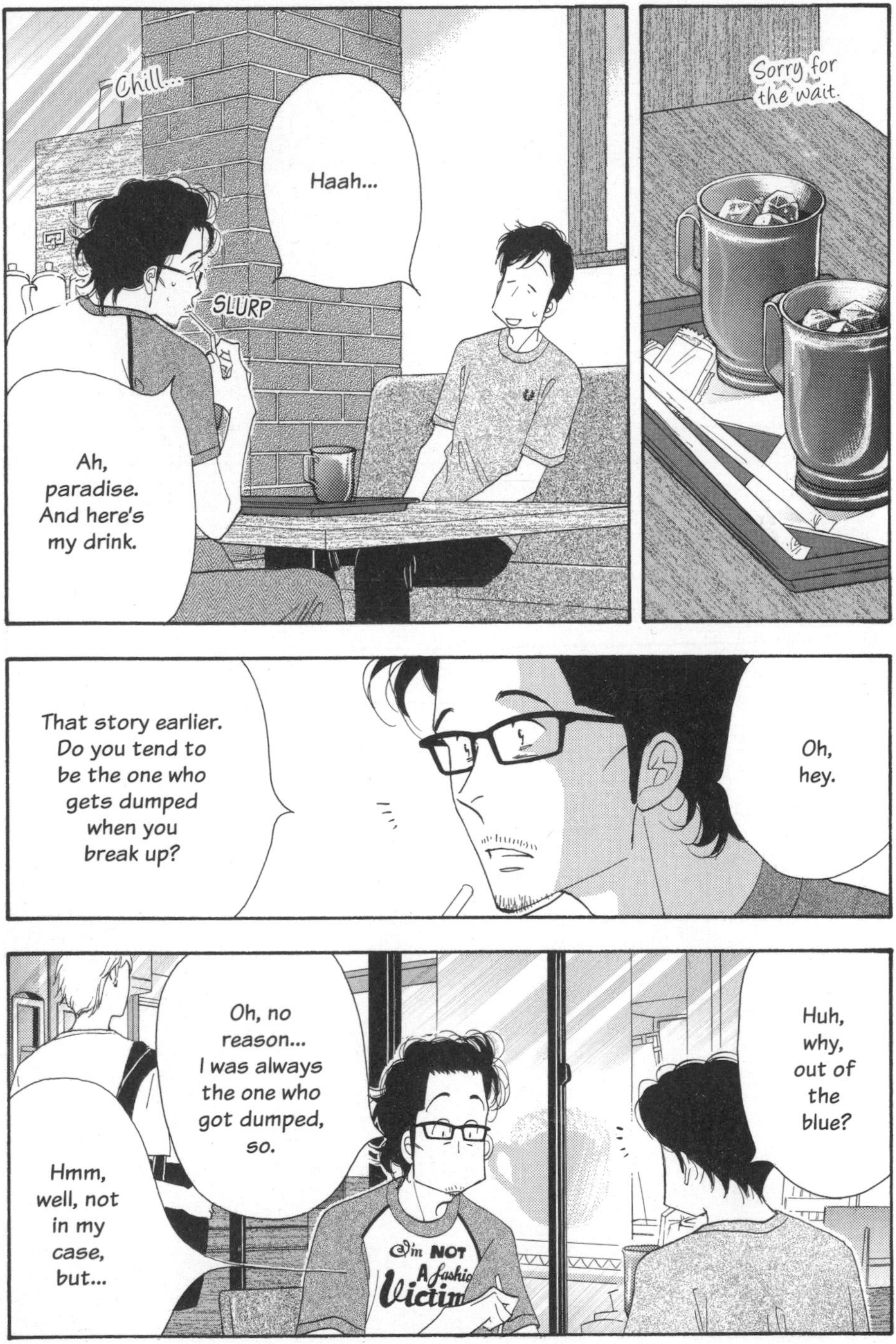
Sorry for the wait.
Haah...
Chill...
SLURP
Ah, paradise. And here's my drink.
Oh, hey.
That story earlier. Do you tend to be the one who gets dumped when you break up?
Huh, why, out of the blue?
Oh, no reason... I was always the one who got dumped, so.
Hmm, well, not in my case, but...

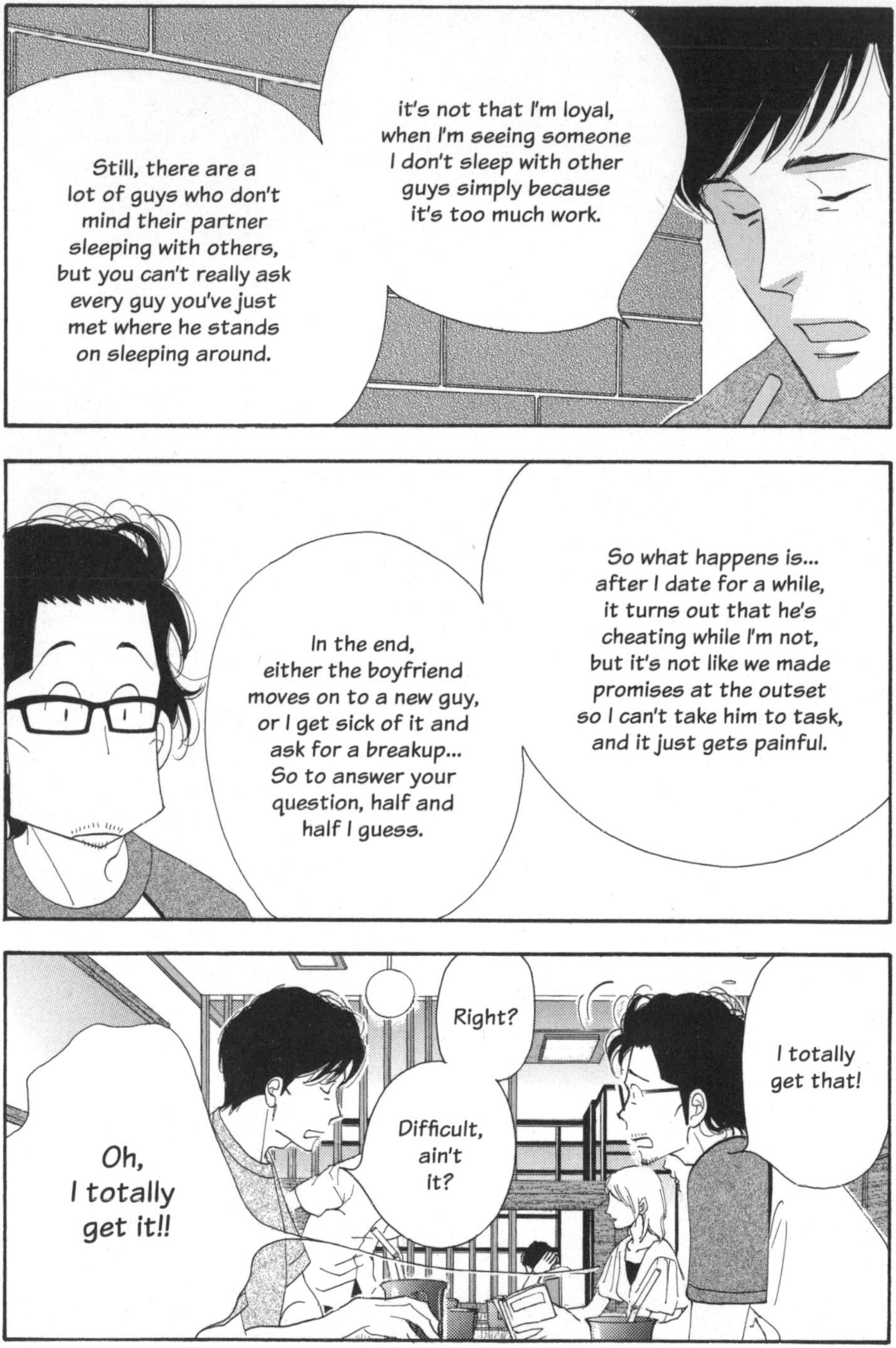
it's not that I'm loyal, when I'm seeing someone I don't sleep with other guys simply because it's too much work.
Still, there are a lot of guys who don't mind their partner sleeping with others, but you can't really ask every guy you've just met where he stands on sleeping around.
So what happens is... after I date for a while, it turns out that he's cheating while I'm not, but it's not like we made promises at the outset so I can't take him to task, and it just gets painful.
In the end, either the boyfriend moves on to a new guy, or I get sick of it and ask for a breakup... So to answer your question, half and half I guess.
I totally get that!
Right?
Difficult, ain't it?
Oh, I totally get it!!

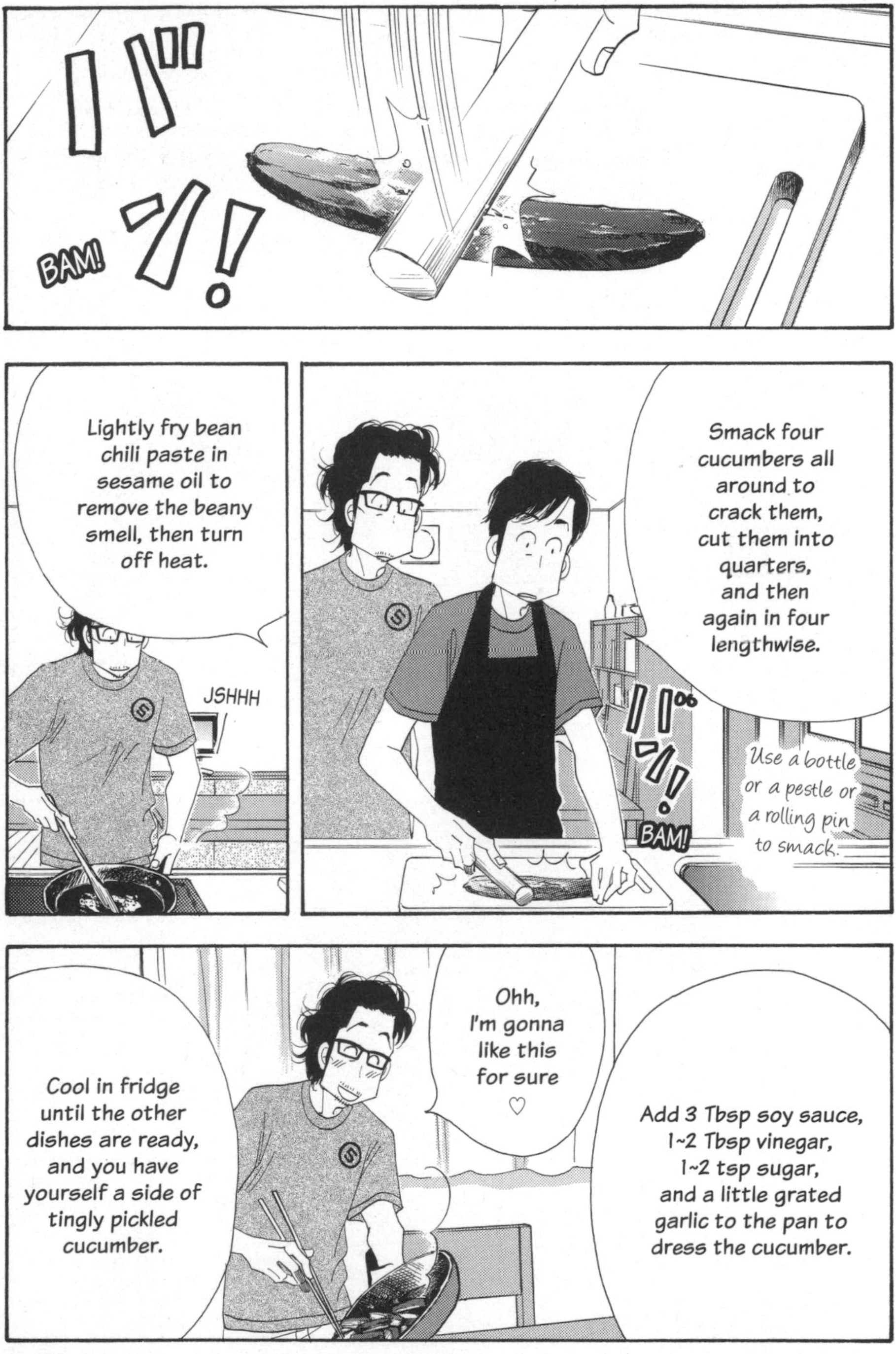
BAM!
Smack four cucumbers all around to crack them, cut them into quarters, and then again in four lengthwise.
BAM!
Use a bottle or a pestle or a rolling pin to smack.
Lightly fry bean chili paste in sesame oil to remove the beany smell, then turn off heat.
JSHHH
Add 3 Tbsp soy sauce, 1~2 Tbsp vinegar, 1~2 tsp sugar, and a little grated garlic to the pan to dress the cucumber.
Ohh, I'm gonna like this for sure ♡
Cool in fridge until the other dishes are ready, and you have yourself a side of tingly pickled cucumber.

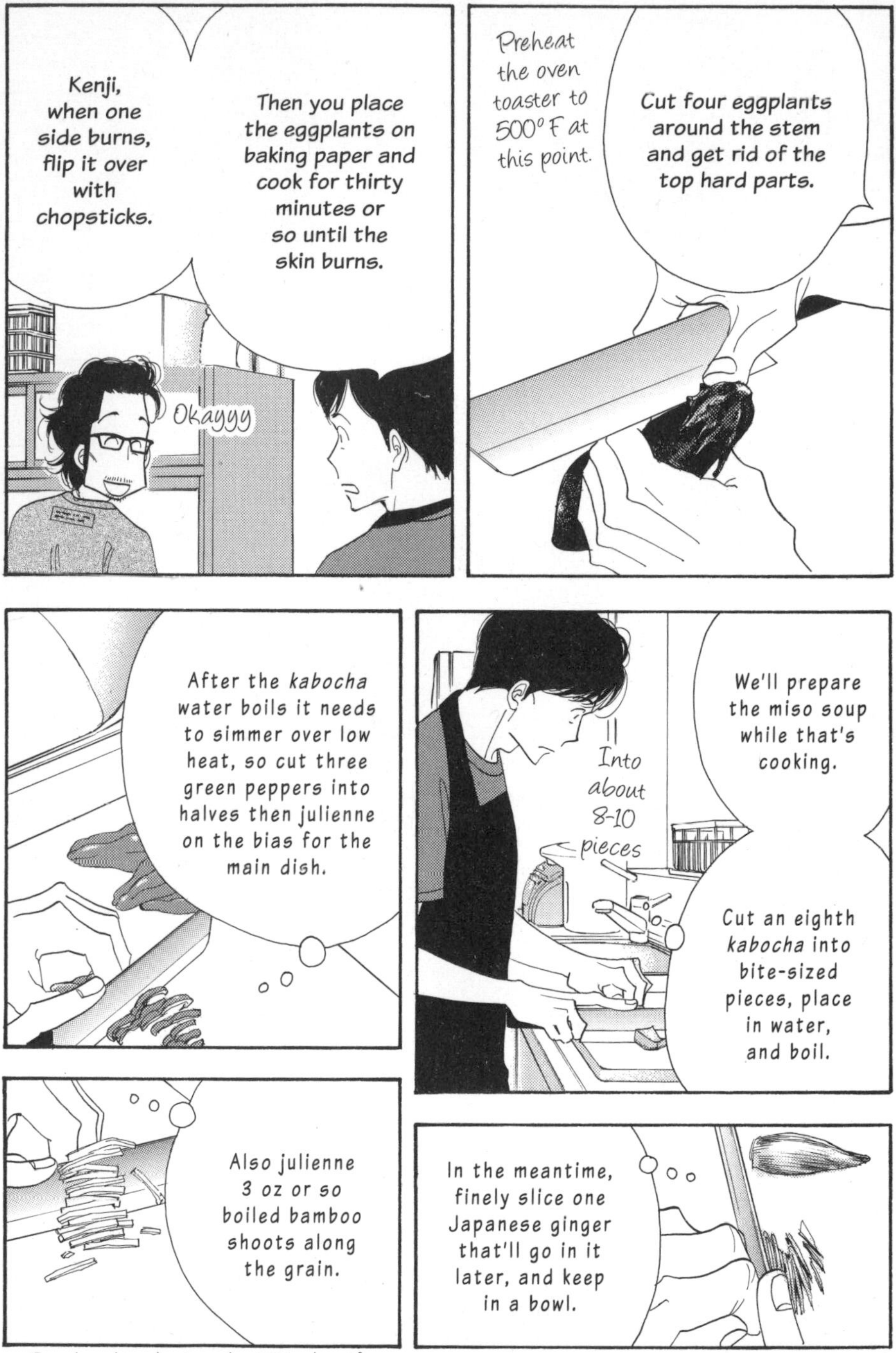
Cut four eggplants around the stem and get rid of the top hard parts.
Preheat the oven toaster to 500° F at this point.
Then you place the eggplants on baking paper and cook for thirty minutes or so until the skin burns.
Kenji, when one side burns, flip it over with chopsticks.
Okayyy
We'll prepare the miso soup while that's cooking.
Cut an eighth kabocha into bite-sized pieces, place in water, and boil.
Into about 8-10 pieces
After the kabocha water boils it needs to simmer over low heat, so cut three green peppers into halves then julienne on the bias for the main dish.
In the meantime, finely slice one Japanese ginger that'll go in it later, and keep in a bowl.
Also julienne 3 oz or so boiled bamboo shoots along the grain.

3 oz bamboo shoot = about 2 inches of the bottom cut round and then into half.

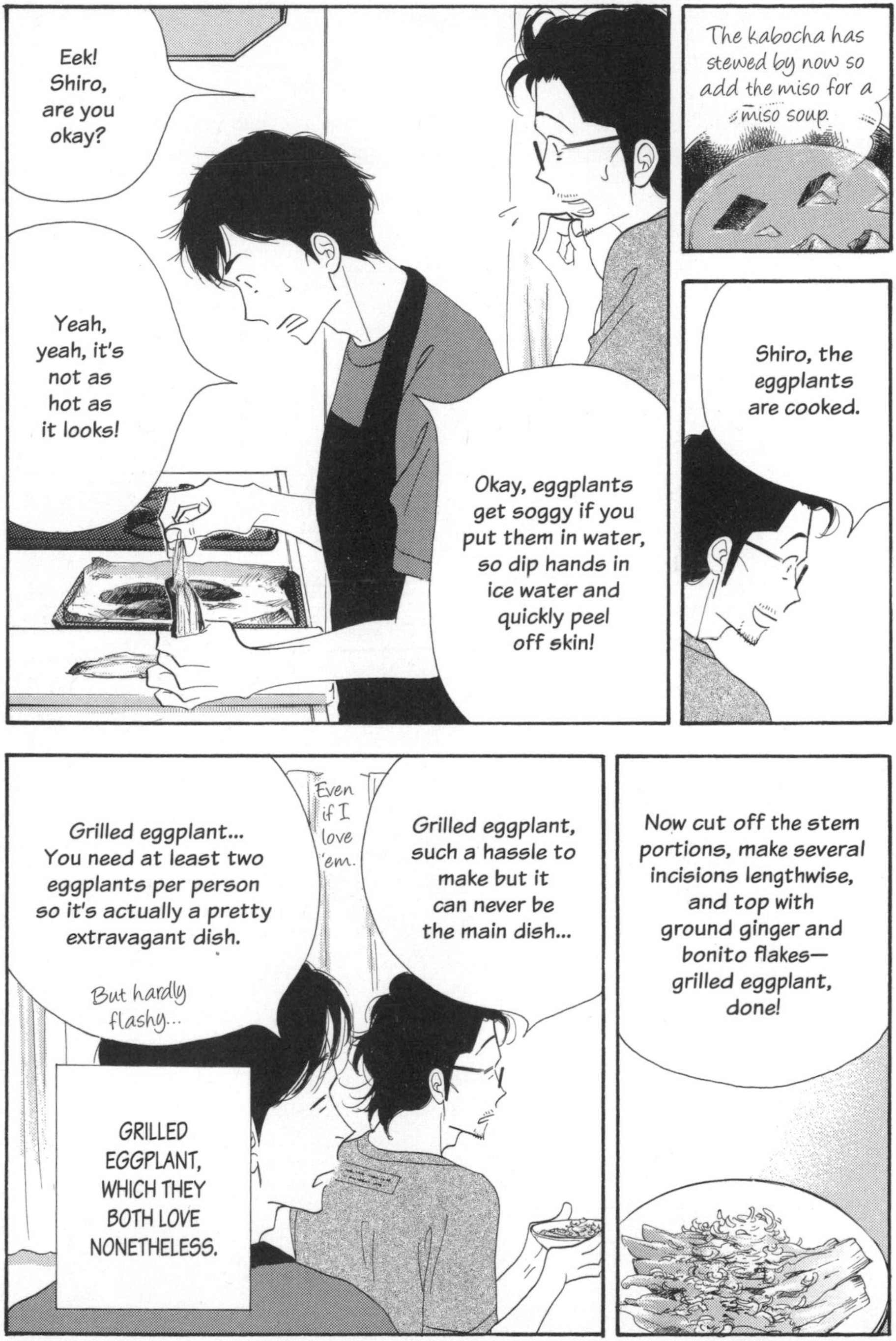
The kabocha has stewed by now so add the miso for a miso soup.
Shiro, the eggplants are cooked.
Okay, eggplants get soggy if you put them in water, so dip hands in ice water and quickly peel off skin!
Eek! Shiro, are you okay?
Yeah, yeah, it's not as hot as it looks!
Now cut off the stem portions, make several incisions lengthwise, and top with ground ginger and bonito flakes—grilled eggplant, done!
Grilled eggplant, such a hassle to make but it can never be the main dish...
Even if I love 'em.
Grilled eggplant... You need at least two eggplants per person so it's actually a pretty extravagant dish.
But hardly flashy...
GRILLED EGGPLANT, WHICH THEY BOTH LOVE NONETHELESS.

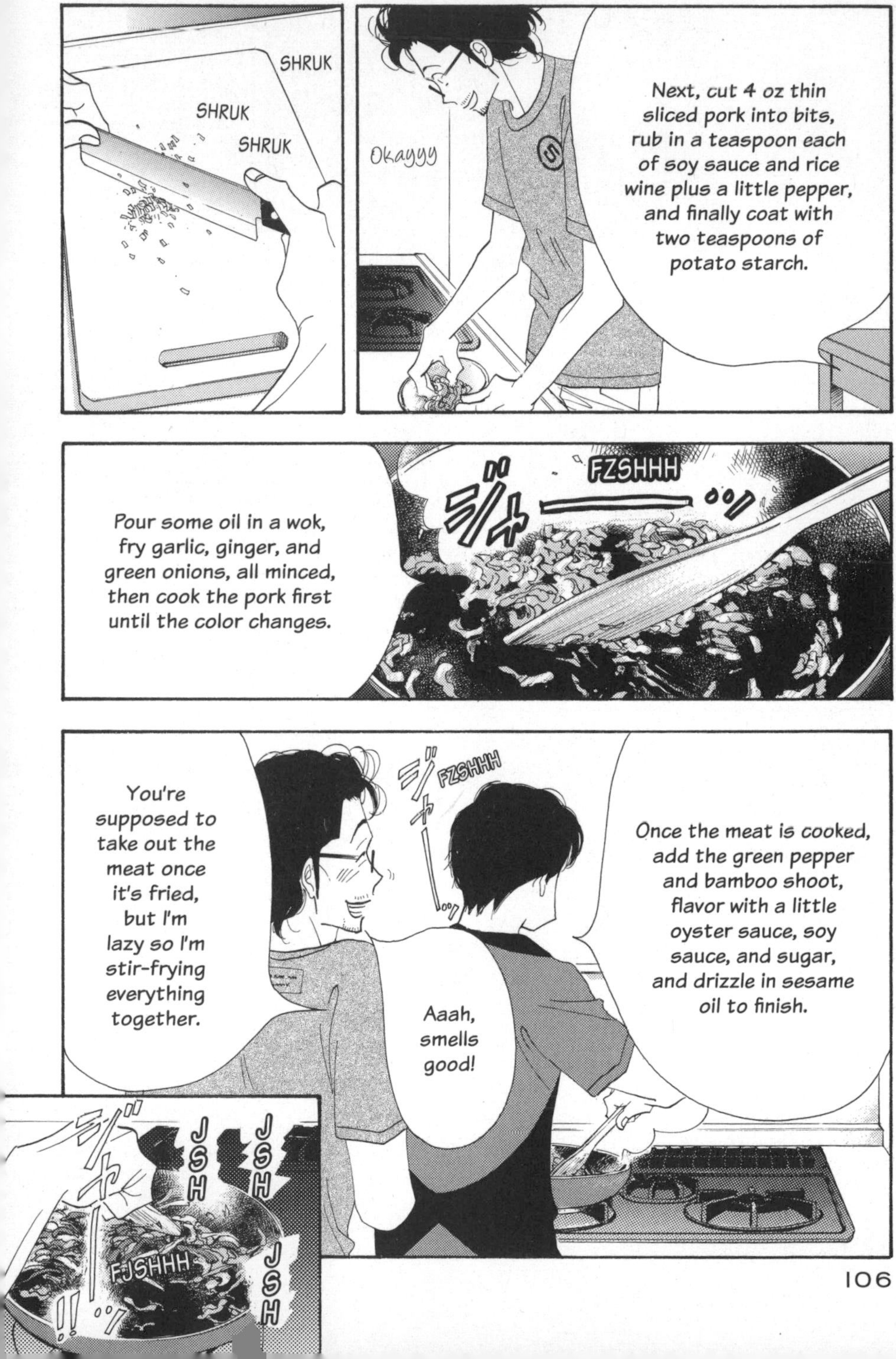

Next, cut 4 oz thin sliced pork into bits, rub in a teaspoon each of soy sauce and rice wine plus a little pepper, and finally coat with two teaspoons of potato starch.
Okayyy
SHRUK
SHRUK
SHRUK
FZSHHH
Pour some oil in a wok, fry garlic, ginger, and green onions, all minced, then cook the pork first until the color changes.
Once the meat is cooked, add the green pepper and bamboo shoot, flavor with a little oyster sauce, soy sauce, and sugar, and drizzle in sesame oil to finish.
FZSHHH
You're supposed to take out the meat once it's fried, but I'm lazy so I'm stir-frying everything together.
Aaah, smells good!
JSH
JSH
FJSHHH
JSH

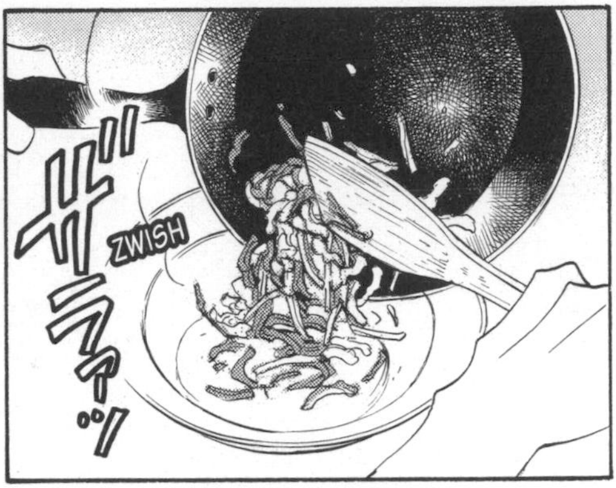
ザラァッ
ZWISH
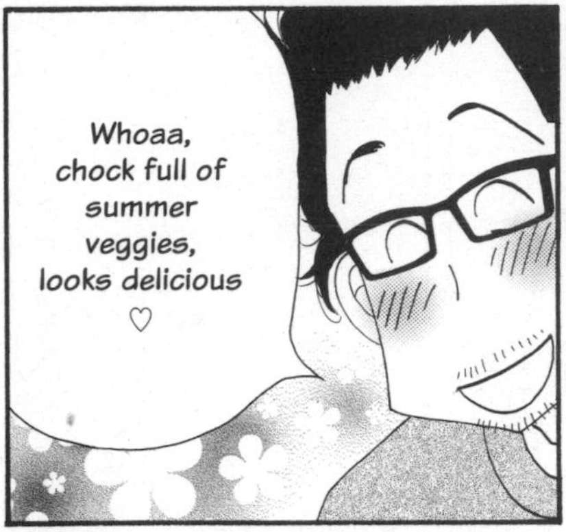
Whoaa, chock full of summer veggies, looks delicious ♡
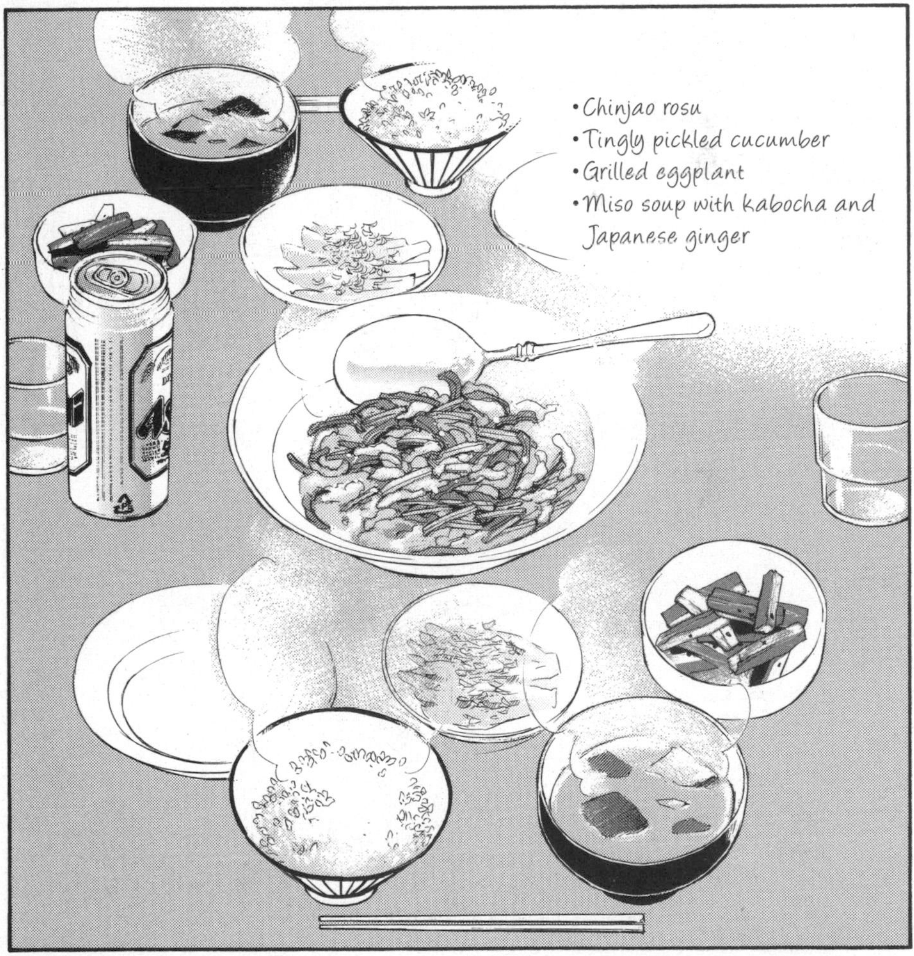
•Chinjao rosu
•Tingly pickled cucumber
•Grilled eggplant
•Miso soup with kabocha and Japanese ginger

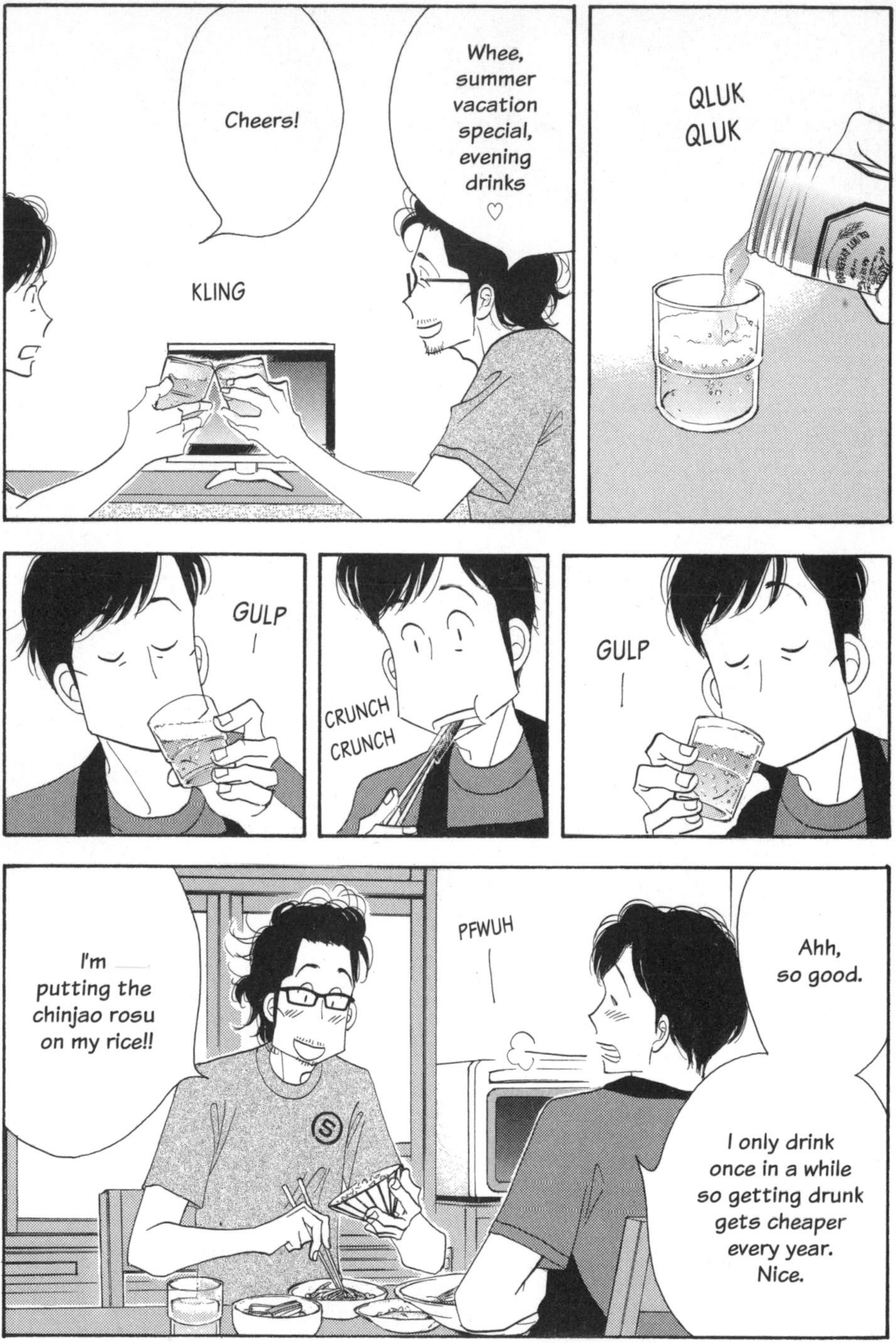
QLUK
QLUK
Whee, summer vacation special, evening drinks ♡
Cheers!
KLING
GULP
CRUNCH
CRUNCH
GULP
Ahh, so good.
PFWUH
I'm putting the chinjao rosu on my rice!!
I only drink once in a while so getting drunk gets cheaper every year. Nice.

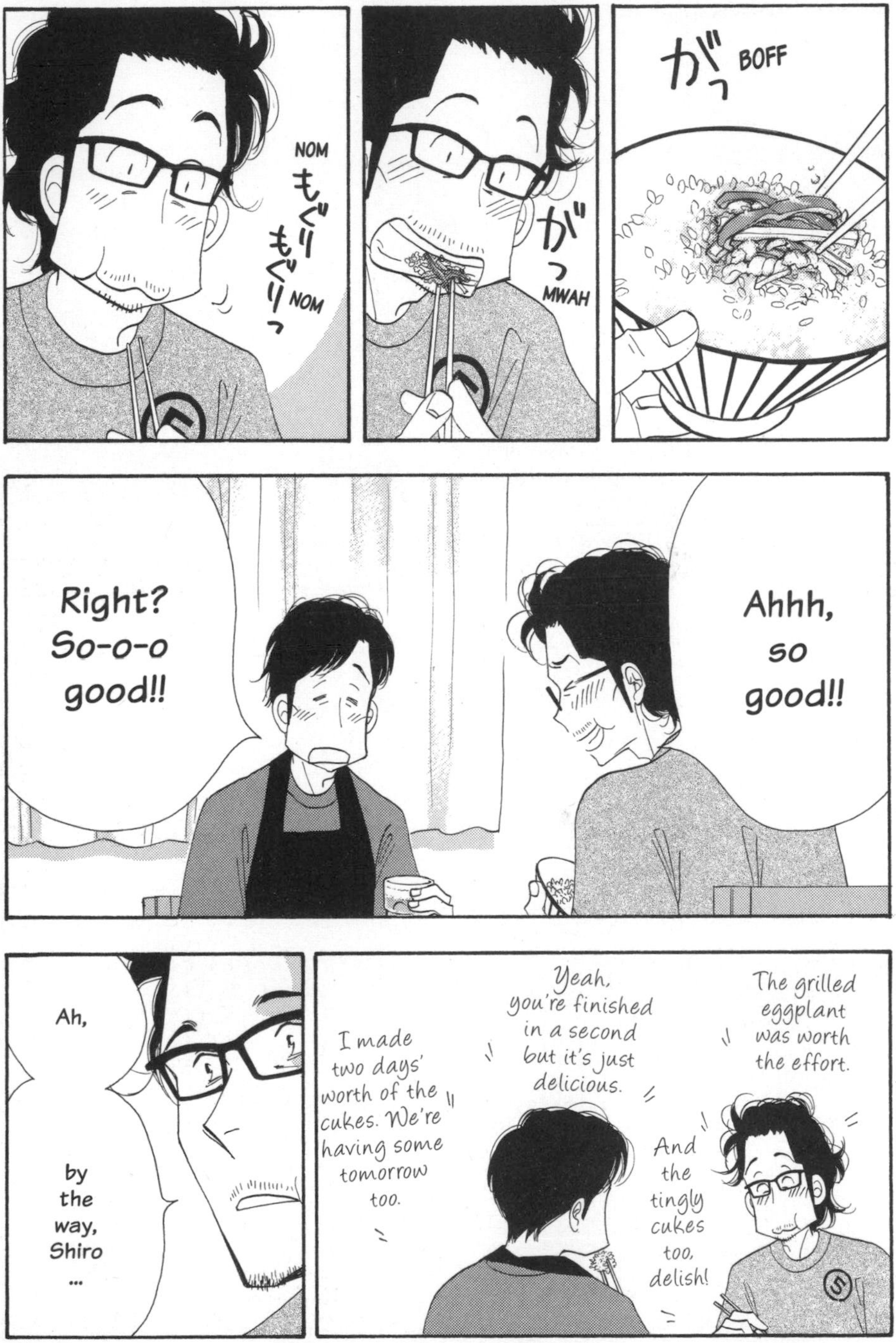

がっ BOFF
がっ MWAH
もぐり もぐりっ
NOM NOM
Ahhh, so good!!
Right? So-o-o good!!
The grilled eggplant was worth the effort.
And the tingly cukes too, delish!
Yeah, you're finished in a second but it's just delicious.
I made two days' worth of the cukes. We're having some tomorrow too.
Ah, by the way, Shiro ...

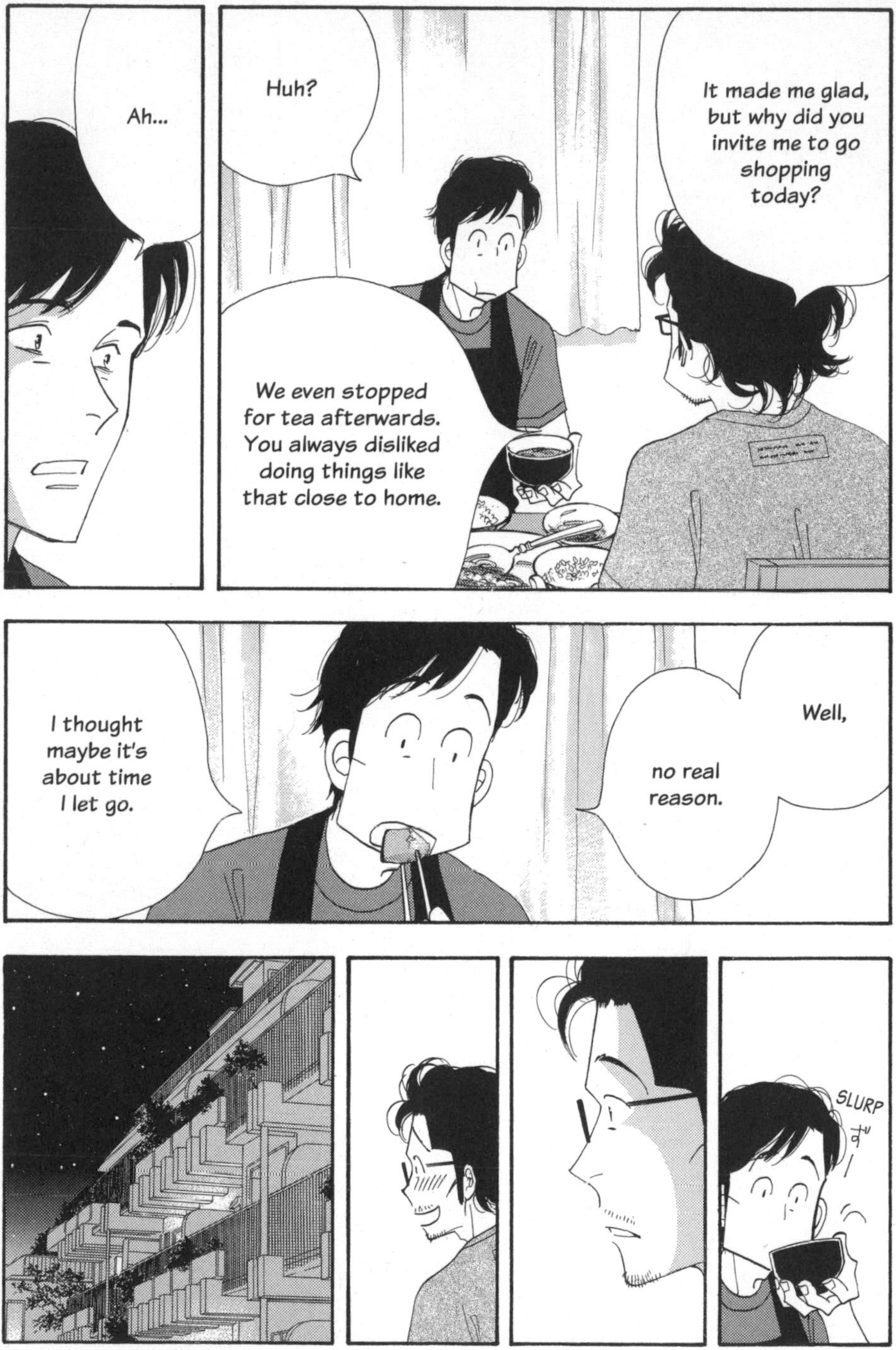

It made me glad, but why did you invite me to go shopping today?
We even stopped for tea afterwards. You always disliked doing things like that close to home.
Huh?
Ah...
Well,
no real reason.
I thought maybe it's about time I let go.
SLURP

The **tingly pickled cucumber** tastes even better
if you scoop out the seeds in the center with a spoon
before you pickle it.

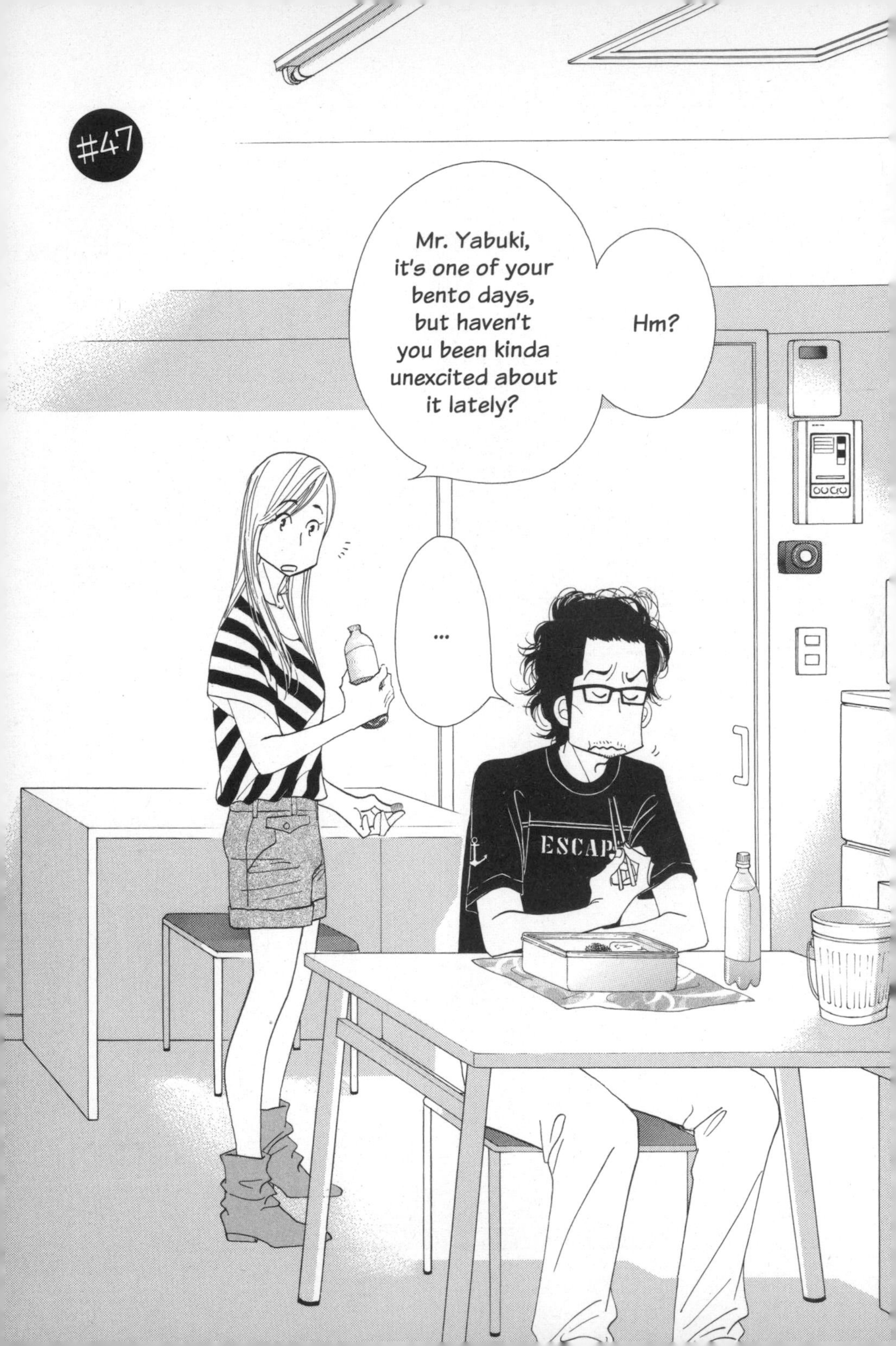
#47
Mr. Yabuki, it's one of your bento days, but haven't you been kinda unexcited about it lately?
Hm?
...

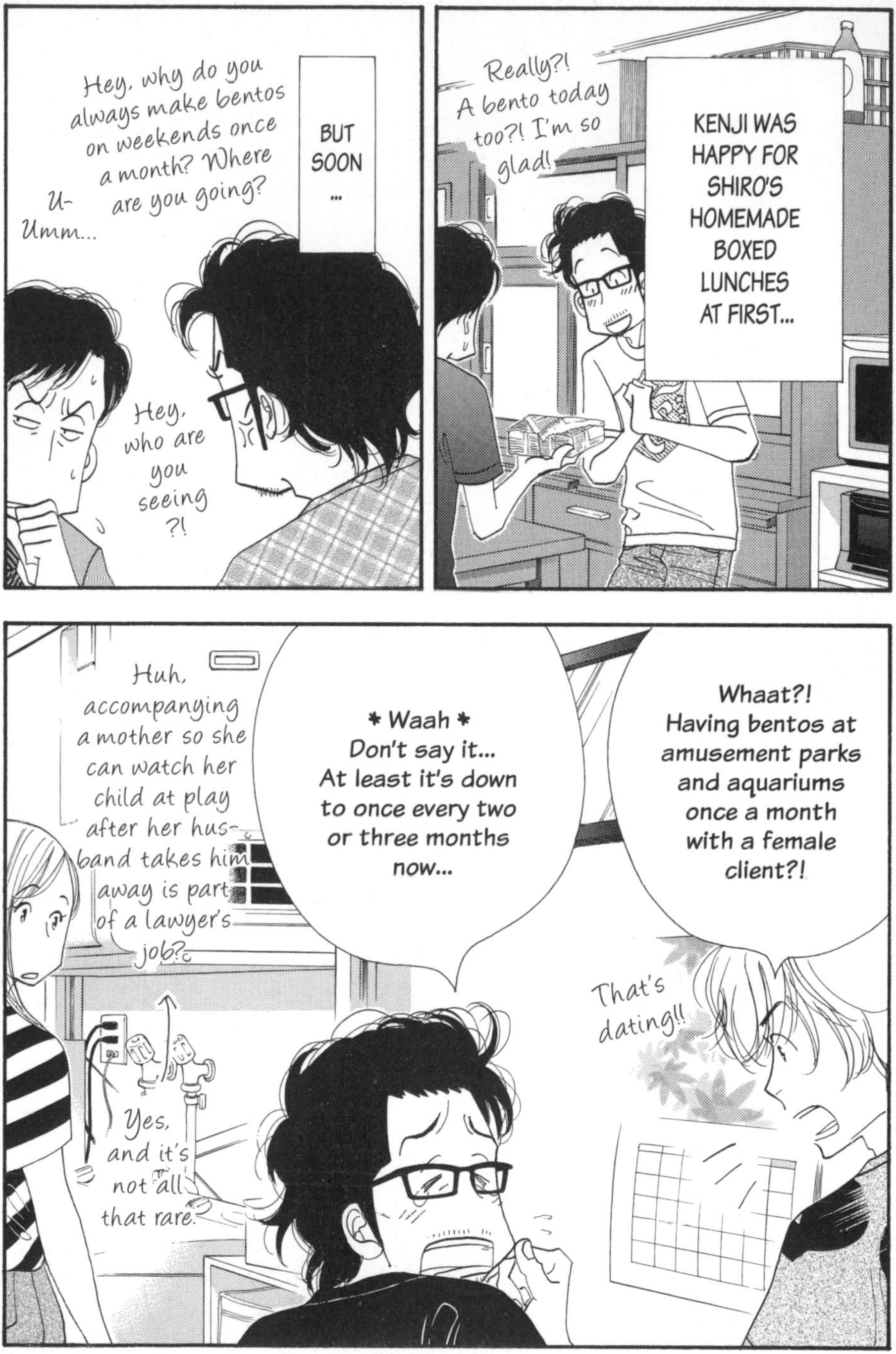
KENJI WAS HAPPY FOR SHIRO'S HOMEMADE BOXED LUNCHES AT FIRST...
Really?! A bento today too?! I'm so glad!
BUT SOON ...
Hey, why do you always make bentos on weekends once a month? Where are you going?
U- Umm...
Hey, who are you seeing ?!
Whaat?! Having bentos at amusement parks and aquariums once a month with a female client?!
That's dating!!
* Waah * Don't say it... At least it's down to once every two or three months now...
Huh, accompanying a mother so she can watch her child at play after her husband takes him away is part of a lawyer's job?
Yes, and it's not all that rare.

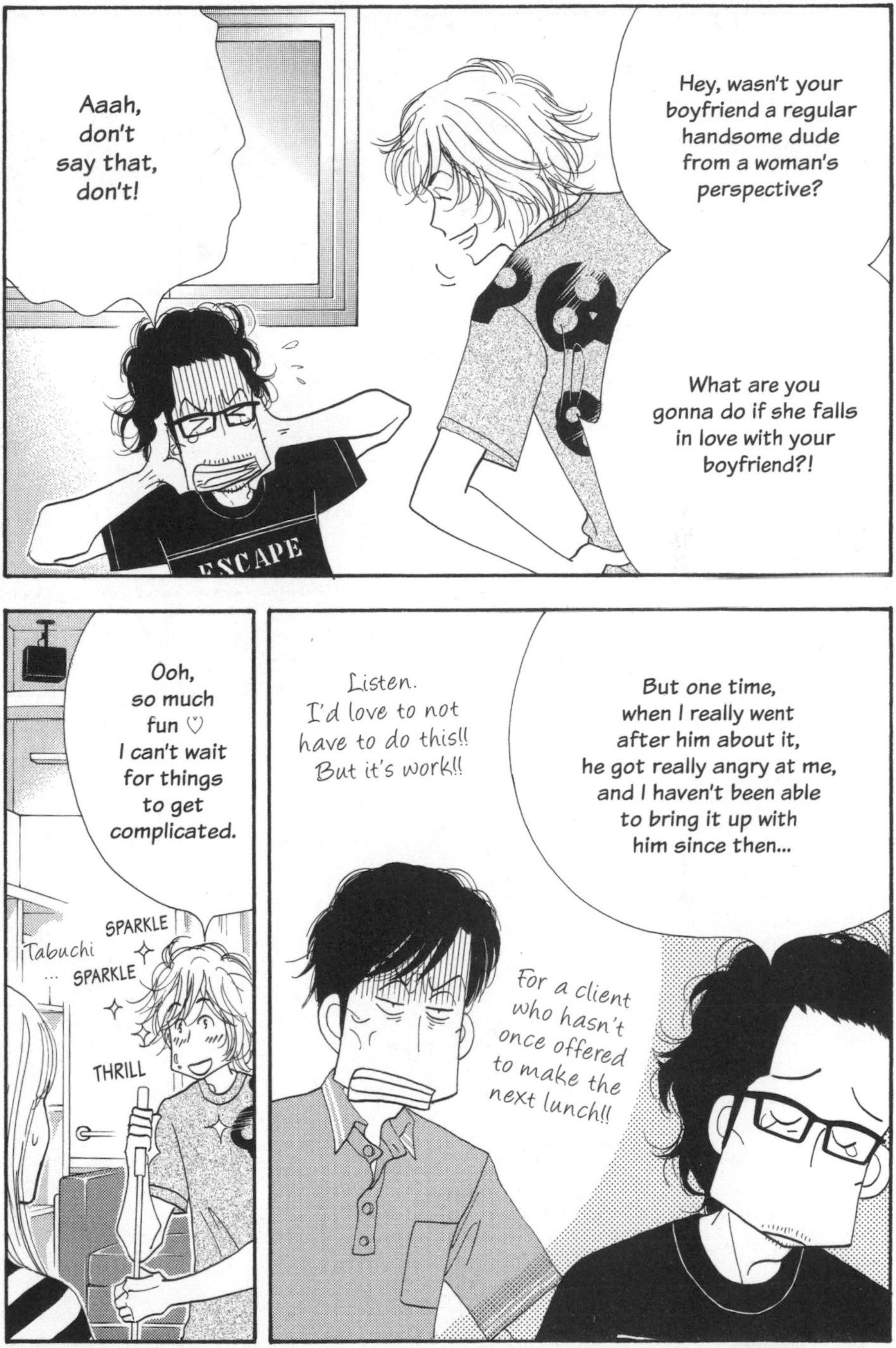
Hey, wasn't your boyfriend a regular handsome dude from a woman's perspective?
What are you gonna do if she falls in love with your boyfriend?!
Aaah, don't say that, don't!
ESCAPE
But one time, when I really went after him about it, he got really angry at me, and I haven't been able to bring it up with him since then...
Listen. I'd love to not have to do this!! But it's work!!
For a client who hasn't once offered to make the next lunch!!
Ooh, so much fun ♡ I can't wait for things to get complicated.
SPARKLE
Tabuchi ...
SPARKLE
THRILL

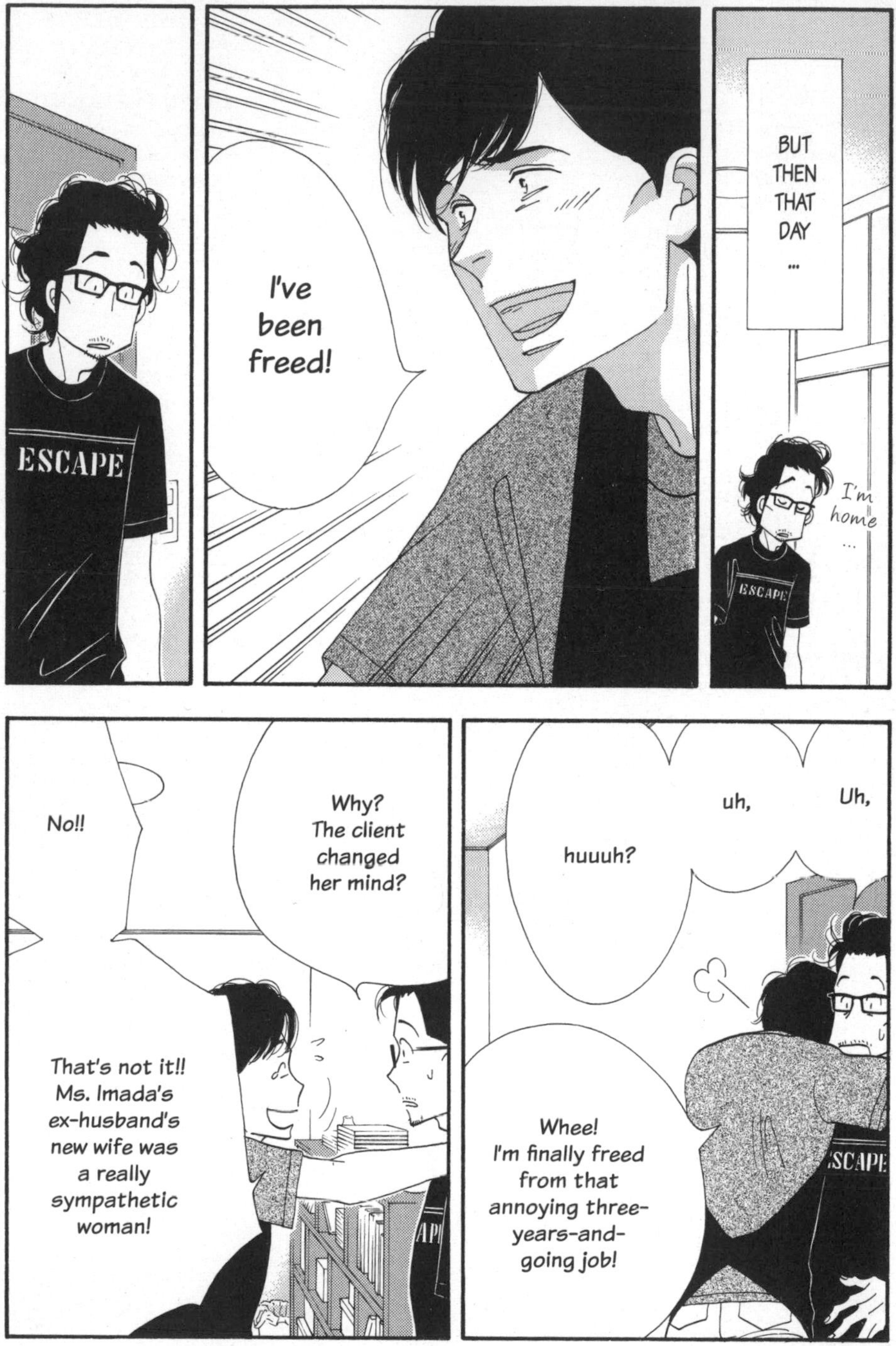
BUT THEN THAT DAY ...
I'm home ...
I've been freed!
Uh,
uh,
huuuh?
Whee! I'm finally freed from that annoying three-years-and-going job!
Why? The client changed her mind?
No!!
That's not it!! Ms. Imada's ex-husband's new wife was a really sympathetic woman!

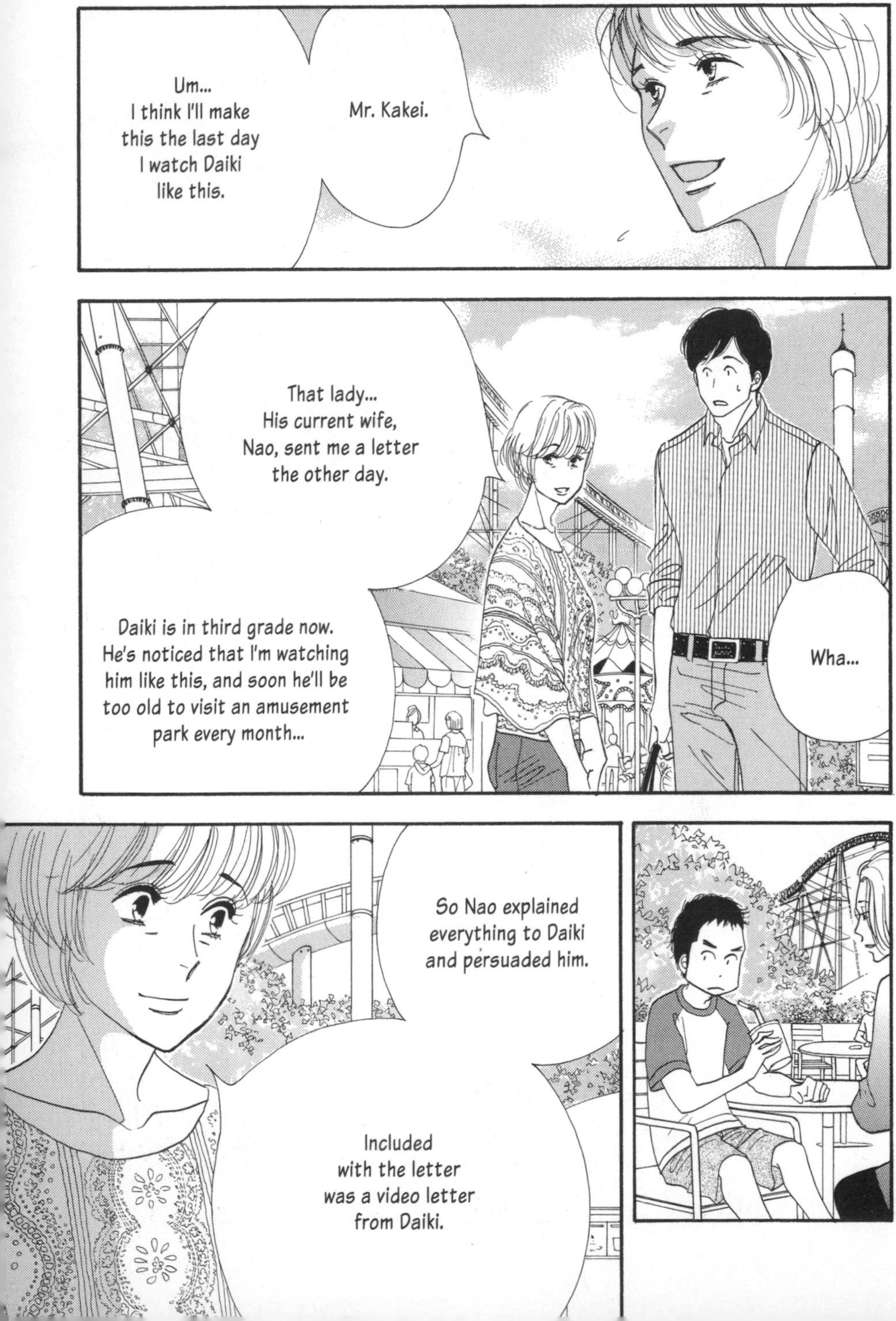
Mr. Kakei.
Um... I think I'll make this the last day I watch Daiki like this.
That lady... His current wife, Nao, sent me a letter the other day.
Wha...
Daiki is in third grade now. He's noticed that I'm watching him like this, and soon he'll be too old to visit an amusement park every month...
So Nao explained everything to Daiki and persuaded him.
Included with the letter was a video letter from Daiki.

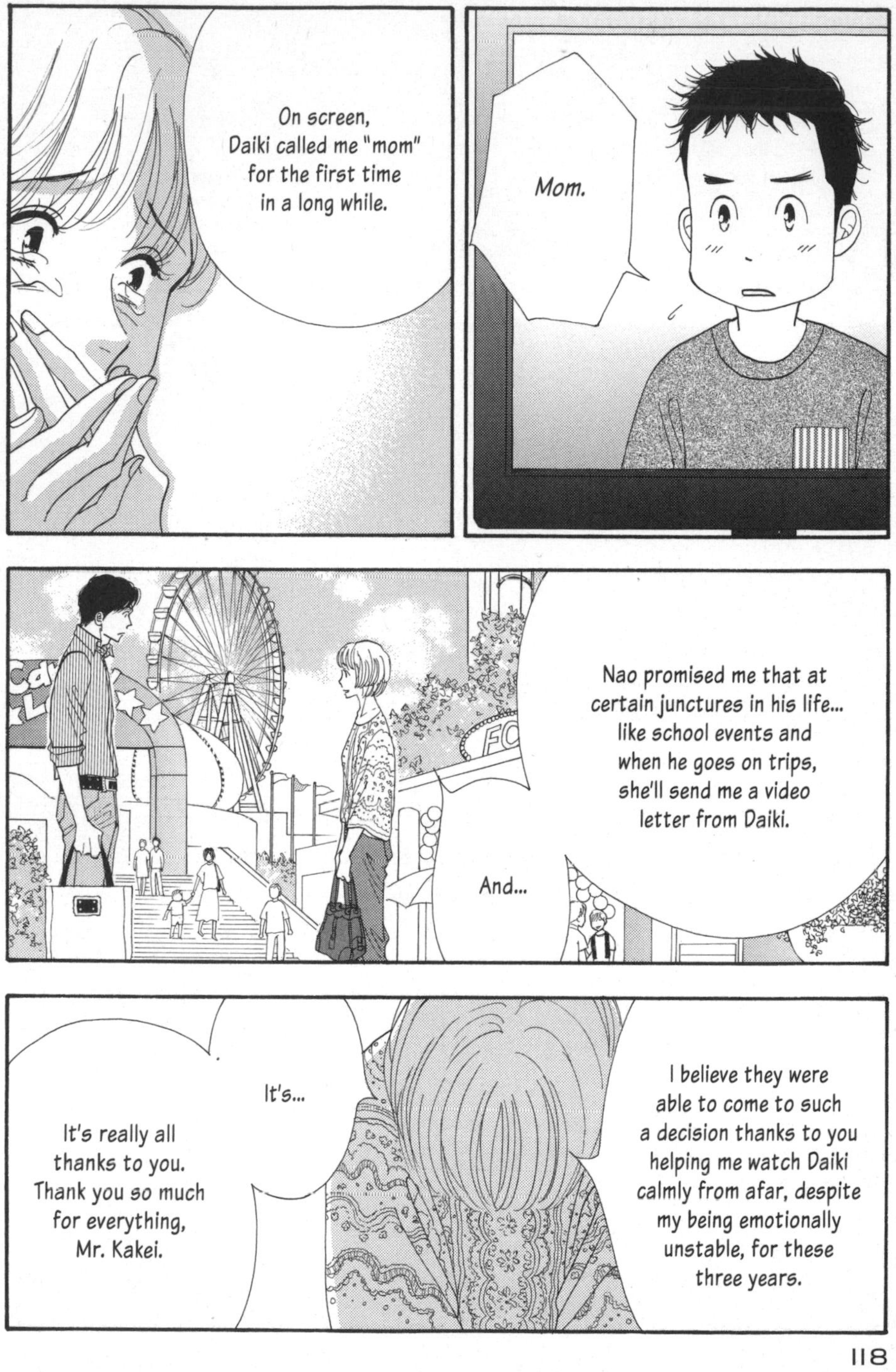
Mom.
On screen, Daiki called me "mom" for the first time in a long while.
Nao promised me that at certain junctures in his life... like school events and when he goes on trips, she'll send me a video letter from Daiki.
And...
I believe they were able to come to such a decision thanks to you helping me watch Daiki calmly from afar, despite my being emotionally unstable, for these three years.
It's...
It's really all thanks to you. Thank you so much for everything, Mr. Kakei.

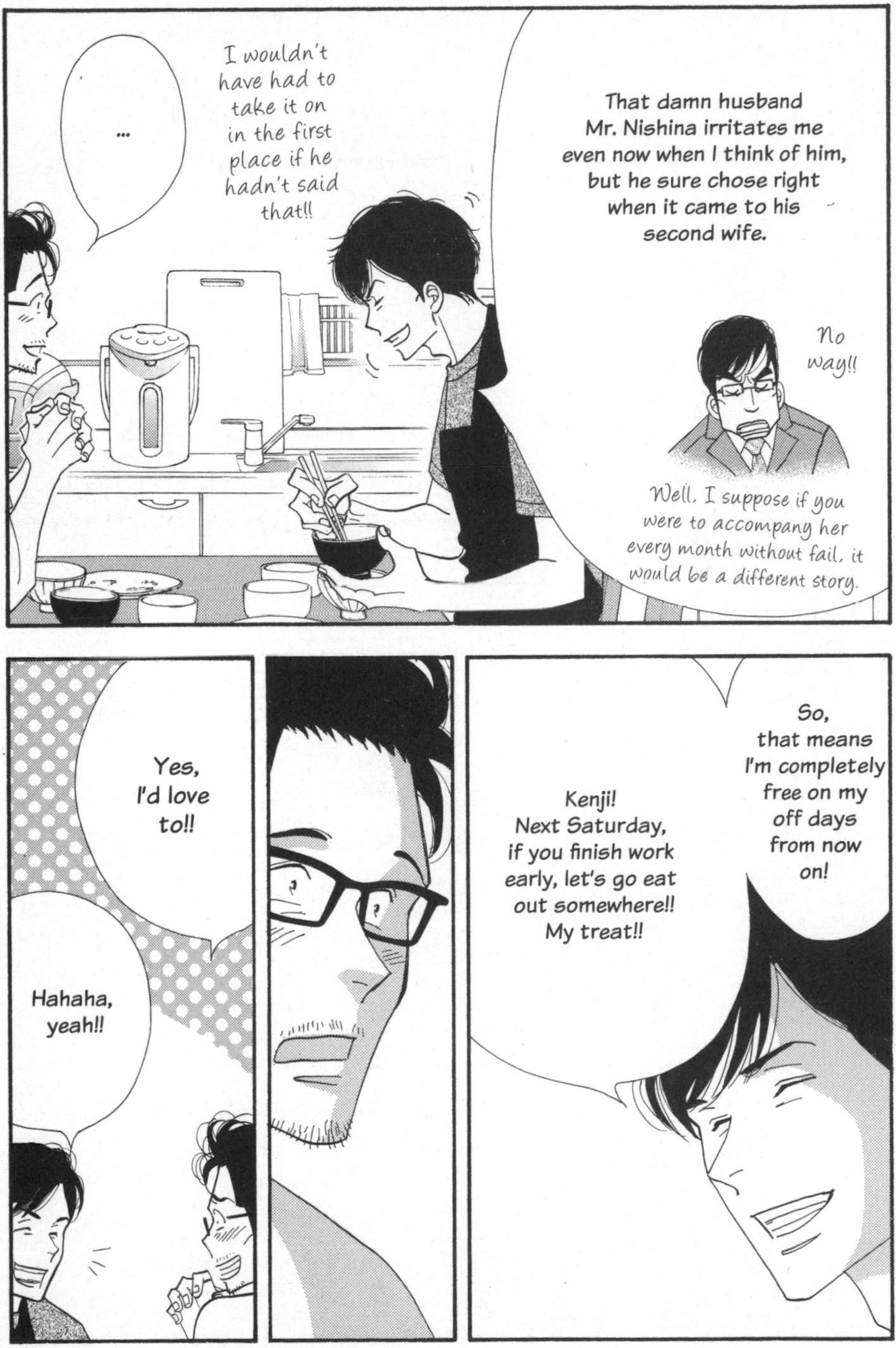
That damn husband Mr. Nishina irritates me even now when I think of him, but he sure chose right when it came to his second wife.
No way!!
Well, I suppose if you were to accompany her every month without fail, it would be a different story.
I wouldn't have had to take it on in the first place if he hadn't said that!!
...
So, that means I'm completely free on my off days from now on!
Kenji! Next Saturday, if you finish work early, let's go eat out somewhere!! My treat!!
Yes, I'd love to!!
Hahaha, yeah!!

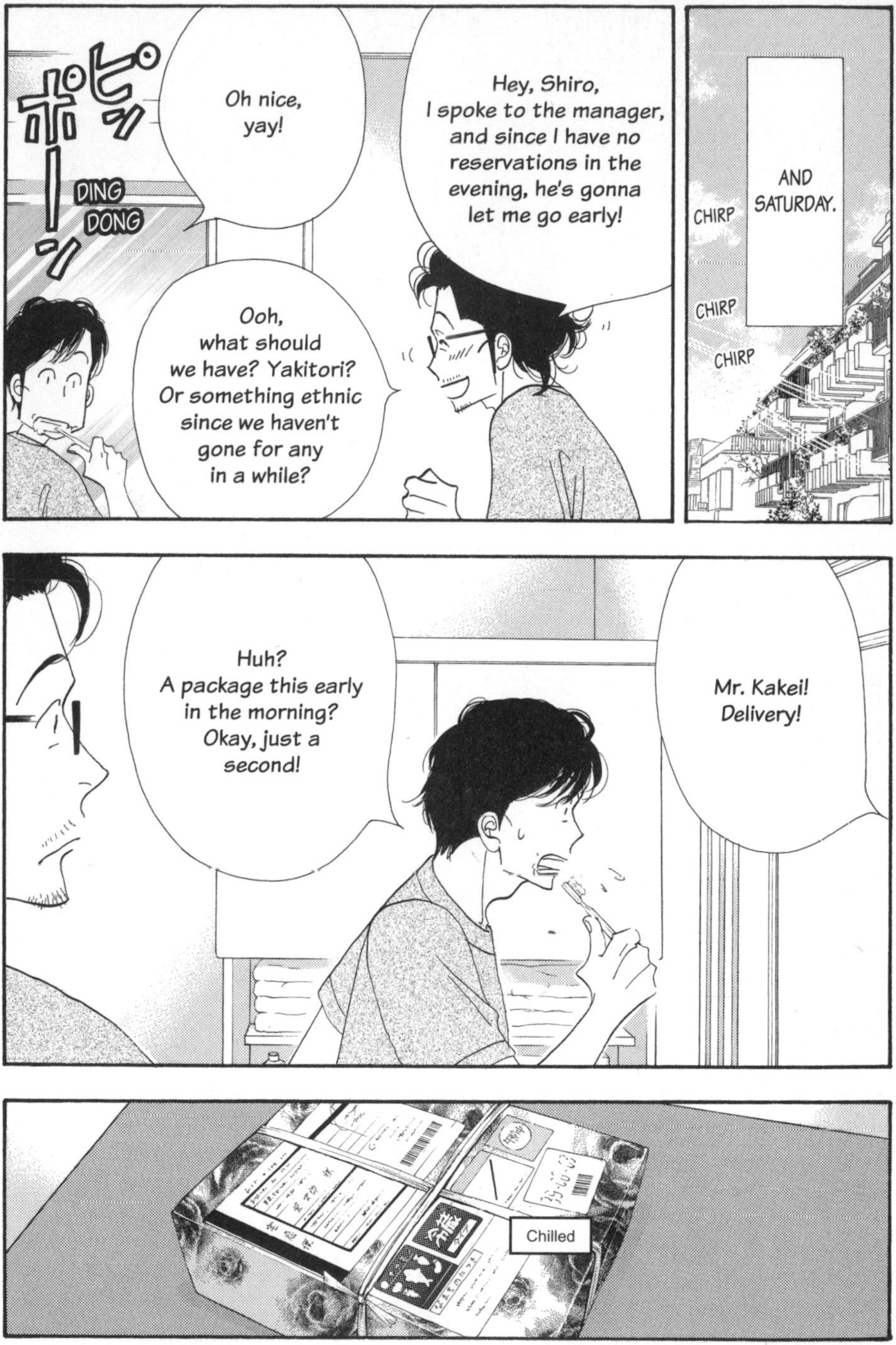
AND SATURDAY.
CHIRP
CHIRP
CHIRP
Hey, Shiro, I spoke to the manager, and since I have no reservations in the evening, he's gonna let me go early!
Oh nice, yay!
Ooh, what should we have? Yakitori? Or something ethnic since we haven't gone for any in a while?
DING DONG
Mr. Kakei! Delivery!
Huh? A package this early in the morning? Okay, just a second!
Chilled

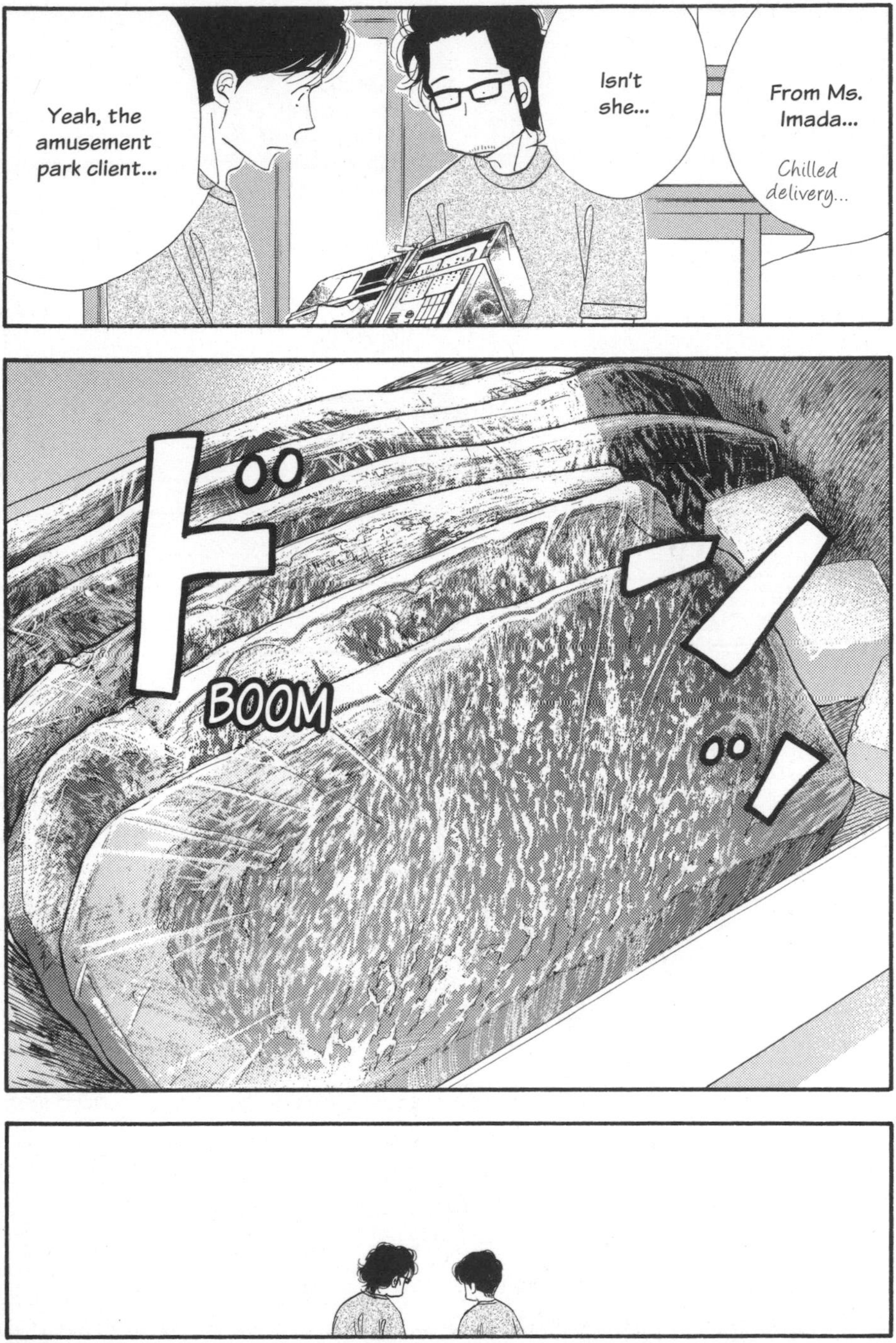
From Ms. Imada...
Chilled delivery...
Isn't she...
Yeah, the amusement park client...
ドーン
BOOM

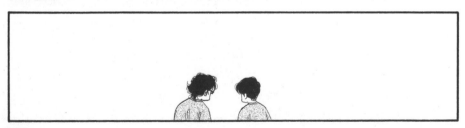

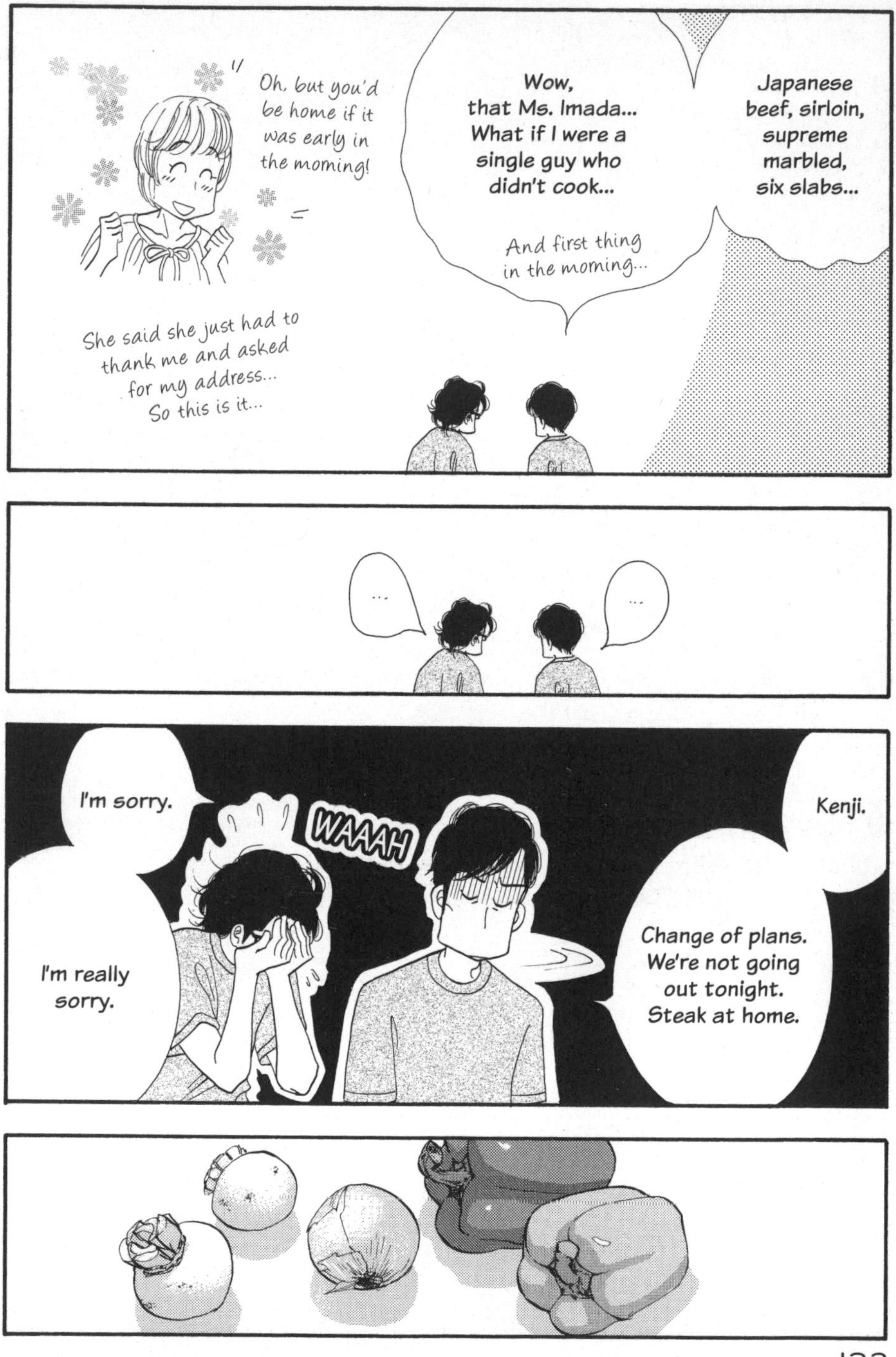
Japanese beef, sirloin, supreme marbled, six slabs...
Wow, that Ms. Imada... What if I were a single guy who didn't cook...
And first thing in the morning...
Oh, but you'd be home if it was early in the morning!
She said she just had to thank me and asked for my address... So this is it...
...
...
Kenji.
Change of plans. We're not going out tonight. Steak at home.
WAAAH
I'm sorry.
I'm really sorry.

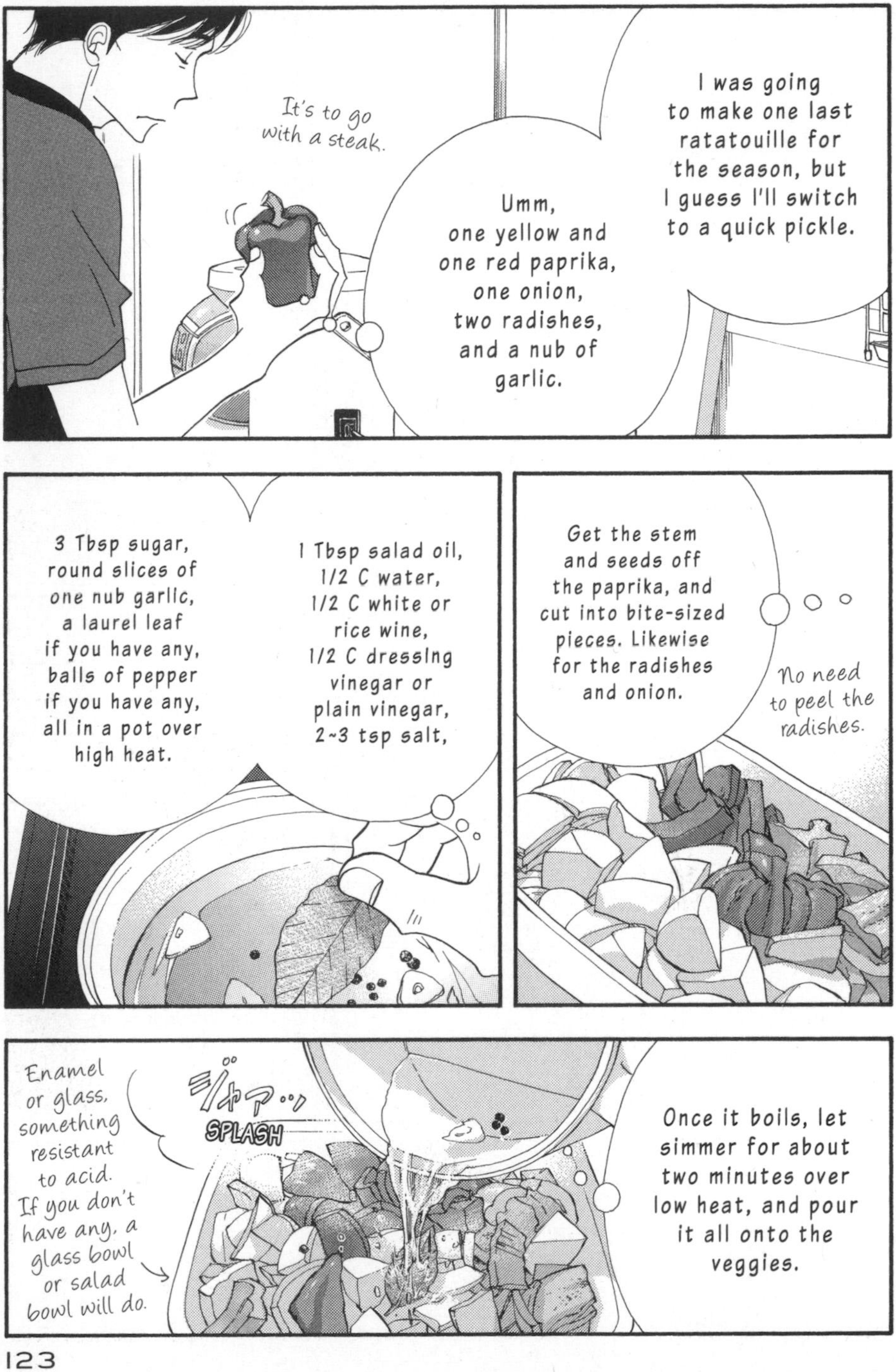
I was going to make one last ratatouille for the season, but I guess I'll switch to a quick pickle.
Umm, one yellow and one red paprika, one onion, two radishes, and a nub of garlic.
It's to go with a steak.
Get the stem and seeds off the paprika, and cut into bite-sized pieces. Likewise for the radishes and onion.
No need to peel the radishes.
1 Tbsp salad oil, 1/2 C water, 1/2 C white or rice wine, 1/2 C dressing vinegar or plain vinegar, 2~3 tsp salt,
3 Tbsp sugar, round slices of one nub garlic, a laurel leaf if you have any, balls of pepper if you have any, all in a pot over high heat.
Once it boils, let simmer for about two minutes over low heat, and pour it all onto the veggies.
SPLASH
Enamel or glass, something resistant to acid. If you don't have any, a glass bowl or salad bowl will do.

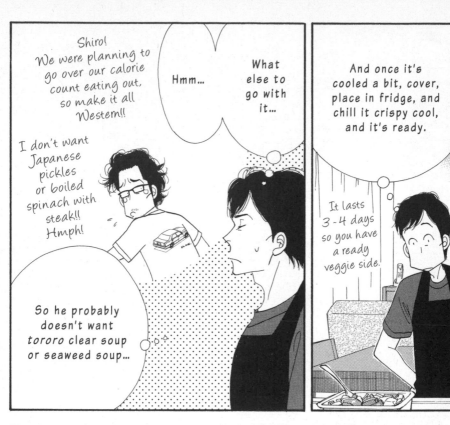

And once it's cooled a bit, cover, place in fridge, and chill it crispy cool, and it's ready.
It lasts 3~4 days so you have a ready veggie side.
What else to go with it...
Hmm...
Shiro! We were planning to go over our calorie count eating out, so make it all Western!!
I don't want Japanese pickles or boiled spinach with steak!! Hmph!
So he probably doesn't want *tororo* clear soup or seaweed soup...
ざく CHOP
ざく CHOP
ざくっ CHOP
Roughly chop an eighth cabbage, cut two strips bacon into half-inch bits, and thinly slice half an onion...
Put it all in a pot, and boil in 2 C water.

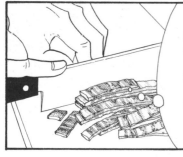

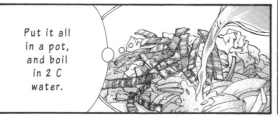

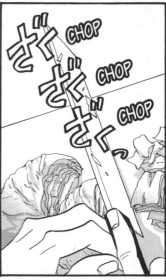

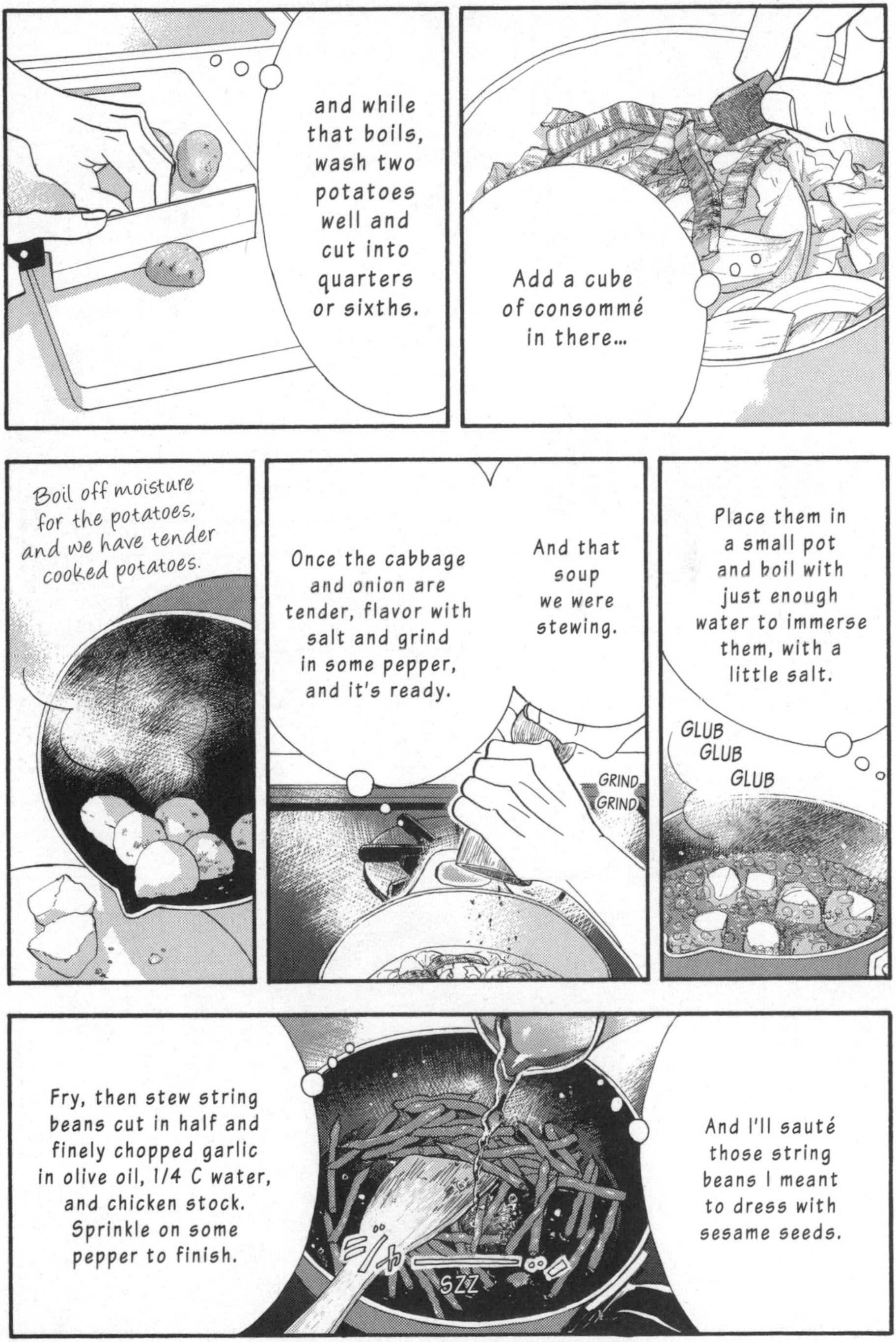

Add a cube of consommé in there...
and while that boils, wash two potatoes well and cut into quarters or sixths.
Place them in a small pot and boil with just enough water to immerse them, with a little salt.
GLUB GLUB GLUB
And that soup we were stewing.
Once the cabbage and onion are tender, flavor with salt and grind in some pepper, and it's ready.
GRIND GRIND
Boil off moisture for the potatoes, and we have tender cooked potatoes.
And I'll sauté those string beans I meant to dress with sesame seeds.
Fry, then stew string beans cut in half and finely chopped garlic in olive oil, 1/4 C water, and chicken stock. Sprinkle on some pepper to finish.
SZZ

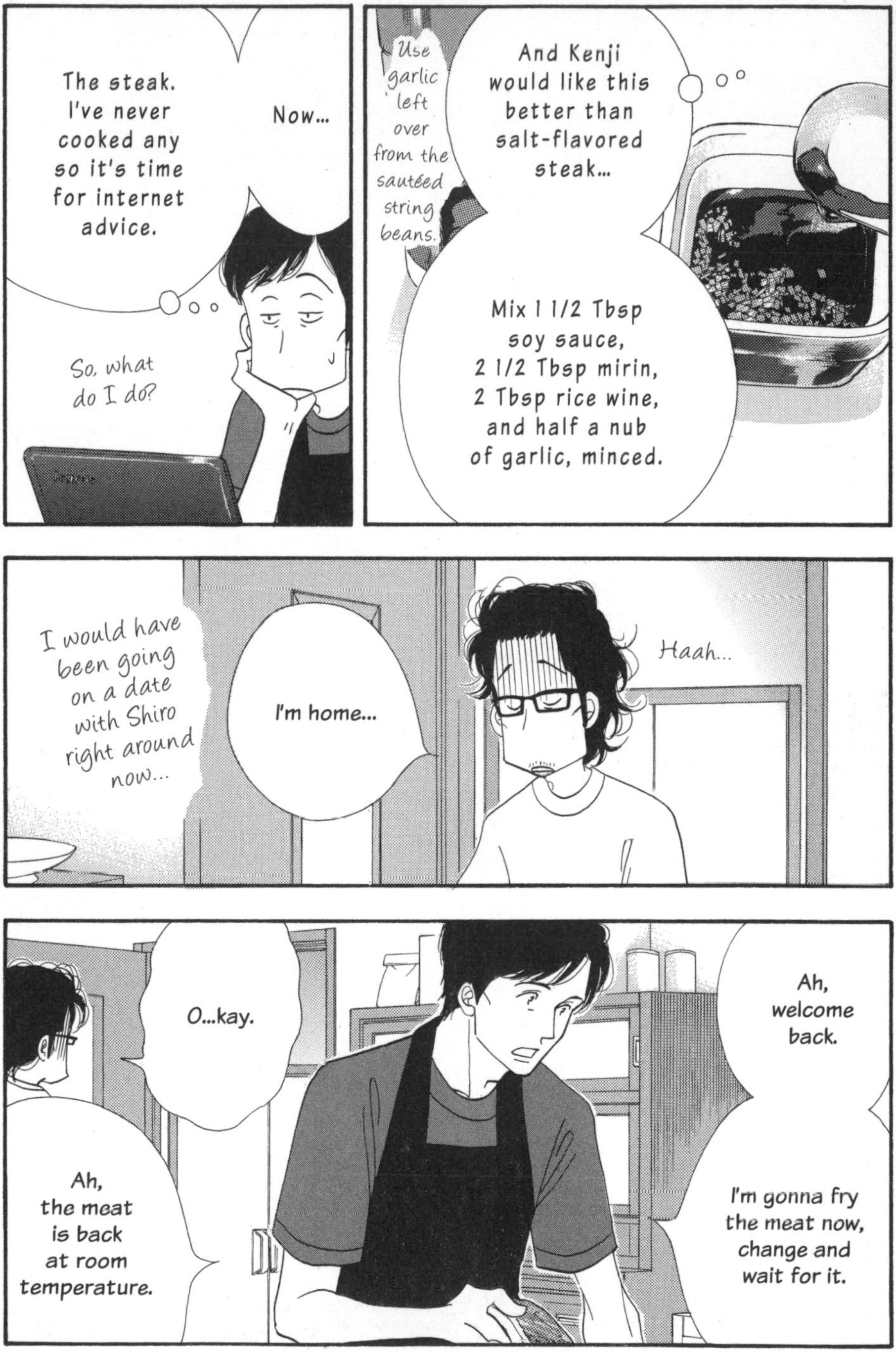
And Kenji would like this better than salt-flavored steak...
Use garlic left over from the sautéed string beans.
Mix 1 1/2 Tbsp soy sauce, 2 1/2 Tbsp mirin, 2 Tbsp rice wine, and half a nub of garlic, minced.
Now...
The steak. I've never cooked any so it's time for internet advice.
So, what do I do?
Haah...
I'm home...
I would have been going on a date with Shiro right around now...
Ah, welcome back.
I'm gonna fry the meat now, change and wait for it.
O...kay.
Ah, the meat is back at room temperature.

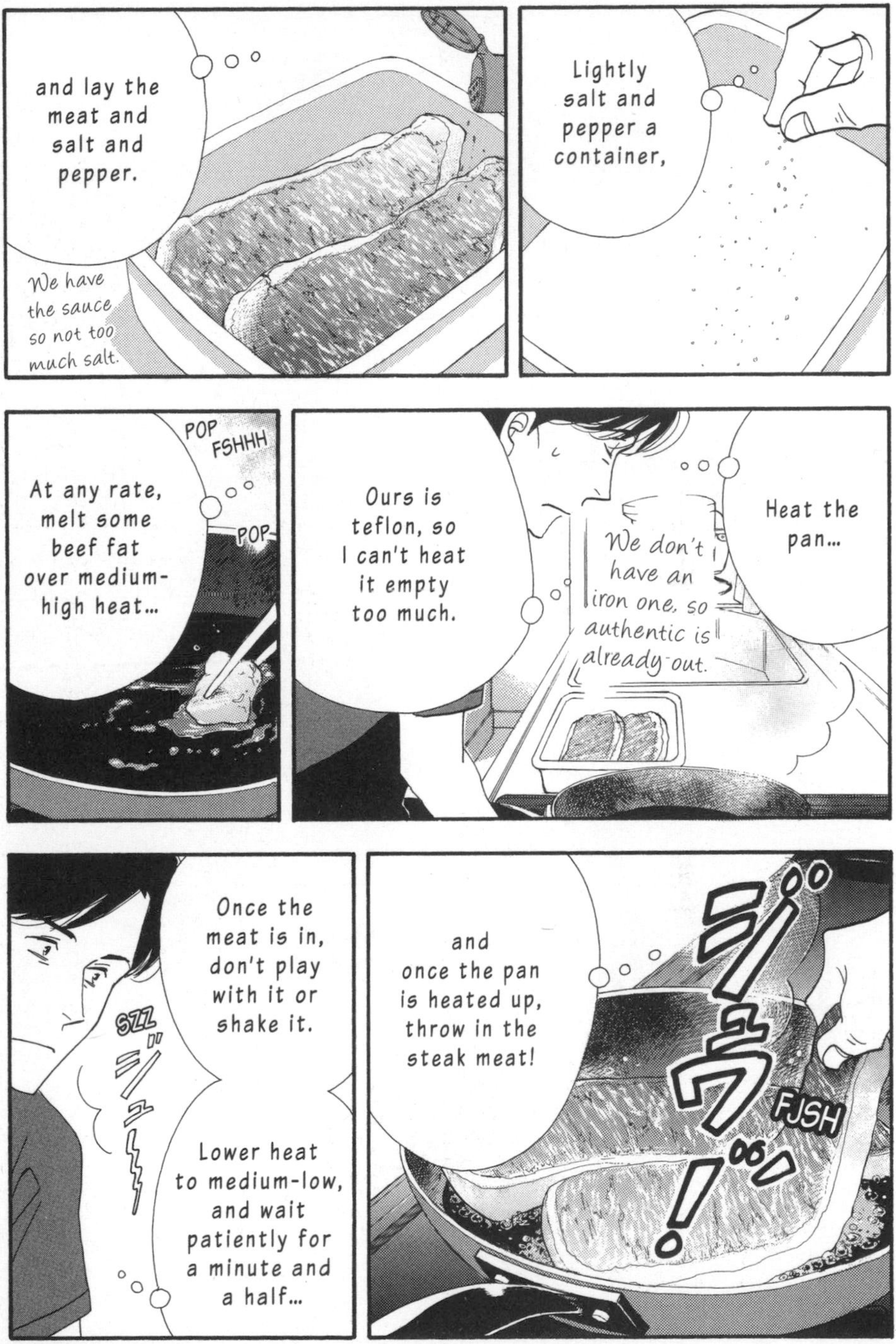

Lightly salt and pepper a container,
and lay the meat and salt and pepper.
We have the sauce so not too much salt.
Heat the pan...
We don't have an iron one, so authentic is already out.
Ours is teflon, so I can't heat it empty too much.
POP
FSHHH
At any rate, melt some beef fat over medium-high heat...
POP
and once the pan is heated up, throw in the steak meat!
FJSH
Once the meat is in, don't play with it or shake it.
SZZ
ジュ
Lower heat to medium-low, and wait patiently for a minute and a half...

Once the back's a good color, flip it over...
SZZ
and cook for another minute and a half, and we have a rare steak!
FSHHH
Then in the same pan, boil the prepped sauce to evaporate the alcohol...
SZZ
wasabi
WRR
It's ready!
...
Wow, impressive...

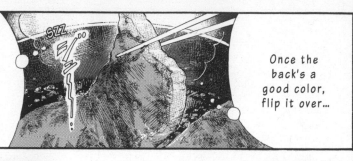

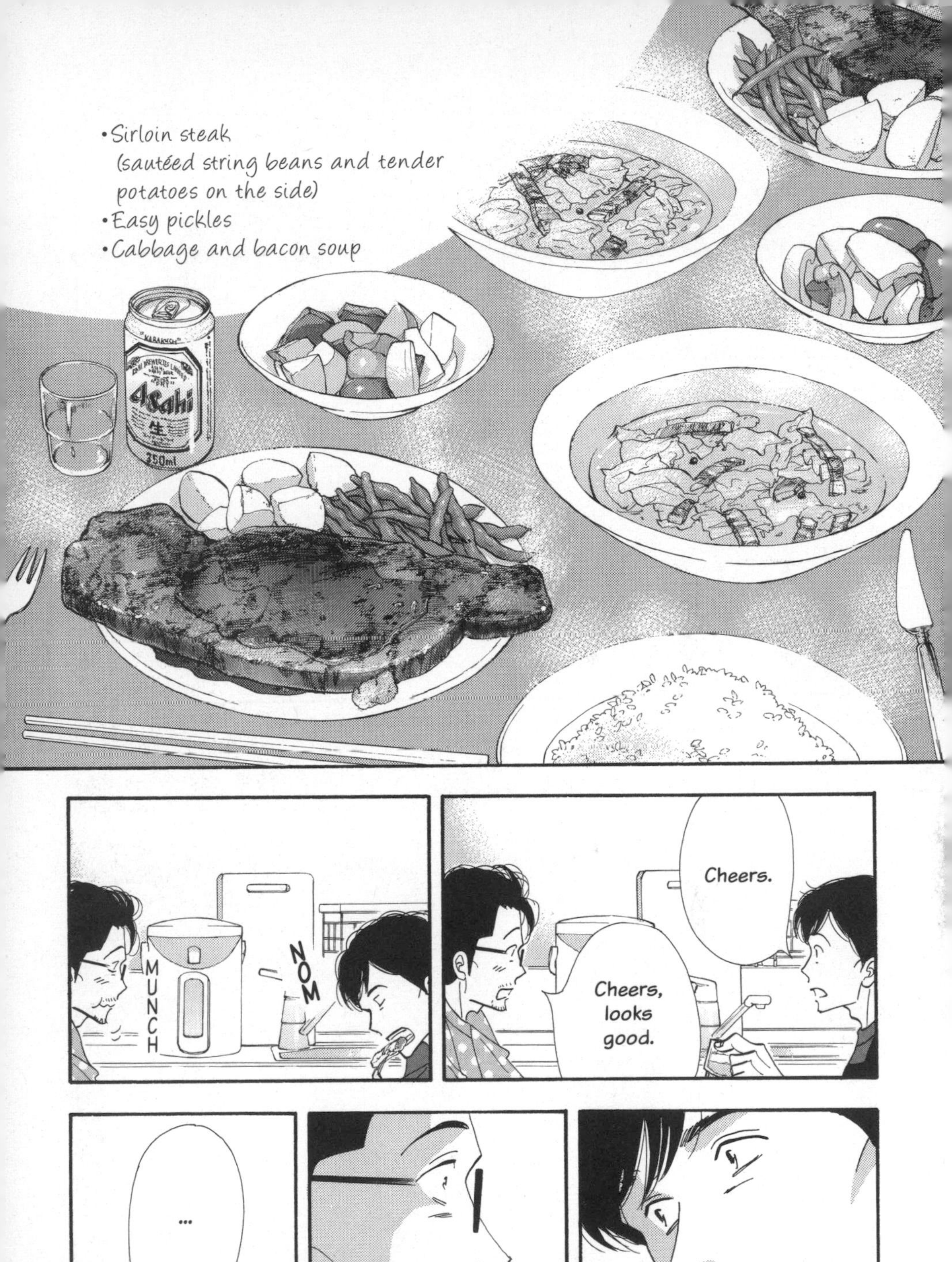
•Sirloin steak
(sautéed string beans and tender potatoes on the side)
•Easy pickles
•Cabbage and bacon soup
Asahi
350ml
Cheers.
Cheers, looks good.
NOM
MUNCH
...

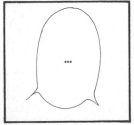

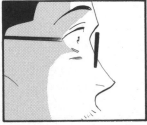

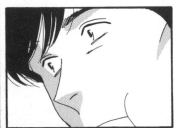

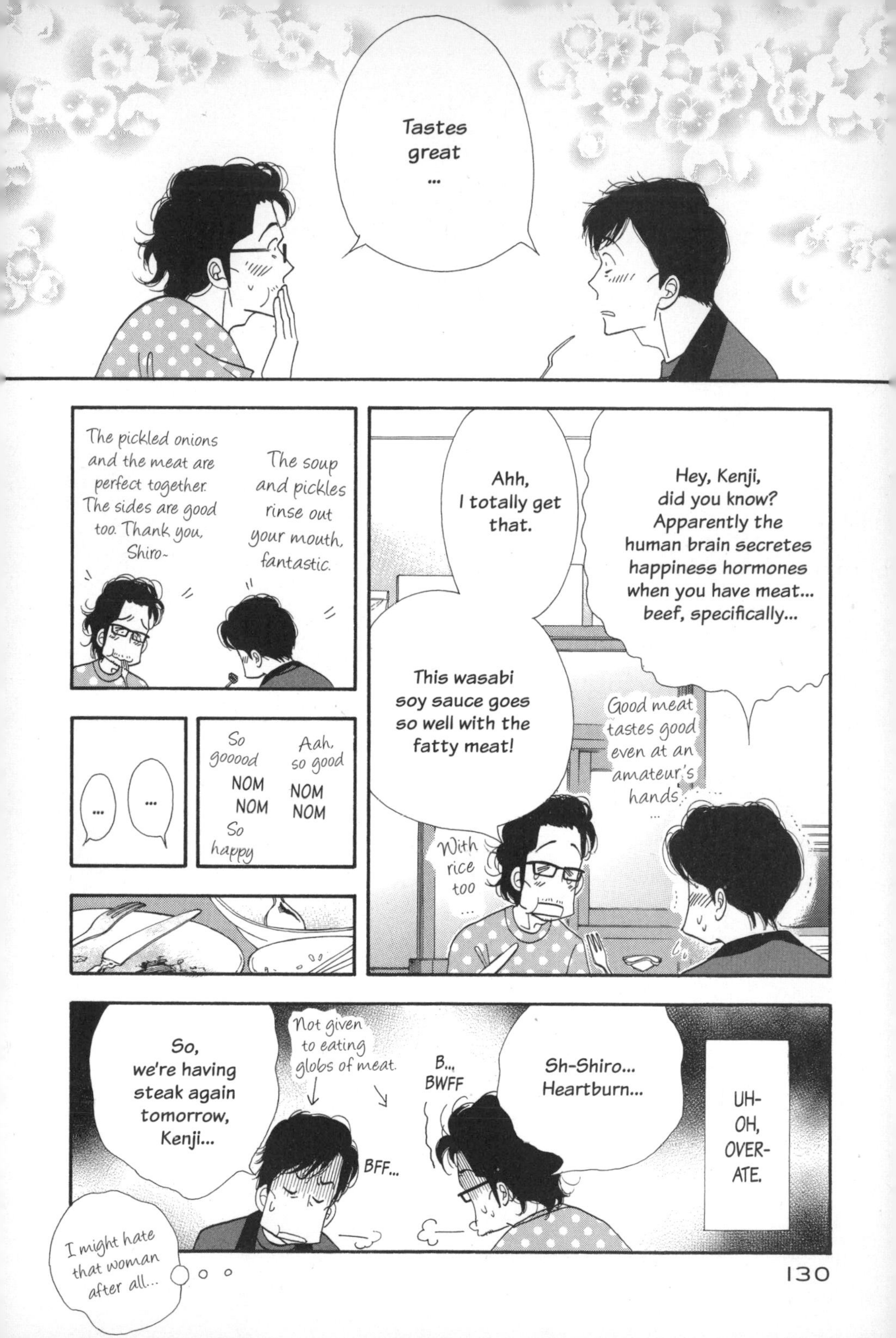
Tastes great ...
Hey, Kenji, did you know? Apparently the human brain secretes happiness hormones when you have meat... beef, specifically...
Ahh, I totally get that.
Good meat tastes good even at an amateur's hands ...
This wasabi soy sauce goes so well with the fatty meat!
With rice too ...
The soup and pickles rinse out your mouth, fantastic.
The pickled onions and the meat are perfect together. The sides are good too. Thank you, Shiro~
Aah, so good
NOM NOM
So gooood
NOM NOM
So happy
...
...
UH-OH, OVERATE.
Sh-Shiro... Heartburn...
B.., BWFF
Not given to eating globs of meat.
So, we're having steak again tomorrow, Kenji...
BFF...
I might hate that woman after all...

I hear the happiness hormone is called **anandamide.**
Oh, and they also say that you can actually freeze
steak meat.

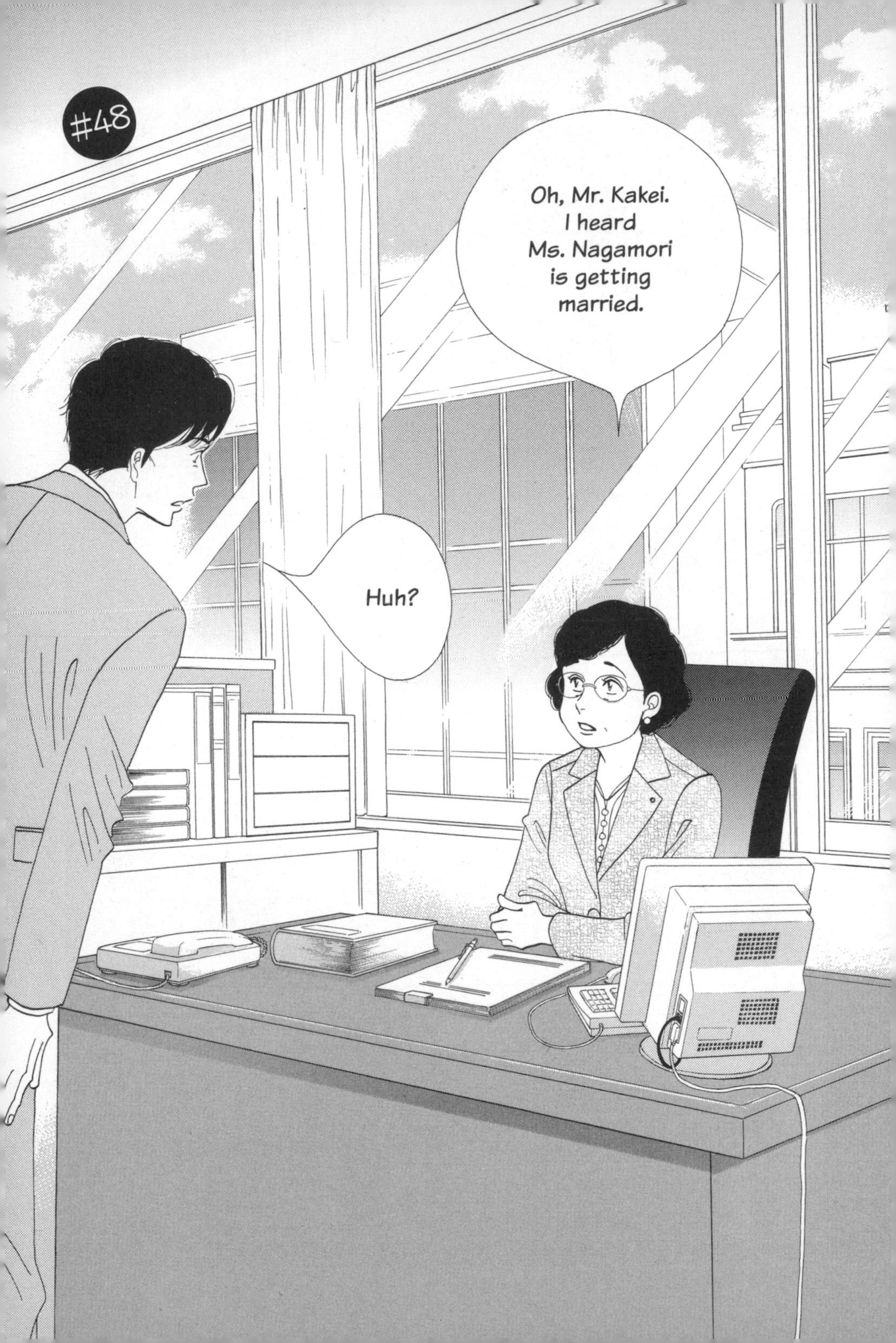
#48
Oh, Mr. Kakei. I heard Ms. Nagamori is getting married.
Huh?

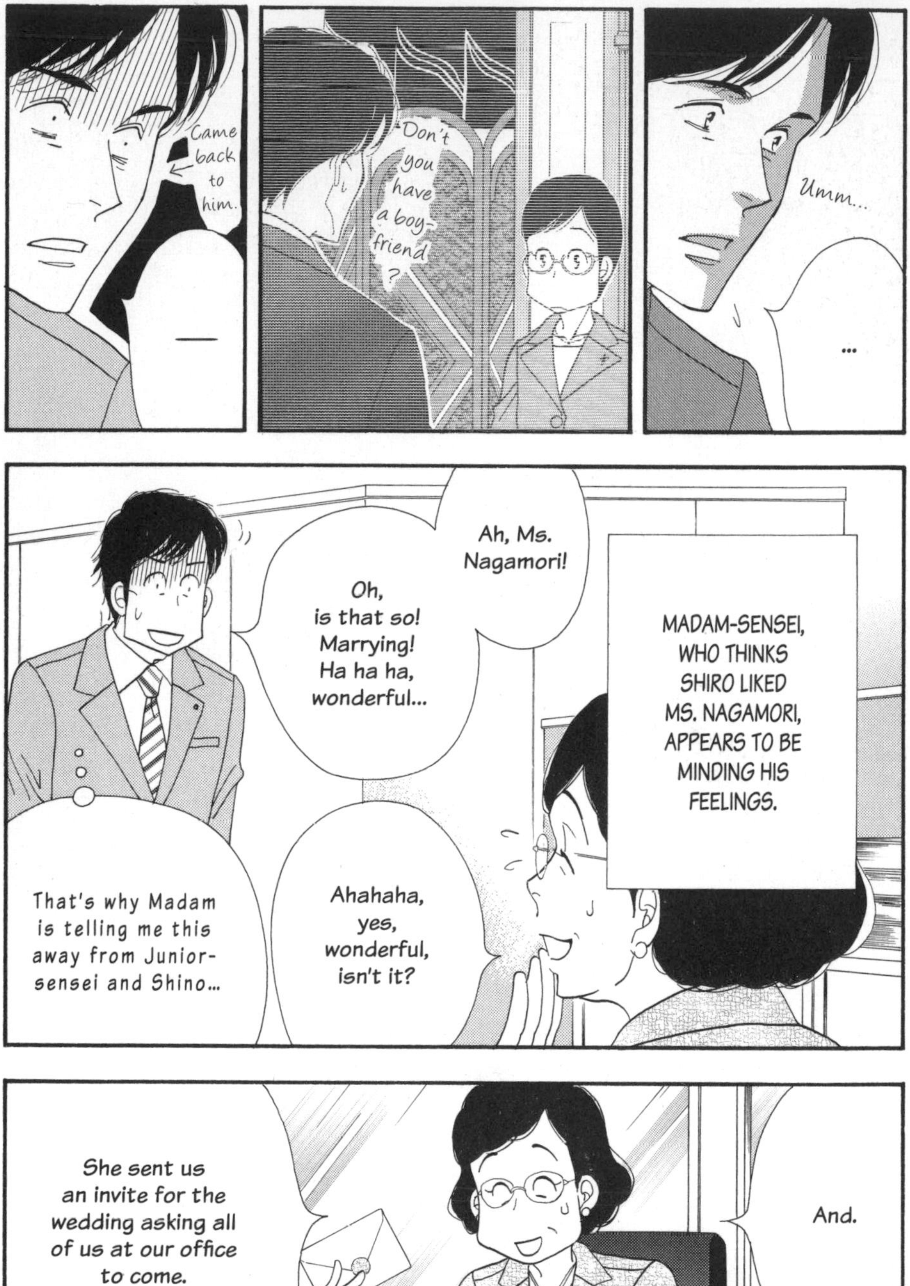
Umm...
...
Don't you have a boy-friend?
Came back to him.
—
MADAM-SENSEI, WHO THINKS SHIRO LIKED MS. NAGAMORI, APPEARS TO BE MINDING HIS FEELINGS.
Ah, Ms. Nagamori!
Oh, is that so! Marrying! Ha ha ha, wonderful...
Ahahaha, yes, wonderful, isn't it?
That's why Madam is telling me this away from Junior-sensei and Shino...
And.
She sent us an invite for the wedding asking all of us at our office to come.

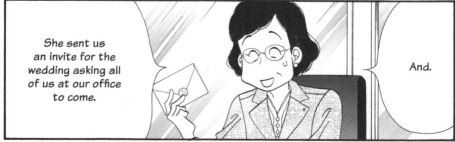

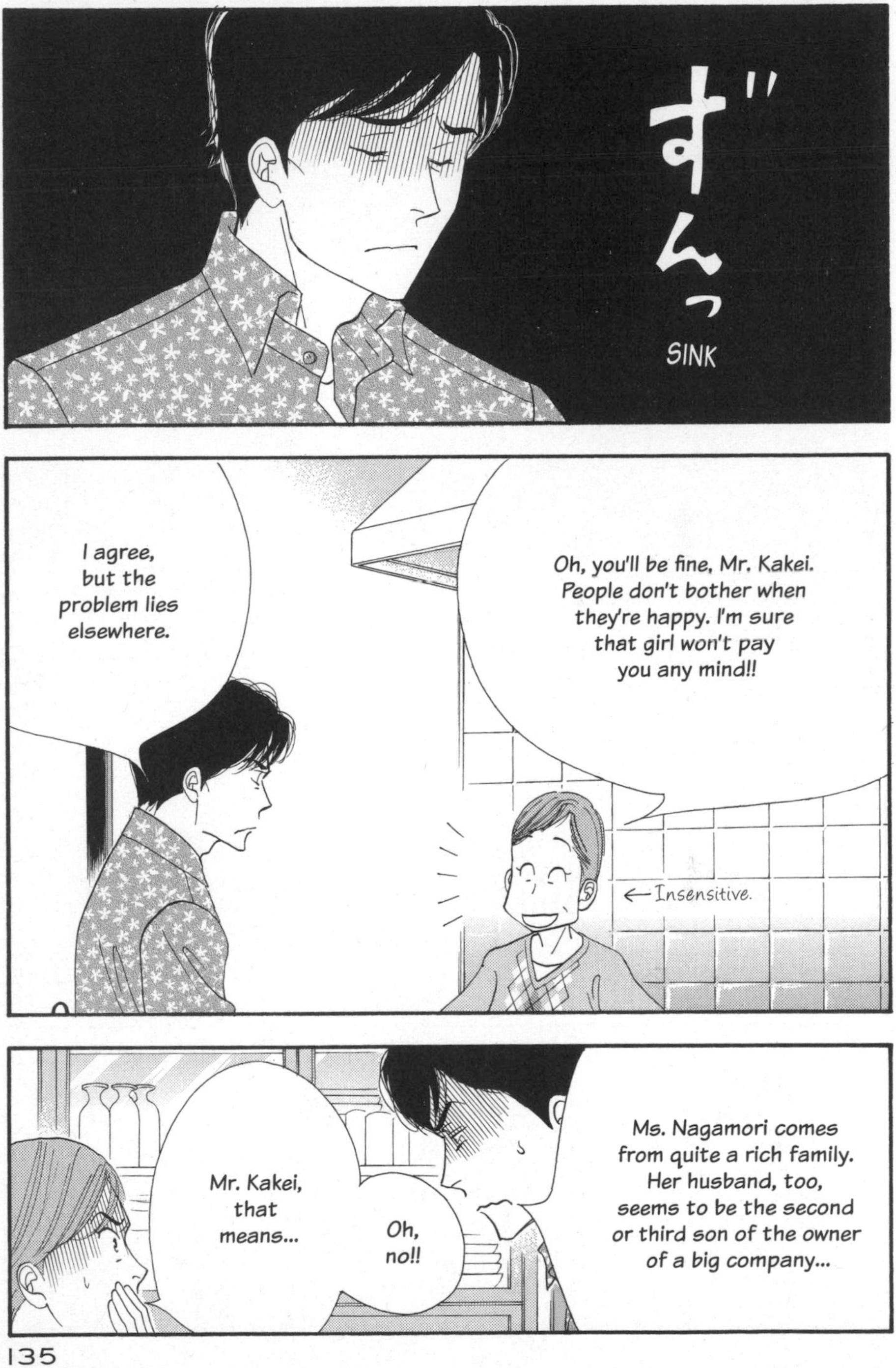
ずんっ
SINK
Oh, you'll be fine, Mr. Kakei. People don't bother when they're happy. I'm sure that girl won't pay you any mind!!
I agree, but the problem lies elsewhere.
← Insensitive.
Ms. Nagamori comes from quite a rich family. Her husband, too, seems to be the second or third son of the owner of a big company...
Oh, no!!
Mr. Kakei, that means...

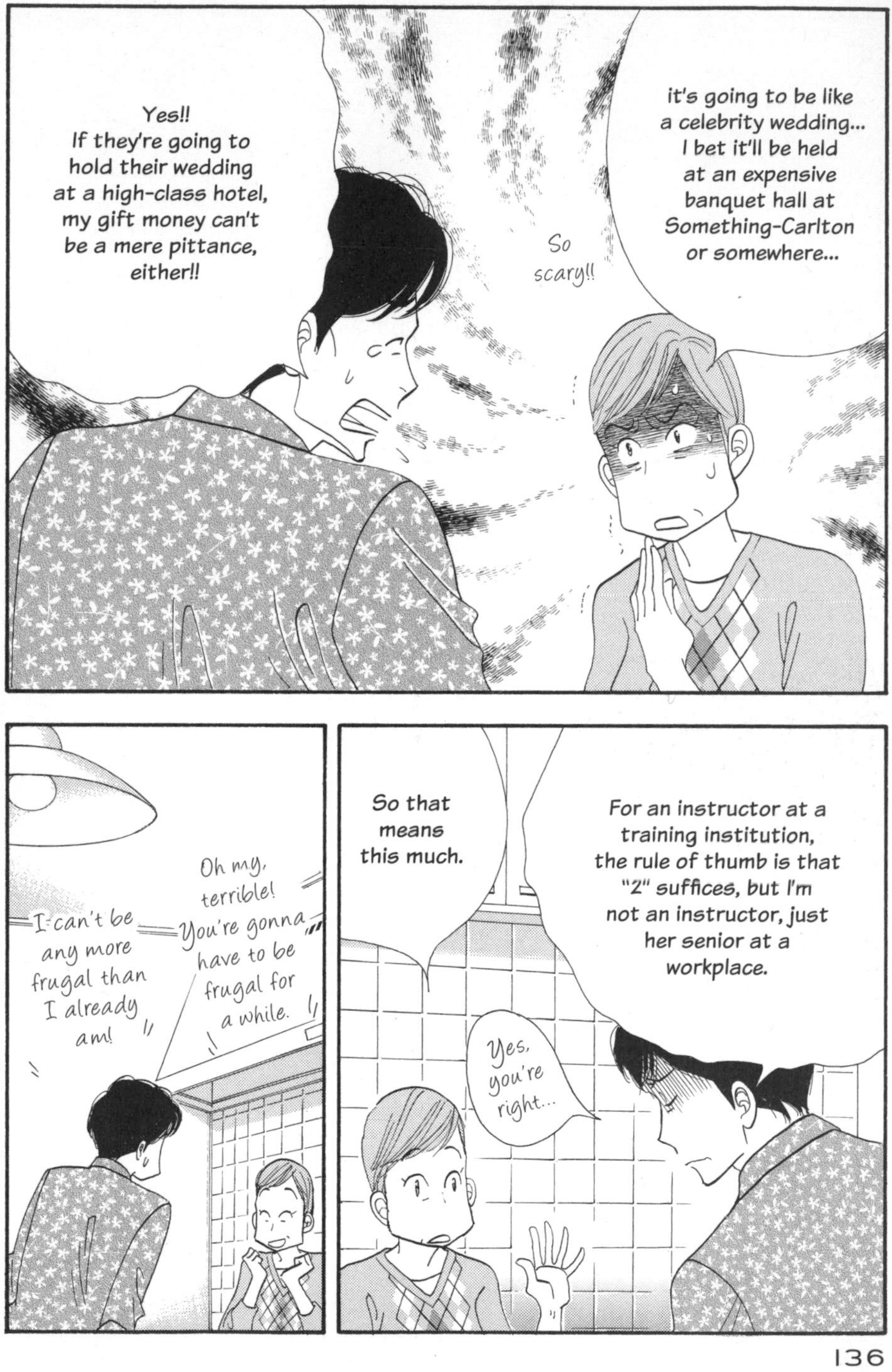
it's going to be like a celebrity wedding... I bet it'll be held at an expensive banquet hall at Something-Carlton or somewhere...
So scary!!
Yes!! If they're going to hold their wedding at a high-class hotel, my gift money can't be a mere pittance, either!!
For an instructor at a training institution, the rule of thumb is that "2" suffices, but I'm not an instructor, just her senior at a workplace.
So that means this much.
Yes, you're right...
Oh my, terrible! You're gonna have to be frugal for a while.
I can't be any more frugal than I already am!

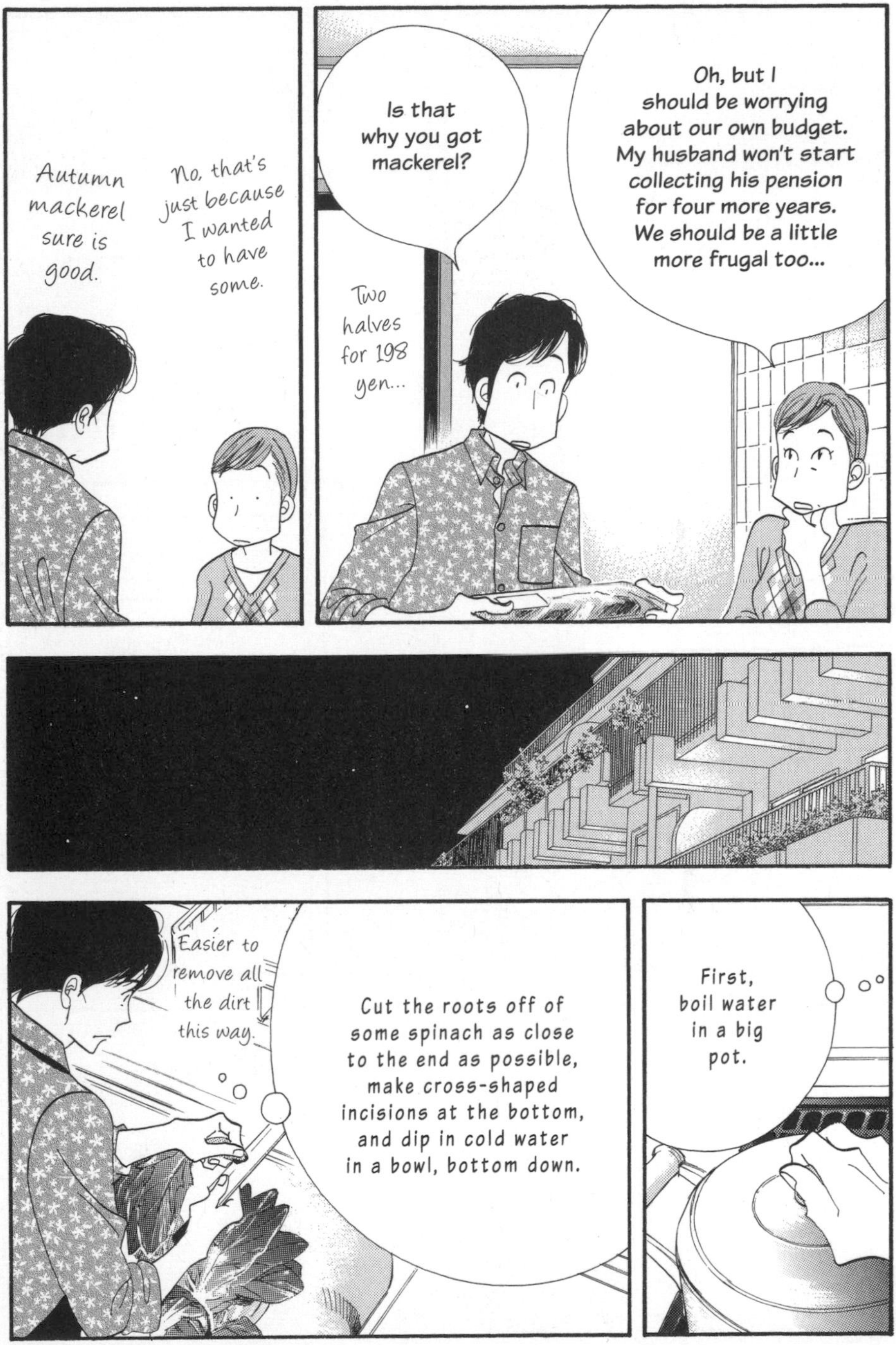
Oh, but I should be worrying about our own budget. My husband won't start collecting his pension for four more years. We should be a little more frugal too...
Is that why you got mackerel?
Two halves for 198 yen...
No, that's just because I wanted to have some.
Autumn mackerel sure is good.
First, boil water in a big pot.
Cut the roots off of some spinach as close to the end as possible, make cross-shaped incisions at the bottom, and dip in cold water in a bowl, bottom down.
Easier to remove all the dirt this way.

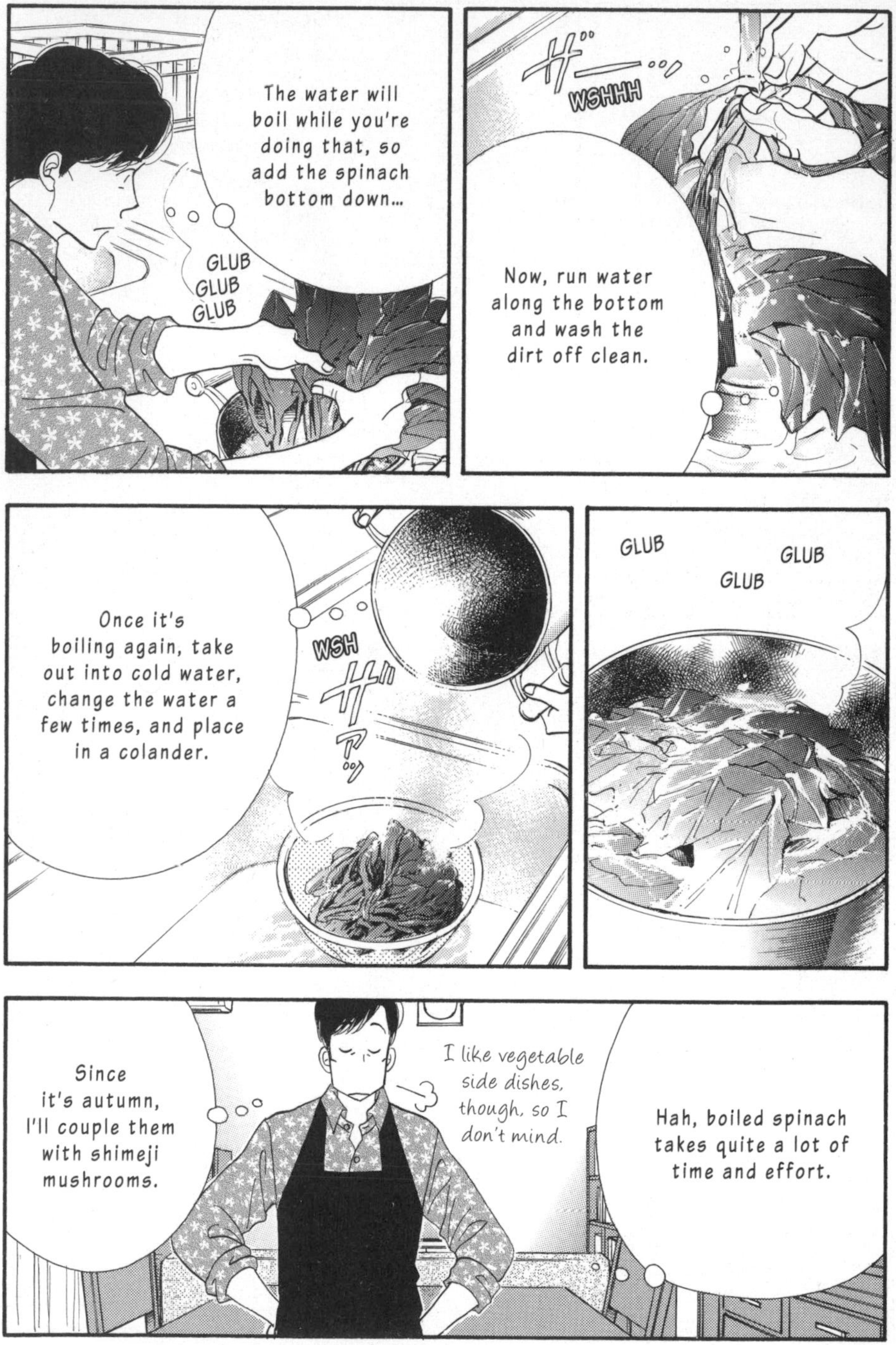
WSHHH
Now, run water along the bottom and wash the dirt off clean.
The water will boil while you're doing that, so add the spinach bottom down...
GLUB GLUB GLUB
GLUB
GLUB
GLUB
Once it's boiling again, take out into cold water, change the water a few times, and place in a colander.
WSH
Hah, boiled spinach takes quite a lot of time and effort.
I like vegetable side dishes, though, so I don't mind.
Since it's autumn, I'll couple them with shimeji mushrooms.

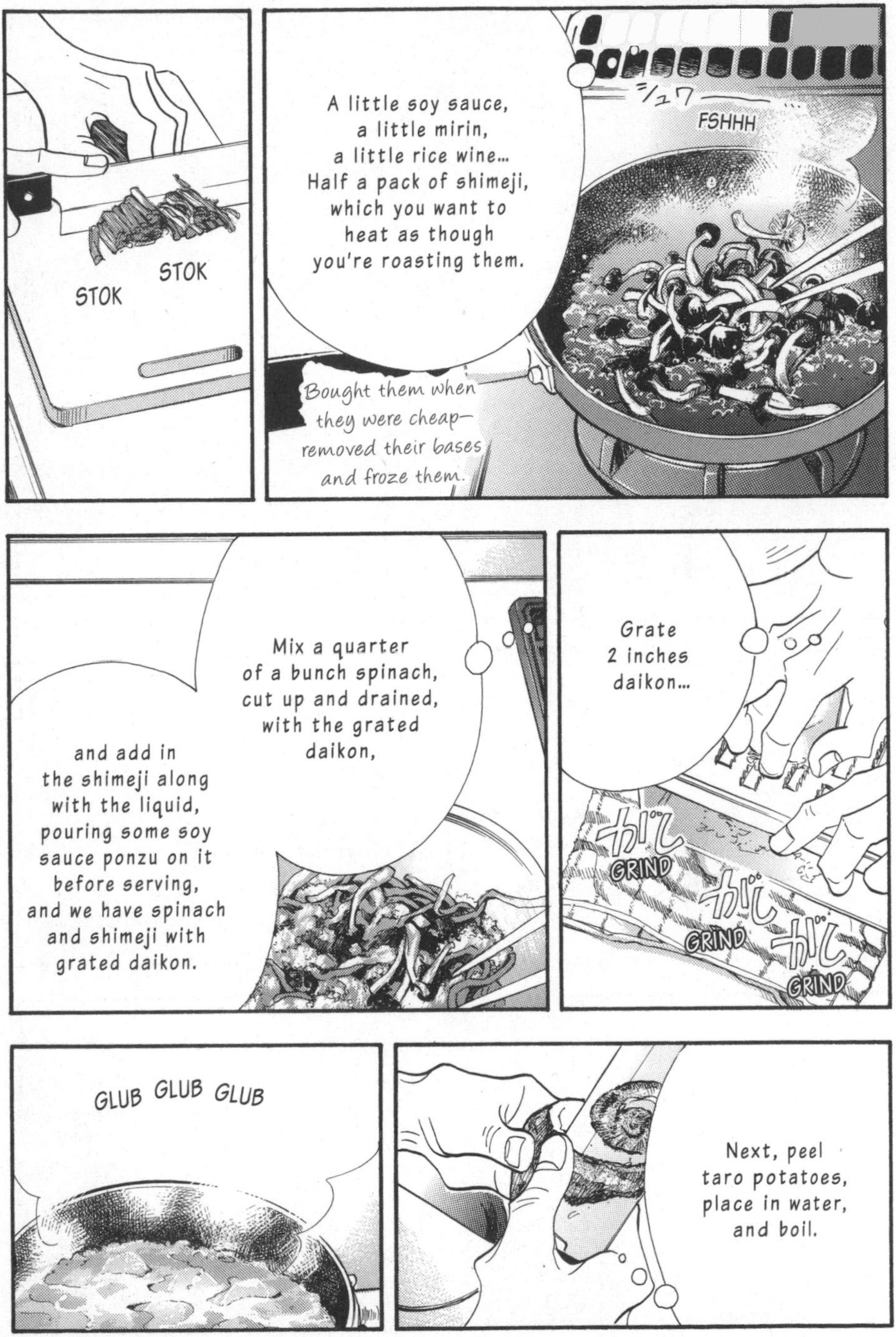
A little soy sauce, a little mirin, a little rice wine... Half a pack of shimeji, which you want to heat as though you're roasting them.
シュワ
FSHHH
Bought them when they were cheap— removed their bases and froze them.
STOK
STOK
Grate 2 inches daikon...
がし
GRIND
がし
GRIND
がし
GRIND
Mix a quarter of a bunch spinach, cut up and drained, with the grated daikon,
and add in the shimeji along with the liquid, pouring some soy sauce ponzu on it before serving, and we have spinach and shimeji with grated daikon.
Next, peel taro potatoes, place in water, and boil.
GLUB GLUB GLUB

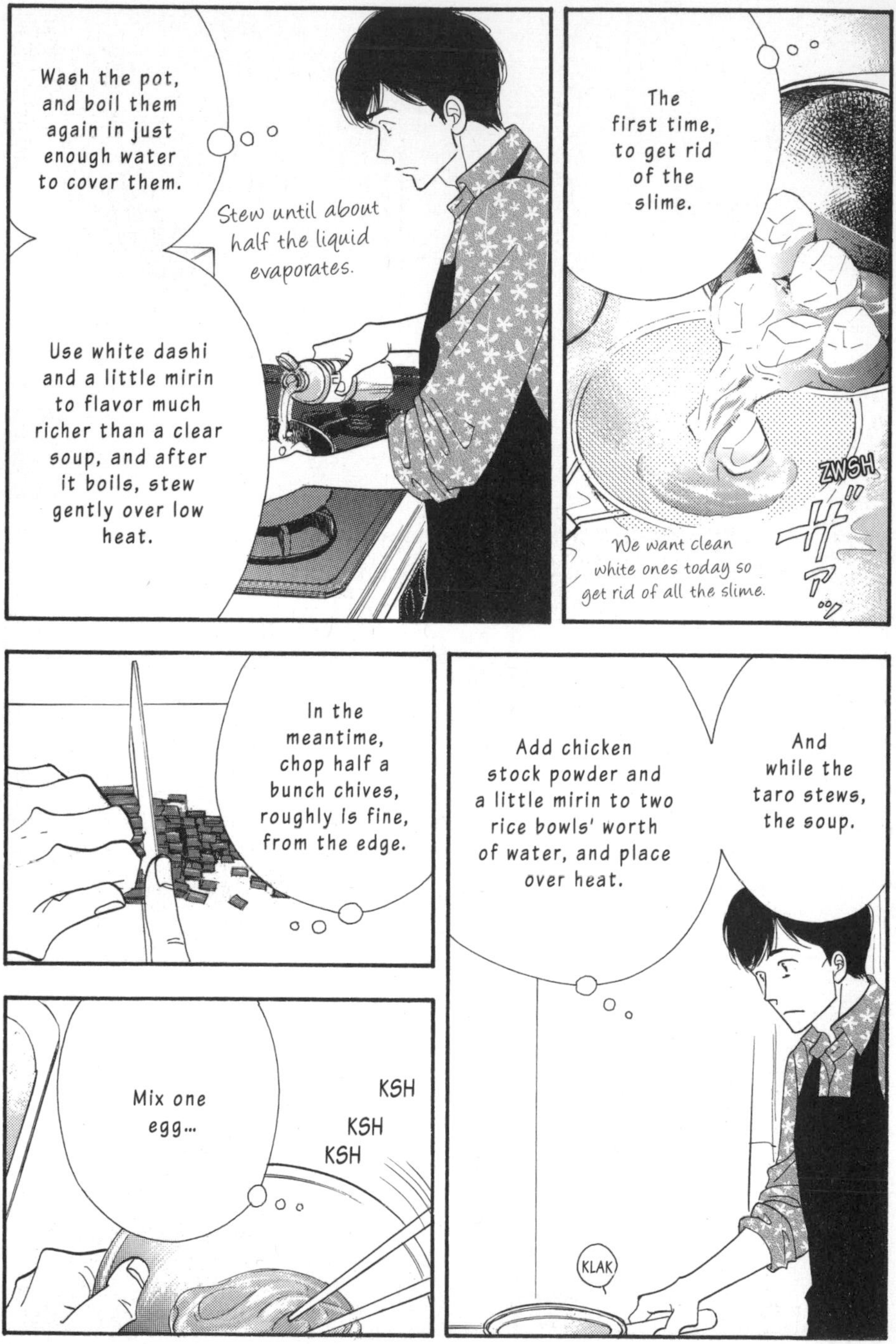
The first time, to get rid of the slime.
ZWSH
ザァッ
We want clean white ones today so get rid of all the slime.
Wash the pot, and boil them again in just enough water to cover them.
Stew until about half the liquid evaporates.
Use white dashi and a little mirin to flavor much richer than a clear soup, and after it boils, stew gently over low heat.
And while the taro stews, the soup.
Add chicken stock powder and a little mirin to two rice bowls' worth of water, and place over heat.
KLAK
In the meantime, chop half a bunch chives, roughly is fine, from the edge.
KSH
KSH
KSH
Mix one egg...

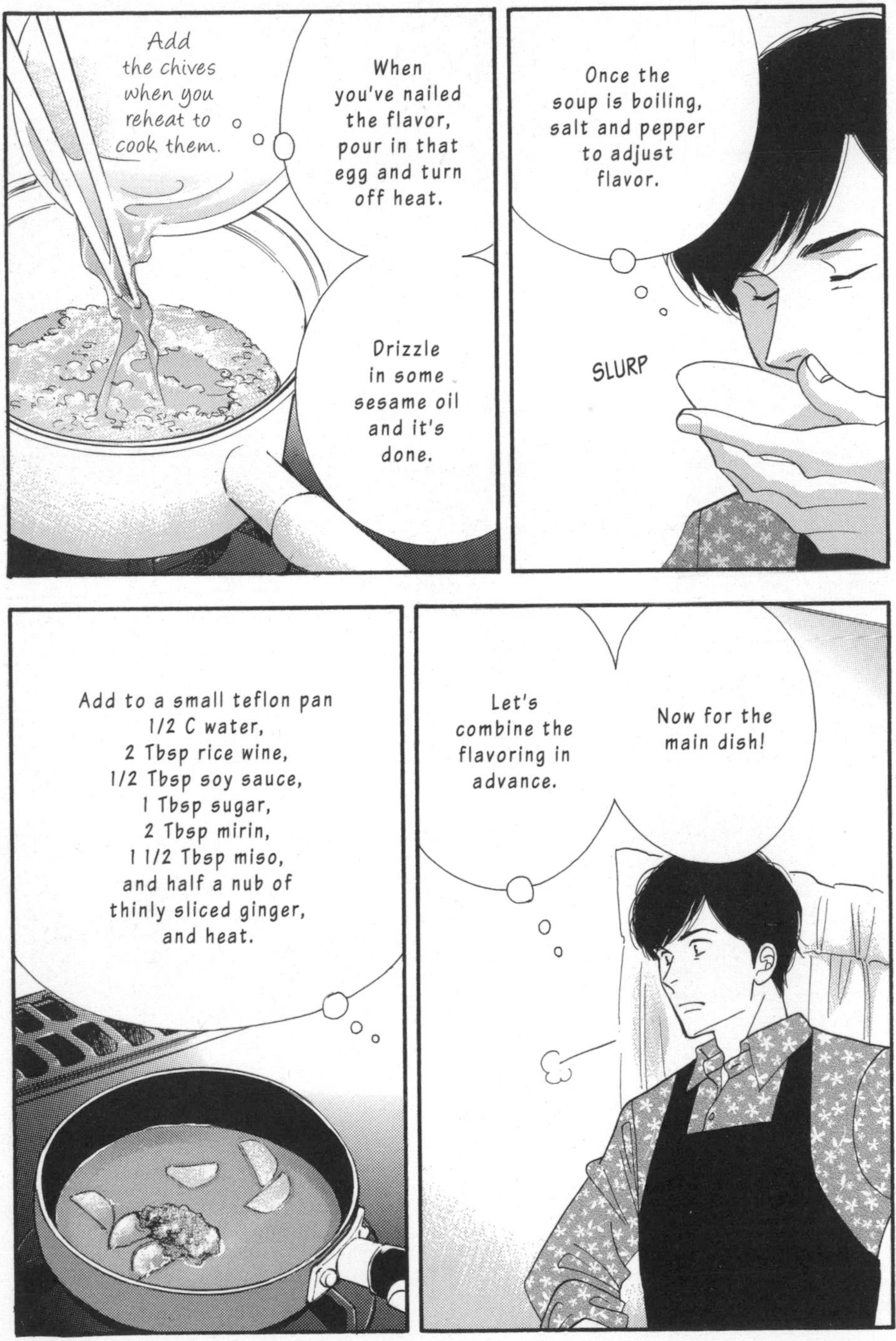
Once the soup is boiling, salt and pepper to adjust flavor.
SLURP
When you've nailed the flavor, pour in that egg and turn off heat.
Add the chives when you reheat to cook them.
Drizzle in some sesame oil and it's done.
Now for the main dish!
Let's combine the flavoring in advance.
Add to a small teflon pan 1/2 C water, 2 Tbsp rice wine, 1/2 Tbsp soy sauce, 1 Tbsp sugar, 2 Tbsp mirin, 1 1/2 Tbsp miso, and half a nub of thinly sliced ginger, and heat.

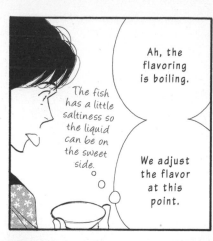

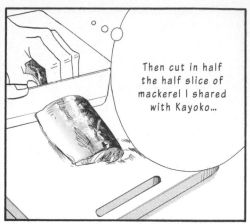

Then cut in half the half slice of mackerel I shared with Kayoko...
Ah, the flavoring is boiling.
We adjust the flavor at this point.
The fish has a little saltiness so the liquid can be on the sweet side.
Toss the mackerel into the liquid just like that.
FSHHH
シュワー
Now put a resting lid on top, and boil for ten to fifteen minutes over medium-low heat.
This is scary easy, Kayoko...
Am I doing this right?
GLUB
GLUB
GLUB
Huh?! You don't need to salt the mackerel first?!
This book also said to put the miso in later so you don't lose its aroma...
Oh don't bother. We're not using fancy miso anyway!
And skip cutting a cross into the mackerel too!!

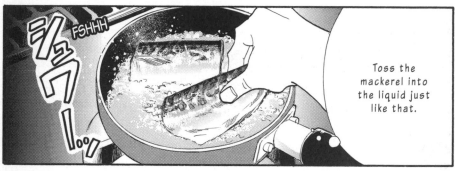

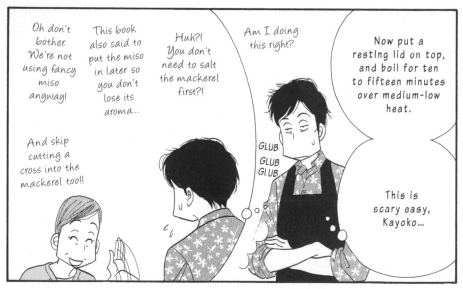

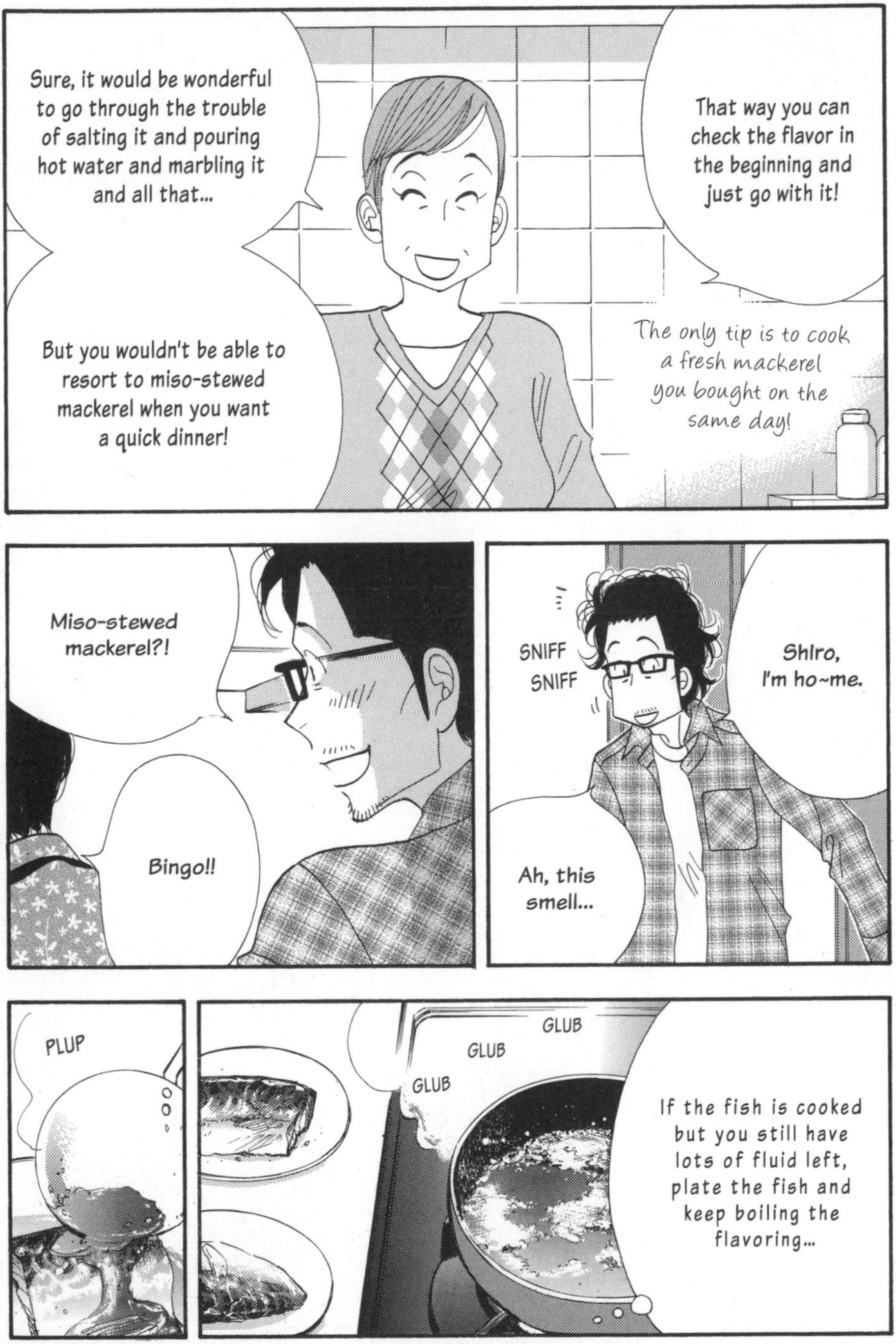
That way you can check the flavor in the beginning and just go with it!
Sure, it would be wonderful to go through the trouble of salting it and pouring hot water and marbling it and all that...
The only tip is to cook a fresh mackerel you bought on the same day!
But you wouldn't be able to resort to miso-stewed mackerel when you want a quick dinner!
Shiro, I'm ho~me.
SNIFF SNIFF
Ah, this smell...
Miso-stewed mackerel?!
Bingo!!
GLUB
GLUB
GLUB
If the fish is cooked but you still have lots of fluid left, plate the fish and keep boiling the flavoring...
PLUP

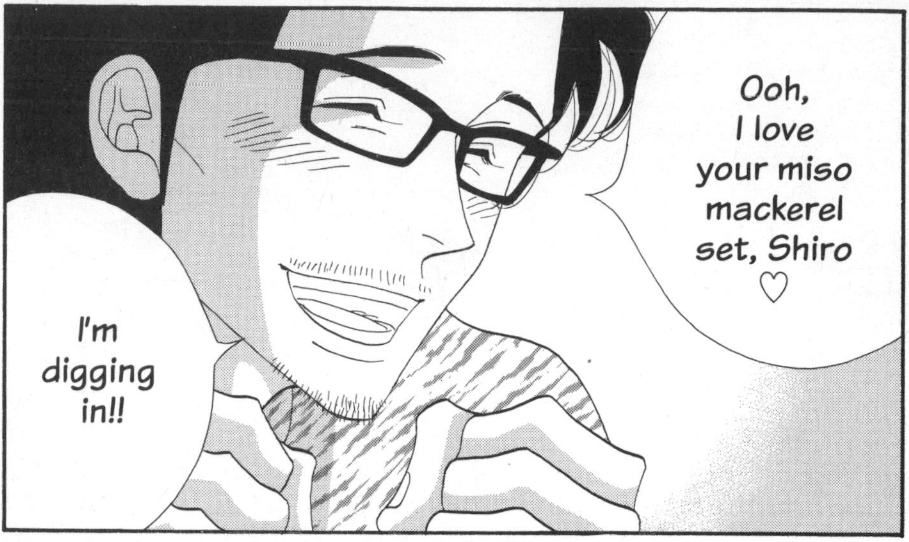
Ooh, I love your miso mackerel set, Shiro ♡
I'm digging in!!

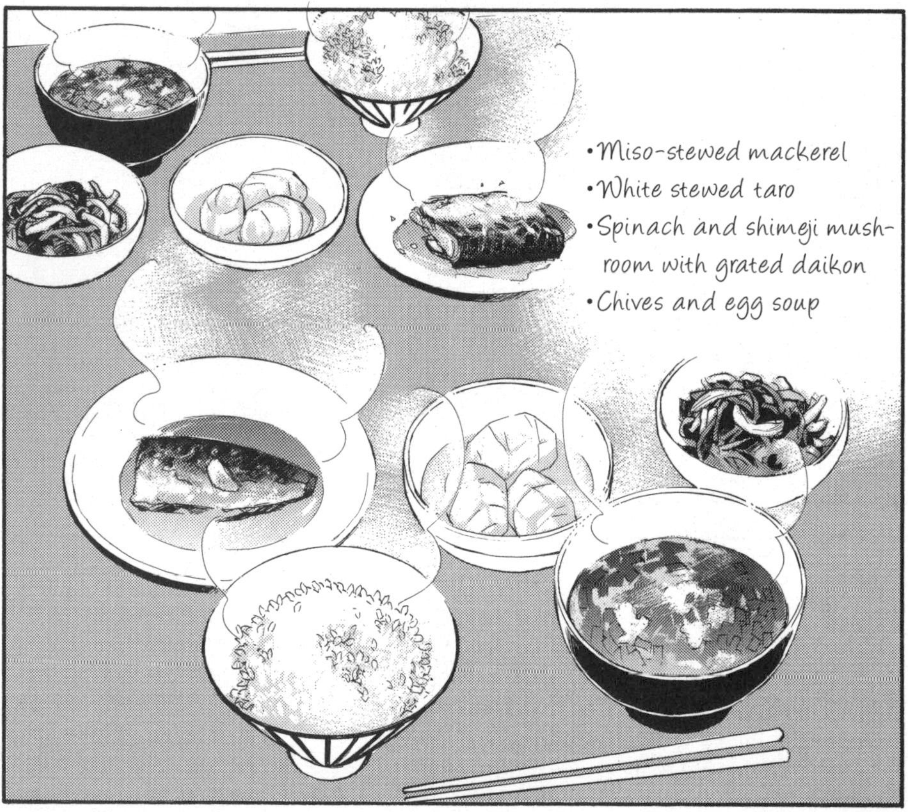
•Miso-stewed mackerel
•White stewed taro
•Spinach and shimeji mushroom with grated daikon
•Chives and egg soup

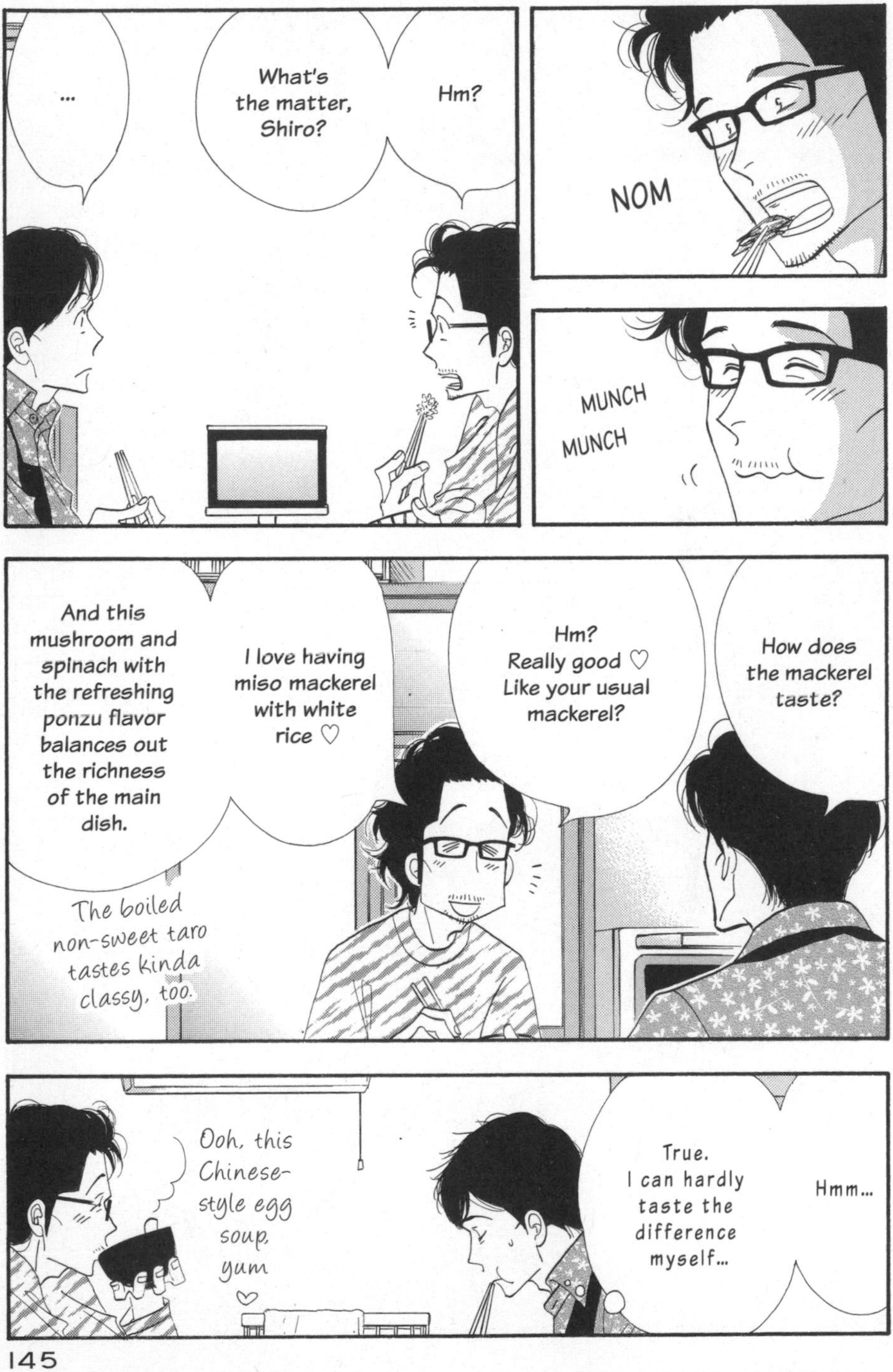

NOM
MUNCH MUNCH
Hm?
What's the matter, Shiro?
...
How does the mackerel taste?
Hm? Really good ♡ Like your usual mackerel?
I love having miso mackerel with white rice ♡
And this mushroom and spinach with the refreshing ponzu flavor balances out the richness of the main dish.
The boiled non-sweet taro tastes kinda classy, too.
Hmm...
True. I can hardly taste the difference myself...
Ooh, this Chinese-style egg soup, yum ♡

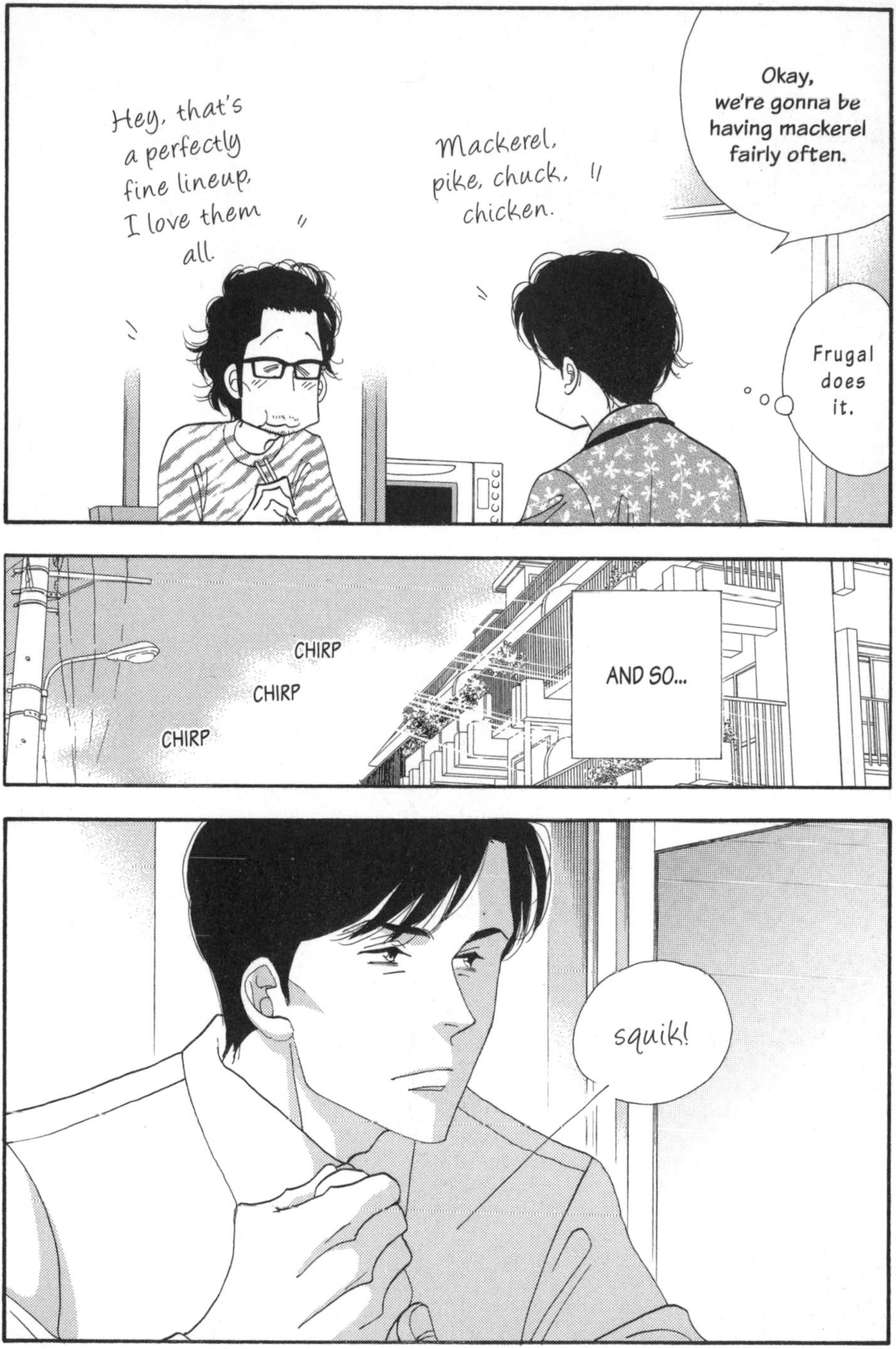
Okay, we're gonna be having mackerel fairly often.
Frugal does it.
Mackerel, pike, chuck, chicken.
Hey, that's a perfectly fine lineup, I love them all.
AND SO...
CHIRP
CHIRP
CHIRP
squik!

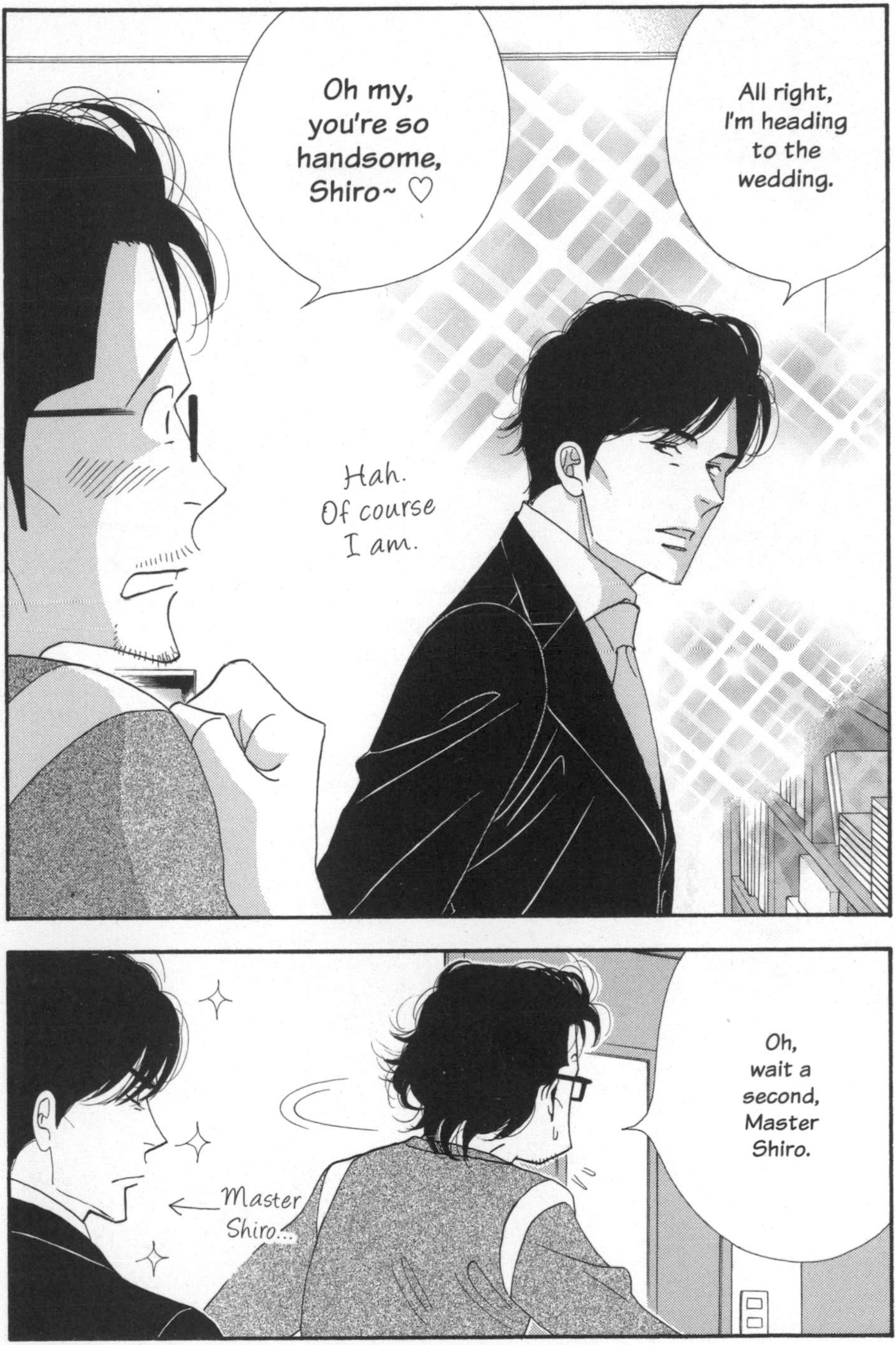
All right, I'm heading to the wedding.
Oh my, you're so handsome, Shiro~ ♡
Hah. Of course I am.
Oh, wait a second, Master Shiro.
Master Shiro...

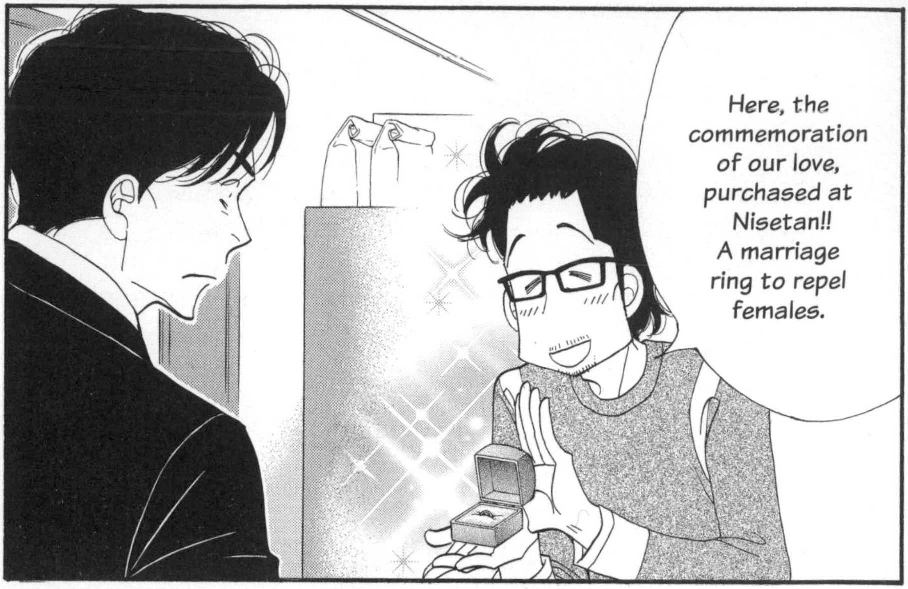
Here, the commemoration of our love, purchased at Nisetan!! A marriage ring to repel females.

* Note: There is a real department store called Isetan, but "nise" means *fake*.

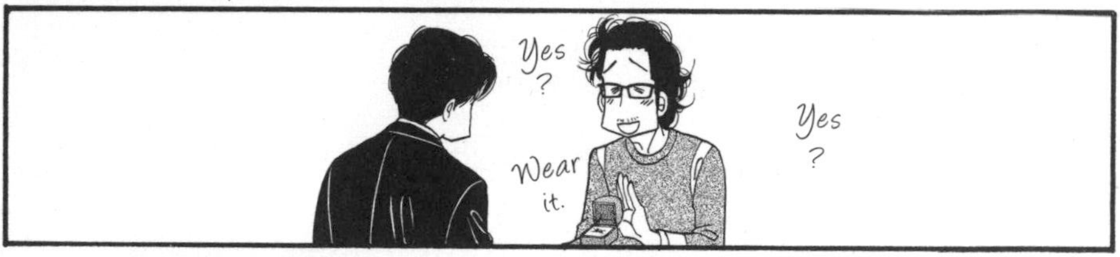
Yes ?
Yes ?
Wear it.

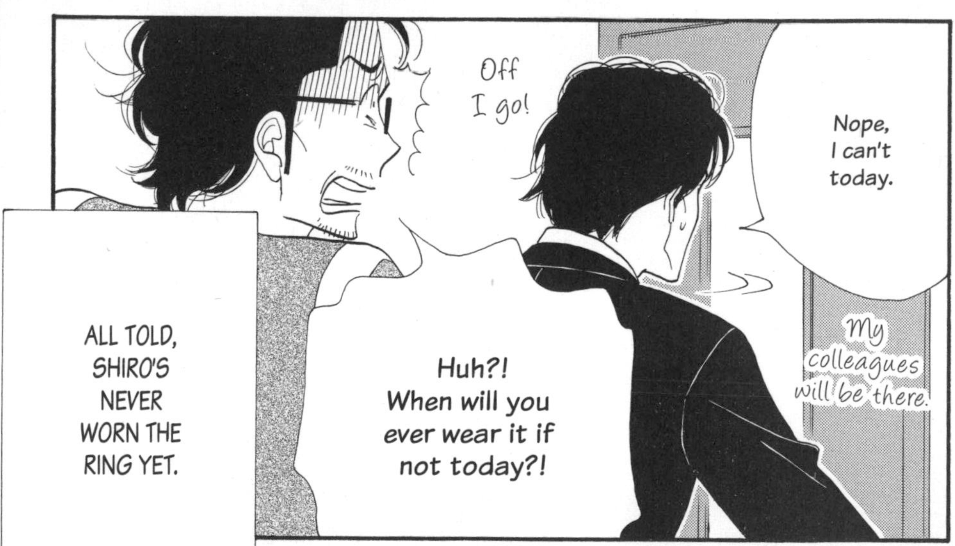
Nope, I can't today.
My colleagues will be there.
Off I go!
Huh?! When will you ever wear it if not today?!
ALL TOLD, SHIRO'S NEVER WORN THE RING YET.

The miso-stewed mackerel requires 1 ½ Tbsp of miso, but it read "1 Tbsp" in the serialized version. I'm terribly sorry.
And when you wash green vegetables like spinach, apparently it's okay to use hot rather than cold water (and I don't mean lukewarm, real hot water being even better).
So, this winter, use hot water to spare your hands and to make things easier on yourself.

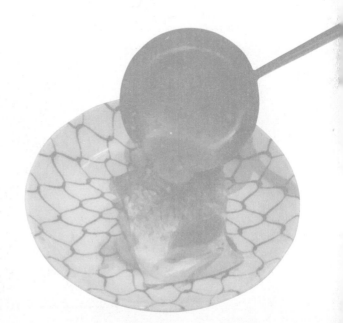

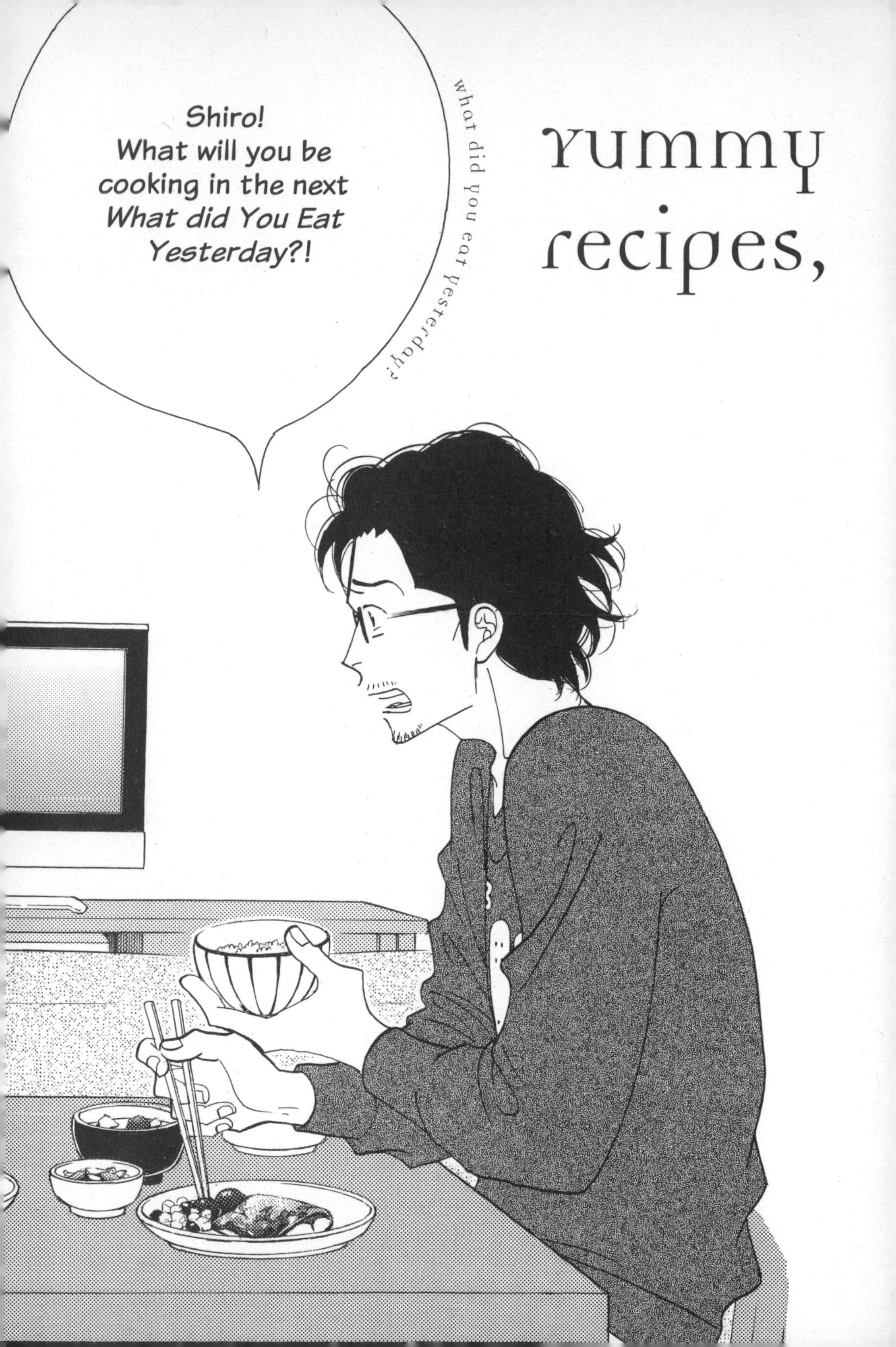
Shiro! What will you be cooking in the next *What did You Eat Yesterday?*!
what did you eat yesterday?
yummy recipes,

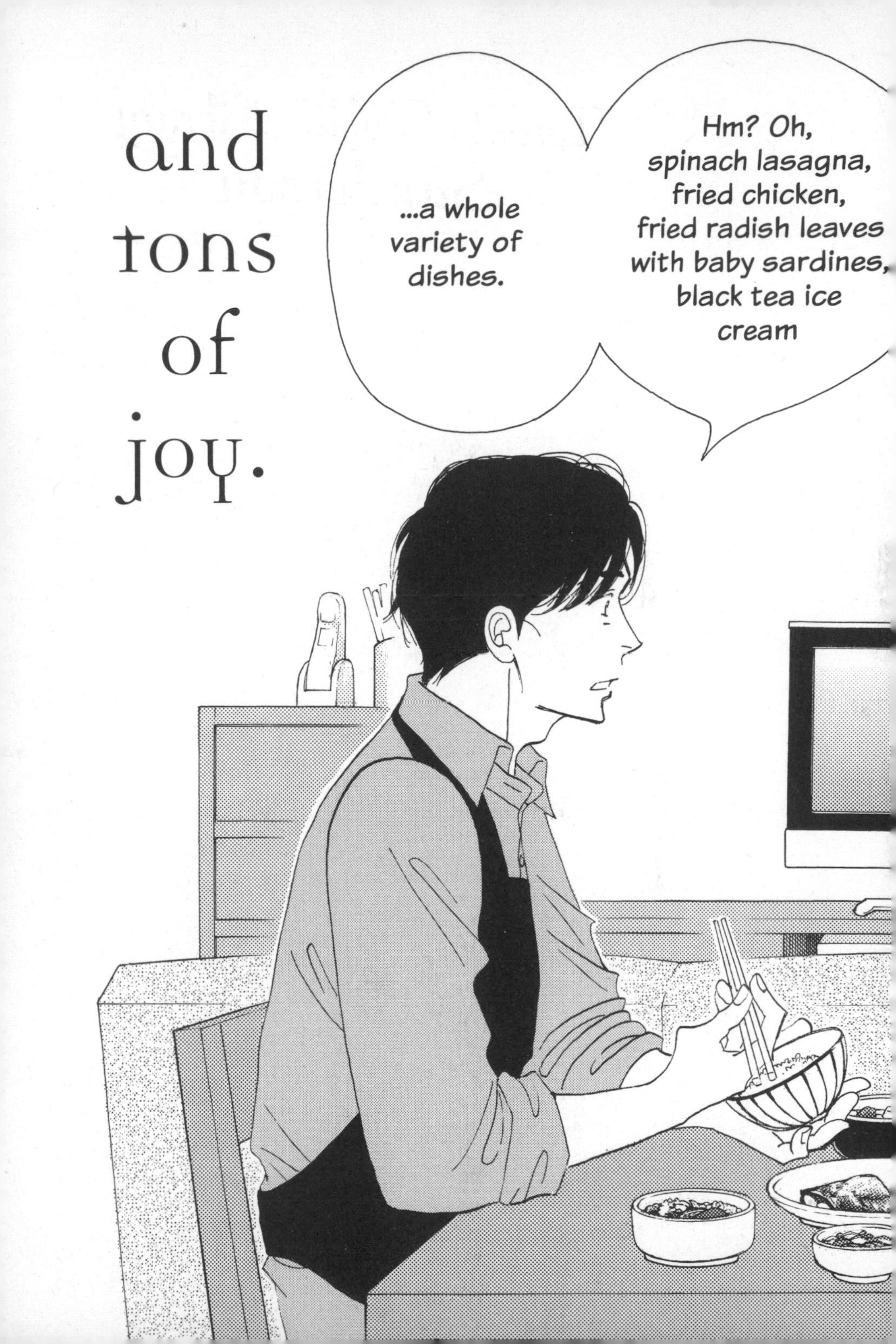

Hm? Oh, spinach lasagna, fried chicken, fried radish leaves with baby sardines, black tea ice cream
...a whole variety of dishes.
and tons of joy.

what did you eat yesterday?, volume 6
translation: Yoshito Hinton
production: Risa Cho
Tomoe Tsutsumi

© 2015 Fumi Yoshinaga. All rights reserved.
First published in Japan in 2012 by Kodansha Ltd., Tokyo.
publication rights for this English edition arranged
through Kodansha Ltd., Tokyo.
English language version produced by vertical, inc.

Translation provided by vertical, inc., 2015
published by vertical, inc., New York

originally published in Japanese as Kinou nani tabeta? 6 by Kodansha, Ltd.
Kinou nani tabeta? first serialized in Morning, Kodansha, Ltd., 2007-

This is a work of fiction.

ISBN: 978-1-939130-81-5

Manufactured in Canada

First Edition

vertical, inc.
451 Park Avenue South
7th Floor
New York, NY 10016
www.vertical-inc.com